T0208989

IN CINQUE:
WHAT WAS,
WHAT IS, WHAT
OUGHT TO BE

RENETTA T. WOMACK HOWARD

BALBOA.
PRESS
A DIVISION OF HAY HOUSE

Modern English Version (MEV)
The Holy Bible, Modern English Version. Copyright © 2014 by Military Bible Association. Published and distributed by Charisma House.

Balboa Press books may be ordered through booksellers or by contacting:

Balboa Press
A Division of Hay House
1663 Liberty Drive
Bloomington, IN 47403
www.balboapress.com
1 (877) 407-4847

Print information available on the last page.

ISBN: 978-1-9822-0694-9 (sc)
ISBN: 978-1-9822-0700-7 (e)

Balboa Press rev. date: 07/02/2018

DEDICATIONS

PART I

This work is dedicated to my mentors,
T. J. Patterson and Eddie P. Richardson
of the *Southwest Digest* of Lubbock, Texas

PART II

This work is dedicated to

Weekly newspaper publishers who believed in me and my work

Emma Crisler of *the **Port Gibson Reveille*** in Port Gibson, Mississippi

Charles Shepherd of *the **Fayette Chronicle*** in Fayette, Mississippi

Alice Tisdale of *the **Jackson Advocate*** in Jackson, Mississippi

Publishers of *the **Madison Journal***, Tallulah, Louisiana

Publishers of ***La Vida* News-THE BLACK VOICE, Fort Worth, Texas**

And several inspirational individuals

My Pastor: Reverend Walter R. McDonald, Ms. Ruth Baker and
Mrs. Opal Lee of *Baker Chapel A.M.E. Church, Fort Worth, Texas*

And *"Cliff" and Harlis*

IN CINQUE

INTRODUCTION

There are many ways to see the world and very often, we see things differently from others, but there are times that it is necessary to be "in Cinque" with the world. These two parts are a collection of essays written in various time, in various places on various topics, by the author and they have been published in various weekly newspapers over a period of twenty years. Each part contains ten years of essays: PART I, 1993-2004 and PART II, 2005-2015.

IN CINQUE reflects the way things are and often how to deal with them. It reveals an historical outlook on the American culture as it deals with the current aspects of life with regards to the economy, politics, education, health, social interaction, family, religion and the arts. These essays herein are reflected chronologically by relevant subjects.

The column, *"IN CINQUE"* was first published in the *Lubbock Digest,* a Black weekly newspaper, currently called the *Southwest Digest,* by Eddie P. Richardson and T. J. Patterson. They encouraged the author to write and T. J. even suggested that the essays be put into a book form. At that point, the author was not certain that she would continue to write, but twenty years later, she is still doing the same thing on a weekly basis and sharing with other weekly newspapers in several states; Texas, Mississippi and Louisiana.

Even though some of these essays were written decades ago, the pertinent information and observations have not changed at all. We can learn how to get *"IN CINQUE."*

PART I - SUBJECT CONTENTS

I-EDUCATION: SCHOOLS, TEACHERS AND STUDENTS

Day One
First published August 9, 1993

Across the nation, schools are beginning the '93/94 school session. Parents and children are busy selecting school supplies and new clothes for the first day of school. Teachers are gearing up to meet their new charges. Enthusiasm fills the air. There are great expectations from every direction.

With such great expectations, what is wrong? Why are we hearing that children, OUR BLACK CHILDREN, in our Black neighborhoods, are not making acceptable scores on the standardized tests?

We are aware that there are many variables which may be contributing to unacceptable performance, but do we know what they are? How can we isolate these variables?

1. All of our teachers have passed the required tests and are certified to teach the curriculum assigned to them.
2. Our students are willing and able to learn.
3. Schools are equipped and conducive to learning.
4. Parents are out there fully supporting the school and their children. WHAT DID I SAY?

I am sorry. I meant to say that they are out there fully supporting the first day of school. Once the preparation is taken care of, it will be celebrated for the next ten months. How do I know?

Teachers buy or solicit pencils, pens, paper, snacks, sometimes

1

eyeglasses and clothing. Many teachers pay for field trips that require admission fees and freely give hugs and words of encouragement every day to children. Often teachers have to babysit after school is ended for the day because children are not picked up from school in a timely manner.

How far do the positive experiences that children have at school take them when they go to a place at the end of the day knowing that they have done the greatest good at home by being out of the house, at school all day?

Being 'in cinque' requires more from parents. Take an interest in what your children are doing EVERY DAY. Find out what they are supposed to be learning. Get to know their teachers and work with the teachers. Remember the teacher takes the place of parent at school. Teachers do not low-rate parents to students and parents should not low-rate teachers. Get 'in cinque' so children may benefit. Go to school and get involved with your children and their education. YOU MIGHT LEARN SOMETHING!

HOME SCENARIOS
First published August 26, 1993

Imagine these scenarios. The first is the home of a single parent who is approximately 23 years old and raising three children ages 8, 6 and 4 years of age. All three of these children are school age and they attend the neighborhood elementary school. This young mom has a job and must be at work at 8:00 A.M. daily. In order to manage her time well, she assigned daily chores to each of her children. She insists that they complete their chores on a timely basis and they respond by cheerfully doing as they are asked to do. These children are in school early each day and they participate in "Y" Care after school because Mom is homebound after school is over.

Once home in the evening, the children play as Mom prepares the evening meal because they did their homework during "Y" Care time. They used their time wisely. Their teachers will be pleased on the next school day. Their social and academic skills are very good and their progress in school is excellent.

The next scenario is very similar. There is one child age 12 and one age 19 in the home of a single mother, age 27. The 13 year old attends a junior high school and the 10 year old attends a neighborhood elementary school. This mother has a job but has left the responsibility of school attendance and discipline entirely up to her two children. They do not have daily chores except to get up and get out to school. Some days they do not make it to school. Mom will give them an excuse to take to school the next day regardless of why they were absent. She works hard to please them and when she does not, they tell her where she can go and what she can do. Mom often has to take off from work to visit the school to defend the actions of her children. They are not working up to capacity. Education has no meaning to them and their teachers cannot understand what the problem is. Their mom is so cooperative, but they are still having problems. They resist attempts to help them.

It is time for parents to get 'in cinque' and teach their children some social skills and responsibility at home. Success in school depends on it.

EDUCATION AND MORALITY
First published October 2, 1993

Educational theory as taught in colleges and universities perpetuate the idea that a school is supposed to reflect the values of the community it serves. In the past couple of decades, the very opposite has been true. The most visible effects of this trend have been in the arena of morality.

When Mrs. Madalyn Murray and her son William J. Murray, Ill, avowed atheist, protested the reading of the **_Bible_** in public schools, it seems that many people felt that they were not supposed to read it anywhere. The country's values as well as personal values began a trek downhill. School had not lost sight on moral values, but it would appear that its constituents had.

Are schools supposed to reinforce callous spirituality in a country which was founded on religious values and principles? Did the justices underestimate the ramifications of allowing the good for two individuals to prevail over the rights of the majority?

It is difficult to teach new ideas and even more difficult when there is no transfer of ideas or motivation to learn new ideas. When children go to school to a set of values which are completely foreign to them, they have a difficult time assimilating the new ideas. Thus, they have a difficult time learning what is taught at school.

It appears that a decline in moral values in the country has affected a decline in the outcome of educations in this country. We need to get 'in cinque' and have a positive effect on raising the level of moral maturity in our communities even if it means going to court to retrieve rights lost to Mrs. Murray and her son. Otherwise, we will be 'without a prayer!'

CRITICISMS OF SCHOOLS AND TEACHERS
First published November 17, 1993

We are only a few months into the current school year and the media has bombarded us with criticism of schools and teachers. Some of the criticism has been based on research and quite astute while most of it has been 'off-the-wall' and ridiculous.

It appears that everyone who has a stake in education has their own schematic drawing of what a teacher is or is not, and the more I read and listen, it dawned on me that everyone wants and has designed an automated teacher for public schools.

School systems have input from the home or the family community/ parents, the legislature, business, religion, labor, politics, educators and plain ole busybodies. Their schematics are similar. The only problem they have is with their circuit board. They keep blowing fuses. There are too many switches and not enough current to make the mechanism operate as it should. But, what the heck, it has got to work somehow. They all need to see their tax dollars at work, right or wrong. **THAT** is what is important. Learning is on the back burner.

When this kind of thinking disappears, school systems and teachers will be able to concentrate on getting the maximum achievement from students instead of hopping from one 'educational' bandwagon to another, without results, trying to prove that they are giving the job of helping students to learn with their best efforts, to satisfy the critics.

Teachers are people. They are human beings with blood running through their veins, with electrolytes but not electrical circuits. They have backbones but not circuit boards. They have hearts that care for the children that they teach, not electrical switches. They love children, not money, because they are the most ***underpaid and over-prepared***

professionals in the world. Teachers live in the community along with those whom they serve, not on a shelf in a laboratory or in a closet.

It is about time that we get 'in cinque' and begin to love, honor and cherish our teachers and let them do the job which they have spent at least four years of college study, preparing to do.

LEARNING DISABILITIES
First published January 5, 1994

Years ago, teachers never heard of 'special education and learning disabilities.' Every child who was able to ambulate on his own, was placed in a regular classroom as well as some who were not able without help of some kind, and were treated as all other children in that room. The child expected to complete all of his assignments just like everyone else. No special allowances were made for him unless he needed help to get his crutches or with putting on a sweater or coat. Self-esteem was maintained and so was respect from friends, family and acquaintances.

As time progressed, along with medical proficiency, all types of child disabling conditions have been discovered. The most popular one is dyslexia or a disturbance of the ability to read successfully, according to Harris and Sipay in How to Increase Reading Ability, (1975) pp. 136-138. According to Funk & Wagnall New Encyclopedia, volume 10, approximately 5 percent of the child population has some kind of learning disability. When it is difficult to pinpoint that disability, it is usually called dyslexia.

A child is said to have a learning disability when his measured ability to learn, such as his IQ, (intelligence quotient) score; (average IQ =90-105) or stanine score (on a 1-9 scale average=5) reflect that he has potential for maximum achievements and there is a discrepancy in actual achievements which are not due to mental retardation, emotional disturbances or sensory disorders.

Two final conditions which greatly attribute to a child being labeled LD is a lack of motivation and pure L-A-Z-I-N-E-S-S; first on the part of the parent who does not take interest in or motivate the child at an early age and later in the child who sees no need to achieve because it is easier not to produce.

Parents, get 'in cinque' and find out what is the REAL situation with your LD child, said to be dyslexic. Is he really dyslexic or plain lazy?

SPECIAL EDUCATION LABELS
First published January 12, 11994

In the educational arena, we have gone from plain special education to 'homogeneous grouping,' to 'mainstreaming,' to 'content mastery,' and the current most prevalent term is 'inclusion.' The experts in the field of education which deal with exceptional children are constantly making 'discoveries' that lead them to make revisions in their dogma and thus rename and re-define what special education is and what it is supposed to do as well as how it is supposed to be taught. Sometime it appears to be much-a-do about what.

Many of the children who are classified as in need of special education would not be candidates if their mothers had gotten adequate prenatal care and been cautious of their environment and the way they took care of themselves during pregnancy.

During the first three months of gestation, the embryo changes to the fetal state after about eight weeks, and the end of the third month, most developmental changes have taken place and growth continues until birth. The fetal environment is pretty much determined by how the mother takes care of herself.

Abnormal situations in the fetal environment are the causes of fetal mortality. When the fetus in an abnormal situation does not die, it develops abnormally. Abnormal results often manifest themselves in mental retardation as well as physical handicaps.

One external agent which is probably responsible for most mental retardation is German measles or rubella. Vaccinations for rubella are a 'must' for girls. Another agent of birth defects is infection from venereal diseases. Radiation and certain chemicals such as drugs, alcohol and tobacco used by the mother can also cause birth defects in the unborn baby. It is time to get 'in cinque' and eliminate the need for 'special education.'

THE PTA: PARENT-TEACHER ASSOCIATION
First published March 22, 1994

There was a time when PTA really meant Parent-Teacher Association. In addition, the Parent-Teacher Association was a vital part of the school community. Meetings were well attended and the topics for discussion focused on issues that would bring about improvements in the learning environment.

The entire community was considered to be the learning environment. The PTA was concerned with the school, the students, and the learning equipment, the moral fiber of the community, the fitness of school personnel and the content of the curriculum. The school board's job usually boiled down to putting its stamp of approval on the work of the PTA.

Lately, in too many schools, the PTA is made up mostly of teachers who serve in a particular school. Daytime meetings are rarely held because parents rarely attend. Most meetings are scheduled for a week night in order to give working parents the opportunity to attend. Some presentations by students are usually made at these night meetings and it is usually the parents of the student participants who show up. Few parents see any worth in an organization unless they see some direct benefit for their child.

It is time for parents to get 'in cinque' and see 'beyond their noses.' Tunnel vision is the downfall of the PTA and too many of our schools. Parents of all students need to become involved in the local PTA. It should not appear that the teachers are more concerned about students than their parents.

PUBLIC SCHOOL BOARDS
First published June 28, 1994

Every citizen, taxpaying or not, feels that they should have some voice in what our public schools do or desire to do. All school systems have some sort of representative board whether it is elected or appointed. The board is theoretically supposed to voice the will of the 'people.'

The people, on the other hand, are not always knowledgeable about how to establish a line of communication between their representative and themselves. They often respond in crises rather than keeping up with current activities and acting before a crisis. One such subject is privatization of public schools.

When school boards have privatization of schools on their agenda, that is the time that concerned citizens should let their board members know how they feel about it, or any other subject, for that matter, before the board acts on it.

There have been positive and negative reports about privatization of schools, across the nation. It seems to be a fact that private businesses taking over public schools make money for the business. It is reported that 'teachers work harder for less pay and if selected by the business, may be less qualified for the job, thus eliminating jobs of better qualified personnel; that some students may profit more from a 'no frill' school atmosphere; that the money given a business to run a school, could be put into site-based administration literally and the community rather than a business could profit. Citizens, get 'in cinque' and let your school board members know how you feel about the privatization of schools before it comes to past. It is not easy to break a business contract!

MAKING LIFE CHOICE IN SCHOOL
First published June 29, 1994

Twenty years ago, I thought that the move to teach career education in primary school was a waste of time and good money. Today, I feel that it is needed now more than ever. Too soon, our children find out about a life career of crime and too late a profitable life career with positive attributes.

Most countries in the world begin to prepare children for a lifetime career when they enter school. The children are aware at the outset of the career that they will pursue. They spend their young lives preparing for their careers. They study to be the best they can be.

It is a sad state of affairs when our young people are seniors in high school, about to graduate and have no idea about their life careers or goals. Making life choices this late in life can be expensive, especially if they plan to go to college.

When students enter college and know what they want to study and what career they are planning for, less time will be spent in pursuit of their career goals. If a student is not sure, changes in majors take place and often more time is needed to complete a particular course of study. More time means more money to be spent on preparation. This expense is generally one born by parents, especially if they are not qualified for the grants and loans. Let us get 'in cinque' at home and at school and help our children to prepare for their futures as adults.

SCHOOL COMMERCIALS
First published September 1994

Well, it is that time again; 'Back to School!' Every hearing, seeing and thinking individual is made aware of this time by school district reminders, fliers and newspaper releases, but the most frequent reminders come through television 'Back to School Sales.'

Everybody who sells anything which is remotely connected to school in any fashion or form, can be found blaring out from any sized television, at all times of the day or night about necessities for going back to school. These attention getters usually start right after the 4th of July and before summer school is over.

Years ago, the commercials were aimed at the teenagers who are now parents. They were hooked by the time they graduated from high school on the commercials. Once the teenagers were hooked, the commercials were aimed at the grammar school aged youth. Now, the commercials are aimed at preschoolers. Preschool fashions shows and other types of exhibits are held to attract attention. Some adult or young adult has to take the preschoolers to these affairs. The cycle is complete. Everybody is hooked.

It is now time to get 'in cinque' and realize that how our children look on the first day or week of school and the name of the school gear that they have, is not nearly as important as the kind of ***attitude and disposition*** about learning that they carry to school with them.

HOME ECONOMICS IN PUBLIC SCHOOLS
First published October 1, 1994

Early academic curriculums in America almost always included a course in sewing and cooking or a combined class called Home Economics. All girls were required to take this course in general high schools. In technical high schools, it was optional. It was sequence choice in vocational schools.

Today, few schools offer Home Economics *per se*. Most offer a course called Home Management or Life Management Skills which are offered to boys as well as girls. Some schools offer a course exclusively for boys called Bachelor Arts.

The number of these courses being offered in schools now has dwindled to a precious few, with only one teacher making the offerings. This would appear to be a reflection on the importance of home and life management skills in our society today.

Students used to learn the mechanics of running a home and a family in the home economics classes. They also learned proper etiquette in the dining room and in the areas of daily life. They finished these classes with more personal confidence and self-esteem. Some students, including *moi,* never learned to sew or cook, but did learn about what the end product should look like and how to make appropriate choices about both the sewing and the cooking, making them more rounded individuals socially and academically. Most of the students who took one of these courses generally approached adulthood and its institutions with a more mature outlook. It is time for us to get 'in cinque' and offer the majority of our students some similar course where they will establish more self-esteem to aid them in life's daily occurrences.

ATHLETIC ACCELERATION
First published October 11, 2004

Throughout the nation, throughout the school year, students, school staff, parents and the general community are caught up in the athletic activities. As a matter of fact, many, sometimes too many, of the school's activities are centered on athletics.

There is a football team in most high and junior high schools as well as basketball, baseball and softball teams. The teams have a cheerleading squad and in many instances, a pep squad as well. This is a school activity of 'togetherness.' The entire school focuses on and cheers for the school's team. Often, the home team wins.

I often wonder why there are no cheerleaders and pep squads for academic winning? Where is the parent pep squad? Parents cheer at the ball games. Where are the cheers for the class activities? Where is the quiet place to study at home? Where are the encouraging words and pats and hugs and whoopee cheers to raise coursework grades and required test scores? What about the parent pep rally at school?

If our children are to excel academically as well as they do on the sports' fields, we must get 'in cinque' and have more overt cheering and pep activities for academia.

CRIME AND PASSION IN SCHOOL
First published November 11, 1994

In times like these when crime is rampant all over the country, each day poses new problems to be dealt with and overcome. Schools like municipalities must also deal with the criminal activities of the community which spill over into its corridors and classrooms. It is this element which is making it more difficult on a daily basis to find qualified public school teachers.

Mandates from state education agencies, local school boards, concerned parent groups, community organizations and student advocate groups put new constraints, higher expectations and stringent evaluations on teachers each year, while students experience improved quality and quantity education on a daily basis. Teachers are becoming more adept at what they do while many students do not CARE WHAT *THEY* DO.

As colleges and universities raise their standards for the educational curricula and some cases, require admittance examinations, and the number of students entering the field of education is far less than in the past. In addition, some of those admitted, do not pass the proper test to exit, cutting the number of educators down even more. At the same time, teachers are exiting the profession as fast as they can, cutting even more into the teaching force. SO, who WILL TEACH OUR CHILDREN in the future? Who will teach our HARD TO REACH HARD TO TEACH children? We need to get 'in cinque' and raise our children to be *teachable and reachable, **NOW!***

PREPARATION FOR SCHOOL
First published January 2, 1995

One writer has said that everything that he needed to know, he learned in kindergarten. I would be thrilled if I could hear someone say, "Everything that I need to know, I learned at home before I went to kindergarten."

If this sounds as though schools are not important, that is not the intention. Schools are designed to reinforce what is taught at home and elaborate upon the principles of humanity which make a peaceful, profitable and happy life possible.

It is the DUTY of parents to prepare their young ones to enter school and willingly abide by school rules. It is no accident when the same students show up in the office of the school principal week after week, day after day for disciplinary purposes. Parental contact in these instances is made and parents are very aware of the student's activities. In some instances there may even be a video of student activity giving an undeniable account of activity.

Students need to know before attending school that though school is designed for them and sometimes by them, it is their duty to follow rules and directions while in attendance.

In yesteryear, a student's behavior at school was often referred to as 'showing home training.' It is time that parents get 'in cinque' and get back to teaching some 'home training.' Students with 'home training' experience more success in school and in life in general than those students without any.

A TIME TO READ
First published February 23, 1995

Most children enter school with a desire to learn to read and write. They are receptive to new ideas and marvel at their progress in acquiring new knowledge. They are enthusiastic and that enthusiasm is fed by their teachers throughout the elementary years. Reading and its merits are lauded for six to eight years. In the meantime, students begin to spend more and more time watching television.

Once a child is addicted to television and the video games, they read less and less. Pretty soon, they find themselves in a situation wherein they do not want to get involved in any type of learning activity that involves reading. Reading becomes chore rather than a pleasure. Parents should set aside daily time for their children to read and use the television and video game time as a reward for reading well done.

Reading is junior high and in high school is mostly offered as a remedial course with the notion that good readers will be exposed to reading in their regular curriculum offerings. This is a true notion but if students can find a way to get around reading or a short cut to reading, they will do so rather than read. It is time that we get 'in cinque' and see to it that our children read and keep that reading enthusiasm alive throughout their school days.

SIDES OF THE BRAINS
First published March 1, 1995

For years, students attended school and teachers trained and untrained, and taught the three 'R's.' There was never a concern about which side of the brain children were learning from. BUT, progress prevailed.

It was the traditional to the modern methods of teaching, with the traditional being the basis of all learning, that formal education has prevailed. It has been from this same vein that the majority of our educators have come, and it is very difficult sometimes to teach 'old educators' new tricks, especially when they have been involved in a multiplicity of new methods which always carried them back to the old tried and true methods. Believe it or not, the LEFT brain HAS it. It always has!

We thank God for our right brains and perhaps the reason for it is to help us to lighten up after hard studying and to put a little 'zip' in our lives. That way, we can utilize our full brains and balance the mental and physical exercises. Our children certainly need the benefit of exercising all of their brains.

The right brain needs some opportunities to be utilized, but the left brain definitely needs to be in charge! Educators as well as parents need to get 'in cinque' and make sure they know what they are in for when they decide to set up schools to accommodate right brain activities without emphasizing left brain control.

13

Renetta T. Womack Howard

TOO MUCH, MUCH-A-DO ABOUT NOTHING
First published March 8, 1995

It is the desire of all communities to see to the young people getting a quality education. Somehow, as hard as educational systems try, there are always those students who are not successful in the system. These are the challenges of the system. Millions of dollars are spent annually to try to prevent the failures. There is usually a simple answer, often overlooked because it is not conventional or does not fit into the system.

In an effort not to discriminate against anyone, since we now live in a 'cause' oriented society, we often end up not giving any student this fair due. No student has a chance to work up to his potential because of the detractions of taking care of the inclusions and intrusions and delusions of what education is all about. We are so busy safeguarding identities and shortcomings, real and imagined, until education is about to become 'much-a-ado about nothing.'

Integration is ideal in every sense of the word if the grouping is homogeneous whether it is academic, physically or otherwise. We cannot make all students equal because some were born with more and some with less God-given talents than others. It is time that we get 'in cinque' and make quality accommodations for all of our students without fear of who is suing whom about where and what they learn.

PARENTAL SCHOOLS
First published April 14, 1995

There is a lot to be said for 'parental schools.' That is, the schools where disruptive students are sent for a short period of time when they have been removed from the regular school, yet too young to be excluded altogether and the district continues to fund their daily attendance. The school from whence the child was removed may feel a release of some of the tension brought on by the child's disruptive behavior. A first time offender may benefit from being placed in such a school for a short time. The second placement is usually a charm. A revolving door is put into action. The majority of these students become 'repeat offenders.' The revolving door syndrome should tell us something.

The removal from the regular school is but a respite for the regular school. The short stay at the parental school is only accomplishing time out for the regular program until the student returns and has time to do something else or the same thing again which landed him in the parental school in the first place.

A 'boot camp' type of program making the parents responsible for their child's behavior and adequate participation may be all some students need, but it may not be sufficient for those whom are placed in correctional institutions. It is time that we get 'in cinque' and ***discipline ineffective parents.*** Parents need training to be effective when they have failed their children too many times. Treating the symptom (the child) and not the malady (the parent), will not, in most instances cure the problem.

STUDENT DRESS CODE
First published August 8, 1995

As school commences throughout the United States, parents are busy making selections for school supplies and school clothing for their children. For some parents, there is not much choice of apparel because many school systems will be using uniforms this year.

Many schools are adopting the use of uniforms to help to curb various kinds of discrimination which lowers self-esteem. Included in the list of reasons to utilize uniforms is a means for elimination of teen gang dress modes.

Teen gang style dress has immensely influenced the way our teens and younger students dress. Students who are not gang-bangers have adopted the gang styles in hope of not being intimidated by gang members. In addition, peer pressure is very important when it comes to how students dress. One thing many parents may not be aware of is the fact that students do not have a great choice when it comes to daily wearing apparel. Most retail stores stock the big,' over-large' apparel which students prefer. They seldom have what we call conventional or tailored clothing, especially for boys, BUT, concerned parents can check out the stores which carry the kind of clothing which is acceptable to the conservative adult population, especially teachers, and select appropriate clothing for their children. Students will soon experience much more favorable situations in their learning environments when their dress reflects acceptable standards of behavior and thinking. Let us get 'in cinque' and help our children to 'dress for success.'

MINORITY MALE STUDENTS
First published September 10, 1995

It disturbs me to see our young minority male students sitting in class on a daily basis as they passively while away their time drawing pictures of marijuana or hemp, forty five magnum guns, gang symbols and their gang names as well as calling themselves 'playas; and /or 'pimp.' This is what can be seen on books, papers, *etc.* on which they should be doing their school assignments. They also wear jewelry portraying these things. The thing that is really disturbing is the fact that when these students are disciplined or chastised, you can see them doing the same thing the next day if not sooner.

What does this tell us about our minority male students? First of all, it says that the young minority male students are consumed with what seems to be gang activities or they are 'wannabes.' Secondly, it tells us that these students have no respect for law and order. Third, these students do not have their minds on academic affairs. Fourth, some type of de-programming counseling is needed for these students.

What can we do to help these minority male students? Plenty can be done, but it will be time-consuming and requires plenty of patience, and in some instances, money. First, parents need to tune in to what their sons are doing or want to do, and either be a good role model or a very persuasive teacher and counselor. Secondly, parents need to find out what their sons are doing at school **before** the school sends for them when they have done something wrong. Third, minority males need to know that they are **expected** to excel in all of their undertakings in the academic arena, not *just in sports*. Making a living at sports is mostly a pipe dream and vocations of substance should be their first line of pursuit. As a last resort, for the hard core, hard-to-turn-around minority males, efforts should be made to place them in institutions where they can learn the value of a regimented lifestyle where they are taught the value of hard work, its rewards and civility. This can cost money, but will be worth every penny in the final analysis. It will mean more to the child in the long run than detention centers, boot camps and schools of intervention which deal with a *part of the child.* They need 'whole child' treatments. It is time that we get 'in cinque' and spend tax dollars for this kind of institution rather than to continue to build places for punishment. Too often, punishment makes offenders become hardened criminals.

SKINNING THE DEAD CAT
First published December 5, 1995

The last person to knock learning more about various subjects to broaden ones horizon in the educational arena is me. However, when it comes to bringing about a change in a person's way of thinking and doing things in a few hours, one wonders if there is a saturation point, especially when one has been around the block enough times to know that there is more than one way to 'skin a cat,' but ultimately, you still have a dead cat.

One wonders why the teaching profession is losing teachers in record numbers and having a difficult time finding replacements. Many people speculate that the school populations, the students of the day are the reason why the teaching profession is being shunned. Others feel that discriminatory entrance and exit tests are responsible for a low number of prospective students entering the field of education. It is a fact that many individuals with degrees in some teaching area are not employed in the area of the degree because of failure to past the exit test. Then there are those who do not want to subject themselves to the scrutiny of one individual's opinion about their performance in the field, after years of study and preparation with master degrees.

On the other hand, there are those leaving the profession because of some of the same reasons that others do not enter the profession. Some teachers have decided that they did not want to watch another child make a mockery of education. Others long to put that last 'in service' behind them and still others want to kiss that annual, usual less than an hour, crucial performance evaluation good-bye. We need to get 'in cinque' and decide as communities and representative members of groups with a stake in education, exactly what is needed to provide our youth, the adults of tomorrow, with quality education and stop 'skinning the same dead cat!'

Renetta T. Womack Howard

LISTEN TO THE CHILDREN
First published February lm 1996

A few weeks ago, the classes which I teach, had the opportunity to view a video which was made in the Harlem community of New York City, showcasing the lives of nine minority young people, who had, in spite of adversities; criminal, social, financial, spiritual and academic, overcome them to lead constructive, positive and productive lives.

Following the film, I had my classes to write about their feelings on the film and what steps they thought could be instituted in our city to keep our youth focused on the kind of goals which would lead them to college, a career, home ownership and better lives for themselves and their children. They were to give me three reasons why steps could or could not be taken to make change and elaborate upon their reasons.

Of all the reasons given in the papers, there was one particular reason in every paper whether it was *pro* or con. *Every student* felt that the greatest obstacle to overcoming adversities was ***parents.*** They said that they either got support from their parents to help stay focused because they were expected to do well or that they did not get any support from their parents, who they felt were not good role models or did not *care* what they did.

Students who felt that their parents supported them expected even more guidance and support. These same students felt that all parents should care more about their children. Those who felt that their own parents did not care about them were the ones who saw no way to overcome adversities. They felt hopeless; that even if they got an education that they would still have a 'hard way to go.' They saw no need to try to learn anything because none of the world's scarce resources would and could not ever be theirs, so why try? Their parents, with little concern for their welfare were doing nothing constructive, so why should they? This theme of apathy was present throughout the papers.

Many sources today, say "we can't blame parents for this...that ...or another,' and place it somewhere else in regards to our children's lack of progress. It is time that we get 'in cinque' and listen to the children! They *KNOW* what is affecting their progress, or lack of it.

TECHNOLOGY IN SCHOOL
First Published March 6, 1996

Our society is becoming more complex with each passing day and with each new bit of technology which is introduced into society. Technology has thrust us into a world community of international knowledge and problems. Many of us still confine ourselves to our *own little world* in our local neighborhoods. 'On line' means standing on a line; 'internet' means one net within another; 'a byte' is 'bite' spelled in 'new speak;' a 'mouse' is that little animal for which we bought a trap last week. "Keyboards' used to be found on pianos, organs and typewriters. They are all obsolete now. Only the keyboard is important. Synthesizers do the job in the hundredth of the space previously allotted to the aforementioned mechanisms. Some people even believe they are more efficient. Time will tell.

As important as technology is and as dangerous as it can be, in the wrong hand, 'hackers,' it behooves us all to find out as much as we can about it. Too many of us are not aware of the dangers lurking in all of the new technology. We need to know. There are schools where we can learn.

Too many students leave school each day about as unlearned as they were upon entry. It is not until they try to find employment that they find out that, "They *don't know nothing!*"They have spent time in school being the best 'hip hopper' or 'gangbanger,' not a good student. Consequently, no job is forthcoming. The moment of truth then arrives. One must decide to **GO BACK TO SCHOOL** and learn what was missed or take the low road to crime.

It is time that *'the whole village'* get 'in cinque' to keep our young people in school, being a part of the world of technology, and encourage our OLDER PEOPLE to also return to school in order to become and remain productive citizens in today's society.

PARENT ACCOUNTABILITY
First published September 10, 1996

There are parents and then there are *parents*. There are teachers and then there are *teachers*. There are parents who want their children to achieve maximum benefits from attending school and cooperate with the school to insure that their children obtain maximum benefits. Then there are parents who fight the school on every turn and corner. They feel that teachers are not qualified to teach and schools are not good enough for their children, but they refuse to pay for a private education or are not qualified to start their own school. These are the 'nitpickers.' They are also a part of the reason why so many teachers are leaving the field of education and not being replaced rapidly enough for the so-called 'baby-boomer echo.'

'Nitpicking' turns many teachers off the educational wave-length and cause early burnout. Early burnout results in early retirement or exodus from education. Most school systems do not have to make early retirement attractive for some teachers, as all many want is an early 'out' without financial penalty.

Accountability for education has fallen on every entity which has a stake in education except parents. It is time that parents become accountable for their children's education. They need to be accountable for teaching their children to be teachable. Until students are teachable, schools are nothing more than daily holding facilities. It is time to get 'in cinque' and see to it that parents are accountable for their children's education and put 'nitpicking' to rest.

'THE CRAZY CHECK'
First published November 20 1996

Ever since Congress passed laws in which money was appropriated to assist in the education of the mentally handicapped, especially the educable mentally handicapped, it has been a fact of life. Schools with EMH classes received federal funds for school supplies and funds to train and pay teachers in addition to what the local entity provided. The EMH classroom had state of the art equipment which was just not available to the regular classroom student or teacher. The money earmarked for these classes had to be spent on these classes or be lost. Misuse of these funds could constitute an act which could be interpreted as a federal offense. Consequently, the money and the items purchased with the money were carefully scrutinized, inventoried and monitored.

The 'so-called' title I schools still receive federal funds to defray the cost of an education for the economically disadvantaged as well as the mentally undeveloped or handicapped students, though in many school districts, these students are no longer mainstreamed but included in the regular classroom to some degree. These students, especially the mentally handicapped or so identified students, get their big reward at home in what has now been dubbed the 'Crazy Check.'

These "Crazy Checks' are sent to the parents of the child, some from birth, to help defray the child's living expenses. If a doctor says that the child is eligible for SSI or federal welfare for the aged, blind and disabled who do not qualify for Social Security benefits, then they can get the 'Crazy Check.' SSI is the abbreviation for Supplemental Security Income which is administered by the Social Security Administration but not paid from Social Security Taxes, but supposedly, from general revenue. Unlike Social Security payments, one does not have to have worked to qualify. In addition, eligibility for SSI can make one eligible for free medical care or Medicaid, the food stamp program and certain social services. In addition, you can keep your car and house without encumbrances.

We need to get 'in cinque and find out what the full ramifications of the 'Crazy Check' is going to be, especially in light of the fact that all welfare is being scaled down. What will it mean for higher education?

USING STANDARD ENGLISH LANGUAGE
First published July 8, 1997

He says, *"Whodat is?"* Then, she says, *"O dat jest my baby daddy."* Then he says, *"Cut out da dram, um going to see my baby mama."* The dialogue continues in such a manner, repeatedly saying, *"O dat jest my baby daddy,"* using a variety of voice inflections to get the point over. These are the lyrics to a popular 'song' which can be heard on the radio of most stations which play pop, rock, soul and rap music.

Sit, walk, stand and be in the path of the boom-box cars, registering about 7.5 on the Richter scale or travel yourself, down a street where there are teenagers sitting on a porch or standing on a corner and you may hear this 'song.' The average student in any class can recite the words along with the artists' and not miss a beat. Yet, that same student cannot memorize the

"Preamble to the Constitution of the United States," or any other academic endeavor assigned by a teacher.

There is a reason why children cannot memorize or learn academic endeavors as teachers and schools feel and want them to. The main reason is because they *do not want to do what is* expected *of them. It has **no meaning for them.*** No one, especially their parents have explained to them why it is important that they speak Standard English and put forth some effort to understand those things that are needed for living, learning, and earning in today's fast-paced society. Ebonics may be great for teenage comradeship but it is not needed in the classroom. The average teacher understands Ebonics and the process of translating this 'language' and any other dialect into Standard English. The so-called W.A.S.P. (White Anglo Saxon Protestants) students also need to have their grammar corrected. If their use of the language and their understanding of the language was perfect, the course would not be offered in the public school or any other attended by W.A.S.P. students, or they would not be required to take the course. This is not the case.

We need to get 'in cinque' and make our children aware of the need to **study and master Standard English.** The world of work revolves around the English language in the United States, spoken in standard terms by everyone.

"WHO IS THE TEACHER?"
First published July 18, 1997

There is a controversy going on about whether school integration has been or still is a worthwhile thing for Black students. One of the reasons for this controversy is the facts that as schools strive to improve test scores that the majority of all minority students appear to be making progress except Black students. With all of the federal chapter funding programs, the **Reading scores of Blacks,** especially, ***have not risen.*** Dr. Granerio from the Equity Center in Florida made this statement on July 15, 1997 as he lectured to a group of teachers taking his course in a Reading Institute.

Based on the premise that Dr. Granerio's theory is correct, what assumptions can educators and parents make from this? The first thing that came to my mind was the fact that Black students are not getting any one-on-one help where and when needed. The second notion that entered my mind was that Black students are not getting encouragement and support from home, and the third idea was that there are not enough Black teachers to teach Black children. The more I thought about it, the more I decided that all three of these assumptions are probably true and may be characteristic of many Black students. These three variables may very well determine how well a Black child learns. It may all rest on **_Who is the teacher?_**

We are aware that too many Black children feel inferior to White teachers or minorities who look White. Based on this knowledge, Black children are slow to ask questions for fear of being called or treated as though they were dumb, when their question might very well have to do with some aspect of their learning which bridges a cultural, social or racial gap and help learning to proceed. Such a gap not bridged could bring learning to a standstill or cause it to lag, showing up on the test report as a lack of progress. Truly, it is a lack of progress.

When schools were not 'integrated,' Black teachers, many with a minimum amount of education, taught Black children and they *progressed*. What has changed? We have more educated Black teachers so what is the problem? We must get 'in cinque' and solve the problem. (To be continued.)

"WHO IS THE TEACHER?" PART 2
First published July, 1997

What has changed the learning abilities and patterns of Black students since the days of integration? It is a common theory that Black children are not learning to read at the same rate as other children in the American school systems. There are isolated cases of tremendous progress of Black children when they have intensive teaching, often one-on-one teaching by Black teachers. Is there a correlation between the progress of Black children and *who is the teacher?* Do Black children in any integrated setting learn better from Black teachers? Do White children learn better from White teachers? What makes the difference?

From my observation of the school systems in which I have worked, in three states, I have noticed concerted efforts on the part of White teachers to have the most apt Black students placed in their classes along with as many White students as they can possibly accommodate. Consequently, the Black teachers are assigned the less capable students of all ethnic groups. There is seldom any homogeneity in these assignments, placing a tremendous task upon the shoulders of teachers often less experienced and educated than their White counterparts. What are the results? The students with the White teachers show progress which would have been manifested regardless to where they had been placed because these are the students who progress *in spite of the teacher!* Unless the less capable students lucked upon an experienced, caring teacher progress is minimum at best.

On the other hand, it is a common consensus that Black teachers just do not know as much as White teachers. They can attend the same school, same classes, same graduation and same job and when White parents have the opportunity to choose the teacher for their students, they will choose the White teacher. Too often, the Black parent does the same thing. This boils down to racism. Who is the teacher?

The notion that Black teachers are not as qualified as White teachers has a lot to do with how well Black children are learning. If the children come from a home where that notion prevails, the children still will not learn as well as they should. They will sit in a classroom with a Black teacher, longing to be with a White teacher and feeling that their counterparts with White Teachers are learning more than they are. Because of this notion of teacher inferiority, the student who believes this, can sit in the classroom of a do-nothing White teacher and feel blessed. This is the kind of parental support which he has received and it can help or hamper his progress. His learning mode was established at home. If integration is to work, we must get 'in cinque' and take racism out of the mix. (To be continued, Part 3.)

"WHO IS THE TEACHER?" PART 3
First published July, 1997

It is clear to many and very vague and uncertain to others in America that school integration has not and is not doing what it should do to help minority students progress. I have concluded that racism is the big factor in the lack of progress. One instance of racism was revealed to me by a Black teacher in a state where the National Teachers Examination is required as a means of securing a license to teach, that she had taken the examination at a predominately White university in order to pass the examination. She stated that she passed though there were too many questions which she knew that she did not know the answers, but passed anyway because the school would/could not afford too many failures on their records. She explained that had she taken the test at a predominately Black university that she would have failed. (As I listened to her usage of the English language, I could understand why she felt that way.) She may be a great teacher and felt comfortable using Ebonics when speaking with me.

In most schools, regardless to the student population, most teachers are **not _Black_.** More Black teachers are needed to teach Black children. Black teachers **DO** understand Black students better on the social and economic ladder, regardless of opportunities on each, *has not changed that much.* Sure, there are great business owners, talk show hostesses, million-dollar sports figures; a few rich and well-to-do Blacks in all walks of life. *And* there always have been some around. They just were not in the national media as often as they are now, but they were in the Black media.

In many neighborhoods, White families move out when 'too many' Blacks move in. This causes a shift in the school population. The White teachers, who can, transfer out also. Those who cannot successfully transfer often stay and do little to teach the minorities. They come, collect a check and often return to the suburbs and students are none the wiser. Some Black teachers are also guilty of the same thing. Integration put them into 'another world.'

Black teachers are systematically tested *out* of educational programs and teaching jobs. There is no wonder that most substitute teachers are Black in some school systems. Some may be rightfully excluded, but a closer look at testing of teachers needs to be made on every level. Are tests for teachers geared to the White middle class? Are Black teachers missing some life experiences which would render them more test-worthy? Should tests determine who is the teacher? We need to get 'in cinque, experiment and plan to have more Black teachers in our schools; eliminate racism and have parental support for **all teachers in all schools.**

TEACHERS NEED RAISES
First published March 4, 1998

It is continuously amazing that every 'politically correct' organization which has or feels that it has a stake in education, cannot see why teachers, especially public school teachers should not be paid more for their services. Every profession, even fortune tellers, go through some type of training program to enter their craft. In every walk of life, there has been a teacher somewhere along the way. Yet, teachers are the lowest paid professionals in the United States and there does not seem to be any positive changes taking place in the future.

The professionals whose services teachers need do not give teachers any special discount because they are underpaid. The dentist charges for a cleaning of your teeth cost approximately one hundred and sixty dollars. If you break a tooth or want one replaced, you are facing a charge of about five hundred dollars per tooth. The average teacher has to work a whole week to pay for that one tooth. If the teacher has dental insurance, there is a certainty that the policy has a 'missing tooth clause' and will not pay for the services.

Get sick. Go to the doctor. You have insurance. Great! **But,** you have a five hundred dollar deductible. That is, you must dig down into your pocket for the five hundred dollars before the insurance will pay a token. Of course, it does not take long to meet your deductible, because your first visit to any doctor may cost well at or above one hundred dollars. Subsequent visits range anywhere from thirty-five to sixty dollars per visit. Plan to spend seventy-five dollars or more for any kind of physical test deemed necessary by your doctor.

The lawyer charges about sixty dollars per hour for his service and rarely is there a case which consumes less than four hours. In instances where you are assisted in securing sums of money for any reason, the fee is usually one third of your receipt.

That loaf of bread, rib eye steak, Grey Poupon, Bibb lettuce, artichoke, and aged dinner wine costs the teacher the same price that the doctor, dentist, and lawyer, pay for it. The teacher has to sacrifice to buy this kind of grocery, while the doctor, dentist, and lawyer can afford to have guest for dinner. It is time that we get 'in cinque' and pay teachers, even when we do not respect them. Unlike the other professionals mentioned, when they leave the job at the end of the day, they take the work home.

INTEGRATION
First published April 20, 1998

As we approach the year 2000, which many like to refer to as the next millennium or one thousand years, it is becoming more apparent each day, that public schools may become a thing of the *past*. There are many factors which point to this. One is integration.

Integration in many, possible most locales are but a farce. In instances where the courts have ordered racial desegregation of public schools, the end result has been that the once 'white only' public schools are **now all Black.** The percentage of White students who remain in these schools is negligible. The other aspect of this factor is that most of the public school teachers are White.

There is really no problem with White teachers teaching Black children *per se* but for most, the approach to teaching is different when the child is Black. The most gifted Black child scoring in the 99th percentile on the Iowa Test of Basic Skills in every area, is seen as a 'gifted child' capable of learning and understanding all that one has to teach or be constructively exposed to, but as a 'smart Black child.' There is a difference in being smart and being gifted!

There are educational programs for gifted children in just about every school district in the nation which prides itself in its curriculum. *But,* look at the participants! What kind of test for a gifted program cannot be passed by a child with an IQ or Stanine in the 99th percentile? Is the hindrance the test or the tester? If schools are not able to accommodate the Black gifted child on the same playing field in a public school as his White counterpart, we need to get 'in cinque' and re-evaluate the public school as we know it. Will it be a necessity in the year 2000?

Renetta T. Womack Howard

TEACHER APPRECIATION
First published June 27, 1998

I have received many verbal and written 'thank you's' and notes of appreciation from students whom I have taught, but the letter which I received just a few days ago from a sixth grader, just sums up so much of what I have labored so diligently to get over to my students on every level:

> Dear Mrs. Howard,
>
> Hi! How are you? I'm fine. I hope you're having a good summer vacation. It was nice being in your classroom this year. I learned a lot of things from you. Now I know why you pushed us so far to learn everything we could to become successful people when we're older. I also learned that the more things you know about the world, the better off you'll be
>
> I just found out that we really do have to set examples for younger kids, like I did Wednesday morning for getting all of those certificates. The kids like us are future congress leaders, governors, presidents, and directors, because we try to get our education in schools from teachers who really care about students becoming successful. Thanks for teaching me all that I know now. Bye.
>
> Sincerely, (Signed) Raquele
>
> P.S. - You were a wonderful teacher.

A better reward, I could ask for? Schools recognize, reward and give special citations to teachers each year, but recognition from students who realize how the educational process has affected them is one of the greatest rewards a teacher can have. It would be most pleasing to see all educators get 'in cinque' and help our children to realize the importance of the reality of schools.

SHORTAGE OF PUBLIC SCHOOL TEACHERS: PART I
First published October 2, 1998

There is a shortage of public school teachers in many school districts and the rumor is that is a nationwide shortage. This should not have come as a surprise to anyone. There are a number of reasons for a teacher shortage: low pay, stringent qualifications for academic education as well as testing requirements for certification, misplaced accountability, legislative funding, political issues, top-heavy administrations, and teacher-pupil ratio inequity.

Low pay has not kept a lot of teachers out of the field. If that were the case, the shortage would be much more widely spread than it is. Teachers are the *only* profession which requires much academic preparation and offers no financial compensation for the preparation. Doctors, dentist, lawyers, accountants, social workers, nurses earn more money than teachers in any year. Professional athletes who ***drop out of school,*** some unable to utter a simple sentence correctly, earn more in one year, (the same season) than teachers earn in five years. Why not play something?

In order to have fewer minority teachers, requirements for entering the field of education were made more stringent, eliminating many potential teachers of all ethnic groups. Many of those were able to work their way through the academic maze, found an obstacle in the certification process. They were unable to pass the required national, state or local tests. This has caused fraud in the test-taking procedures in some locals. Some people just do not test well, yet they are great teachers. While on the other hand, some test very well but *cannot or do not do* a very good job of teaching.

The most probable reason why there is a teacher shortage is due to misplaced accountability. Teachers have been made accountable if students do not learn. One must be able to teach children in order for them to learn. Children who are teachable are rare in these days. If they think that they know everything, they are not interested in learning anything in school. It is boring, they say. So, it is difficult to get their attention. They do not see the need for what takes place in the classroom. If it does not come from the TV or a computer ***game,*** they are not interested. This frame of mind is not an accident.

The frame of mind that our children have today is brought from home

29

with them to the classroom in the early grades. It becomes stronger anti-school as they grow and become older. The anti-school attitude is learned at home; a home where learning and education has no value. It had no value for the child's parents and therefore it has none for him. The greatest value of school is the *'free babysitting'* five days a week which permits parents to keep an eight to five workday or play day, unencumbered. If the child learns anything at school, it is purely an accident. He will have put forth little effort with low expectations and actually feel good that he has learned anything at all. It is time that we get 'in cinque' and make changes in accountability and put it where it belongs; at **HOME!**

PUBLIC SCHOOL TEACHER SHORTAGE: PART 2
First published October 8, 1998

One of the greatest drawbacks to public schools is the funding by the various state legislatures. Schools come in for allocations after appropriate funds are allocated for local jails and county and state prisons. If the money were put into lowering class sizes to a teachable number rather than deciding arbitrarily that 25 or 22 is a good number and decide that the classes of today should contain 15 to 20 teachable children rather than herding 22 to 25 into classes where few if any *really* learn something. The money would be well spent.

If enough money is spent per child to allow teachers to have a decent salary, the teacher turnover would not be so great. This coupled with small class sizes, would permit a teacher to do a wonderful job of teaching and actually see the progress made by students who will learn because they have an environment which permits the greatest achievement.

If students have the opportunity to achieve, they will achieve sometimes in spite of the situation. However, there are students who feel the need for non-traditional teaching and learning. Small class sizes will decrease off-task behavior and promote learning. If the students learn in such a manner as to become good citizens, the jails will be empty. Funding the schools is the proper course to take. More money on schools will mean less money on jails in the future. As it is now, it would appear that schools are designed to fail while jails grow larger and larger. Similar to the movement for businesses to privately run public schools, there is one on foot also to privately run jails. Both use the tactic to make it look profitable to the consumer to be there. They both purport to have a fail proof treatment plan. The end result is often the same. The way they handle and arrive at the resulting data is different. They set criterion which they know that they can meet, regardless to whom they have doing the job. There are instances where there are too many individuals doing the jobs.

Often, if a few administrators are pulled out of the main offices and put on the front line, where the children are, more could be accomplished. If there are a sufficient number of individuals 'pushing papers' at the ground floor, where the children are, and a computer could handle much of the paper work at the top. More administrators are need on the 'battlefield,' not in the neat little cubby-holes, apart from the daily action in the various schools. Administrators are needed to find out exactly what business and the rest of the world of work expects form the graduates of public schools, and then put those expectations into meaningful curriculum plans. This is the real test that our children will pass or fail. It is time that we get 'in cinque' and compensate teachers and children with more pay, better teaching results, smaller classes, better school funding without politics, parental accountability and fewer administrators at the top.

BASIC SOCIAL SKILLLS TAUGHT AT HOME
First published January 15, 1999

One has to wonder about where we are really going as we enter the twenty-first century, new millennium or Y2K. We have seen the onslaught and perpetuation of many new and innovative ideas as well as those that haunt us as we approach the year 2000. Many of us approach it with some trepidation while others have a 'roll with the punches attitude' about everything.

I see a problem of 'rolling with the punches' of *harassment.* There is plain ole *harassment,* usually connected to the workplace, and there is *sexual harassment,* also connected to the workplace. It is difficult to come up with clear-cut evidence of either unless a 'sting' is involved. *Harassment* has left its niche in the workplace. Parents are suing schools alleging that schools are responsible for student to student harassment.

Students are children in grades throughout most of their public school years. There are a few who manage to hang around until they are 21 years of age, but they are the exception. They are also referred to as 'minors.' Being 'minors,' mean that they are under legal age and are in a position to 'mind' someone, usually an adult in charge. When students harass each other, it simply means that a minor is *not minding.* One child harassing another is nothing more than a means to get a child involved in fisticuffs. Children have done this for years and it is natural. Parents know this because they have a tremendous job *in their homes* trying to avoid sibling harassment and actual fights. The number of children in the home is also limited, whereas in the school, classrooms are made up of many families.

Teachers attempt to teach all of the children in a given class how to get along without harassment. Teachers discipline children within the limits of the law. Children ***need to be taught at home,*** before they get to the school, how to get along with others.

Too much blame and responsibility is placed upon schools. Children are home with their parents for five to six years before they enter school. It is during these years, the formative years, that basic social skills should be taught in order to prepare children for school and ***Life!*** Let us get 'in cinque' and commence to 'do the right thing' in Y2K.

AMERICAN TEXBOOKS AND CULTURAL LAG
First published July 23, 2002

With forty-two years of employment behind me and the utilization of two master's degrees in my cap, it was upon retiring from the world of work and the decision to treat myself to a couple of week of rest and relaxation, that I learned something new. I learned firsthand, the kind of information that you cannot get in a classroom. The first thing that I learned was that our textbooks in Social Studies, especially those dealing with world and European history, need to be revised.

The revisions need to be made by someone who has current knowledge of the countries studied from firsthand experiences, using primary rather than secondary sources. Furthermore, it would not hurt if teachers of Social Studies also had some firsthand experiences regarding the area in which they taught. This is not only true for History, Geography, Political Science and Sociology, but for Economics as well, especially during these times of mega-company bankruptcies and the declining value of the dollar. It takes more U.S. dollars to equal the value of other countries' currencies these day, ranging from $$1.04 to $1.20 in some countries. Everyone is capitalizing. In many European countries, the median salary is about $4000.00 per month. The working people own their home, usually a condominium, a couple of cars, a bicycle and a boat.

Capitalism is the current form of economics in most European countries these days, even countries once considered 'behind the iron curtain.' Business as usual is capitalism, but some still have socialized medicine and free education. It rings of something that the United States should begin to look into as there are all kinds of schemes in the works for Social Security and Medicare and the PPOs (Primary Physicians Options) and HMOs (health Management Options) are the pits for the most of us. At best, you spend as much for the insurance as the services are worth in the first place.

Our past first lady, Mrs. Hillary Clinton, tried to help this country institute some form of national health insurance, but it was 'blown out of the water!' Various states are working to try to have health insurance for all children in the state, which is good, but will this initiative be graduated to all of the adults in the various states?

Most doctors and health care workers would like to keep medical expenses sky high in order to garner high salaries and get to Club Med from time to time in addition to living like the 'rich and famous' already. They are pushing for tort reform in some states for that same reason, as most of them can more than afford the malpractice insurance they gripe about. They need to realize that lives and the quality of life are more important than money. As a matter of fact, it is time that we all get 'in cinque' and realize that the countries which have been ravished by world wars are moving at a supersonic speed to be modern main players in today's world and that our country needs to get busy removing the obstacles that are making us stagnant.

POLLUTION AND LEARNING DISABILITIES
First published April 5, 2003

Everyone is aware that efforts have been made to reduce the level of pollution in the United States. Of the many new occurrences present in this country which was not apparent in earlier times, pollution is the one steady variable. It seems apparent to anyone who takes the time to observe, that with the advent of pollution and its increase from various sources that certain diseases in this country are on the increase as well. The irony is that the occurrence of the diseases which may or may not be related to pollution is affecting greater segments of our population every day. There does not appear to be any known cause of Attention Deficit Disorder, the high incidence of diabetes and uncontrollably high cholesterol. There may be other variables that add to the increase in these ailments, but the high correlation with pollution needs to be explored. As a start, let us delve into Attention Deficit Disorder.

About thirty-seven years ago, many educators were introduced for the first time to the study of the activities of the kinesthetic child; the one who could not be still, be quiet or concentrate on anything for a long period of time; the child who appeared to be driven by a strong force which he could not control. It was felt that this was a physical problem which was in some way related to one's nerve. Later, it was called Attention Deficit Disorder or ADD.

Nerves or synapses seem to figure in the definition of Attention Deficit Disorder and hyperactivity, which was once given the name 'kinesthetic child.' The common term used for this disorder is ADD, ADDH or HADD. Medical experts have decided that the brain failed to develop a general for the electrical impulses which are transferred from one nerve to the other. Therefore, chemical drugs have been used to help to give directions to the nerves and help the victim of this disorder to function as a normal individual instead of one who cannot concentrate, be still or make split decisions without thought to the consequences.

Prior to the attention given pollution, the only attention deficit we knew about was when children ***did not get enough attention.*** It was at these times when they were prone to 'act out' and make their parents take notice to their behavior. We know that pollution, especially second-hand smoke is responsible for many diseases of the lung and consequently death. We need to know if pollution has a role in the conception, gestation and birth of babies which causes so many of the diseases that we DO KNOW about. It is time that we get 'in cinque' and do more extensive research on the extent of the adverse effects of pollution on the human body.

"NO CHILD LEFT BEHIND"
First published September 1, 2003

The new national law, "Leave No Child Behind," mandates that schools in the United States put in place, educational programs that guarantee that no child is left behind in the learning process. Schools are being rated on the success of individual groups of students. When a school fails to measure up, it will be put on a list of low performing schools or what will be known as priority schools.

There will be consequences for being cited as a low performing school. Teachers can be dismissed and so can principals. Superintendents and school board members will also be under fire. This could become a very explosive situation, especially if there are personality conflicts in the arena. "Heads will roll' will probably become a very commonplace saying.

For years now, state and local school systems have been busy trying to bring programs into play which enhances student achievement. California led the way with its California Test in the early seventies to measure the achievements of its public school students in order to determine if they were on target with what they were expected to know when they finished high school. Soon afterwards, Chicago Public Schools initiated the Chicago Test.

The Chicago Test was designed to determine if its seniors were qualified to graduate from high school. They were tested during their junior year. Any student who failed the test had to take a remediation course which covered basic mathematics, reading and social studies. A social studies credit was given for the course if the student passed. If the student passed the test in the course, he had satisfied the requirement for passing the Chicago Test and would be permitted to graduate as long as he satisfied all of the other requirements for graduation.

In its quest to educate students, Texas has implemented several tests to insure that its graduates from high school were capable and ready to graduate, the more recent version being more difficult than the previous two. School ratings and teacher pay are both based on the school and teacher performances.

We know for a fact that all children are ***not born equal.*** Some have a higher l.Q. than others and will naturally perform better than others on all levels. For this reason, we know that some children ***will be left behind.*** Therefore, it is time that we get 'in cinque' and take necessary steps, as parents, teachers and concerned citizens to insure that no child is left behind. We need to stop 'playing school' and really be accountable for roles we have in educating our children. Every stakeholder needs to make every effort to do his part.

NEEDED: QUALIFIED TEACHERS!
First published May 18, 2004

Fifty years ago, in 1954, the United States Supreme Court handed down a landmark decision designed to end racial segregation in the public schools of America. The many cases from various states were made into a class action suit in the name of the plaintiff whose name began with a 'b', first on the list in alphabetical order. *Linda Brown verses The Board of Education of Topeka, Kansas* was the name of that case.

Today, some of us wonder if the case has been fruitful in bringing about the integration of public education, racially, as it was designed to do. During the days of mandatory bussing to achieve integration, there were some positive aspects for many students of all races. There were downsides as well. Ironically, many of the negative aspects remain. Public school is offered to all, regardless of skin color, but the quality of education in the public schools is still NOT EQUAL. Many people interpreted the decision to apply to all areas of life in America though it pertained to education. An equal education al opportunity could have eventually led to equality overall, but it still has not happened. The *Ayers* Case is a point in fact.

Jake Ayers, Jr. brought a suit against the state of Mississippi to dismantle the *dejure* segregation system of the Mississippi State colleges. Such a provision would have made it less difficult for Black students to enter the all-White universities and would have provided more funding to the historically Black universities.

Students in the schools, especially in states where integration was not gleefully accepted, are basically populated by African Americans. The few students of other races who attend public school are basically those students who parents cannot afford to send them to a private school.

Private schools also have the teachers who can afford to live on a salary smaller than that offered to teachers in public schools. They often employ teachers who have not been certified by the required examinations as well. Many of these teachers, however, are able to function better in a situation where the number of students is much smaller and conditions are ideal and conducive for learning, again proving that Faculty/Staff cliques have grown making it impossible to really understand and evaluate good teaching. Consequently, non-clique teachers lost in the job market.

There is improvement in education and race relations, but far from the ideal hoped for fifty years ago. Black Americans are still on the bottom rung of the ladder of success in society in every area except crime. Seldom is an African American involved in crime involving great sums of money. When they are, it is the 'crime of the century.'

Students in the public schools would have much more fruitful attendance years if adequate funds were made available for their education. Classes are too large and students are too difficult to discipline. Too many parents are difficult because equality in public schools in essence, quickly spread to all aspects of life for people of color and they quickly began to assert themselves about what they wanted for their children without adequate knowledge of the mechanics of education.

White parents went to school in droves to be room mothers and formed strong PTA's to watch what happened to their children because they lost the trust which they previously had in all-white public schools. They did not feel that Black teachers were qualified to teach their children and in some instances they were right. In that same vein, there were White teachers who were not qualified to teach Black children and some still are not, though they make up the majority of public school teachers in many school districts with only Black students. Therefore, we need to get 'in cinque' and put more trust and money and *qualified teachers* in our schools and help our children to grow academically regardless of their race or country of origin.

II-GOVERNMENT AND THE ECONOMY

WELFARE REFORM
First Published September 17, 1996

A welfare reform bill has been passed by Congress and signed by President Clinton. This new bill limits the time that families and individuals can receive welfare benefits. It also requires states to put a certain number of these recipients to work over an extended period of time **or lose some of the block grant money meted out to states each year.**

Finally, everyone who has felt that there were too many people on welfare, feel good. Sadly, too many people on welfare know that this is _not true_. The first reason being that _there are not enough jobs to go around_. Secondly, if there were or will be enough jobs, most welfare recipients who are able-bodied will need training or re-training to be employable. Thirdly, other recipients are either unable to work or too young to work.

The too young to work are our children of all ages who because they receive welfare benefits of some kind, also receive free breakfast and lunch at school each day during the school year. For some children, these are the _only_ meals which they receive during the day. Denial of benefits should not be categorical.

On the other hand, there are a number of welfare fraud cases. Every effort should be made to remove these cases from the welfare rolls. Ironically, these cheaters do not profit as well as thought, because they have to hide and cover everything that they do. This can be frustrating and hard work. They face criminal charges _when caught._ These are federal charges because federal money is involved.

Because the time has come for communities to *'put-up or shut-up,'* it is time for us to get 'in cinque' as individuals, community organizations and businesses to make families viable and self-supporting again. Stronger families will put an end to much of the crime we face today.

WISE BANKING BUSINESS
First published October 8, 1996

I have never been known as a financial expert or a mathematician, but through life's experiences, I have found that there are too many adults who are not aware of many minute maneuvers which deal with everyday finances. One much overlooked maneuver is the little situation where you borrow your own money at a low rate from your financial institution.

Most people save money and many save in the form of a certificate of deposit wherein you put a specified amount of money in the bank for a specified period of time at a specified rate of interest. If the money is withdrawn from the bank before the specified period of deposit, a financial penalty is levied. Though your money is tied up, so to speak, you can borrow on it. Generally, you can borrow an amount which equals your deposit on it. The interest rate that you pay on your loan is about two percent higher than the interest that you earn on your CD. Your loan payment is usually a one-time payment, due at the end of the loan period. *You can still save money on the loan.* Instead of making payments to the loan institution each month, put the payments in a savings account and earn interest on your payment deposits. When the loan payment is due, you will have earned interest on your money in the savings account and on the CD which may cancel out the interest on the loan.

Another profitable angle on CDs is to get a variable rather than a fixed interest rate. The variable rate is tied to the Federal T-Bill and the interest earned is only a few points lower but goes up or down with the T-Bill and is usually higher than the fixed rate. Let us get 'in cinque' and make our money work for us and insure our families a 'good life.'

COMPUTERS: SIMPLE AND COMPLEX
First published November 11, 1997

It is becoming more evident every day that, we *must* learn to live with the computer in the twenty-first century. There does not seem to be any way around it no matter how much we try to avoid it. Just about everything that we do in a day's time is somehow involved with some type of computer.

Most of us get up to some type of alarm. Very few of us use an alarm today which is purely an alarm. We have radios that we can set to alarm at two or more times during a twenty-four hour period. They may beep, buzz, play music or just play the radio. Then we proceed to the bathroom to brush our teeth with the electric or electronic tooth gadget. Many of us bathe in our Jacuzzi which is no ordinary bathtub. By the time that we are dressed, we go into our kitchens and zip out a quick breakfast with the coffee maker which we programmed before we went to bed last night and put a few other items like bacon and maybe some grits or other quick cereal into the microwave oven and in a matter of minutes, we are eating breakfast. By now, that beeper watch on our arm is telling us that it is time to punch the remote control to take the burglar alarm off our car so we can get started and on our way to our job.

Many of us arrive at a parking building, tailor made just for employees. We drive into the gateway and slip our parking 1.0. ticket into a box which tells us that it is 0.K. for us to enter and park. We enter the workplace, often with an electronic key and then if our job does not call for us to use a computer all day, we still need the services rendered by the computer at some time during the workday.

When the workday is over, we reverse our operations and often take a few moments at home to watch some television program which we recorded on our video cassette recorder (VCR), while our children play the video games on another VCR in a different room. Computer technology is changing daily and by the time we think we have usage under control, new changes are made which makes it imperative that we get 'in cinque' and be prepared for the twenty-first century which is only a couple of years away.

POVERTY ECONOMICS
First published January 11, 1998

As we move closer to the twenty-first century, there is a continuously growing concern about the lack of progress and achievement among minority students who reside in the inner city. It is known that most of these students are living on or below the poverty level. Consequently, they are often the recipient of rent subsidy such as Section 8 administered by the Housing and Urban Development Agency (HUD). They generally are also recipients of USDA food stamps which render them eligible for the free lunch program at public schools, a monthly check, federally funded, and often matched by the state government in the form of Aid to Dependent Children or SSI (Supplemental Security Income). The benefits do not stop there. If one receives the ADC or SSI checks, one is also eligible for health benefits, called Medicaid.

Medicaid is not to be confused with Medicare. Medicare comes in two parts, A and B for recipients of Social Security benefits once they have reached the ripe old retirement age of 65 years and have either paid for the coverage or signed up to pay before retirement. There is a deductible to pay for use of this coverage and there are limitations to how much coverage one can obtain. In addition, one needs a supplemental health insurance coverage policy to avoid further out of pocket expenses. On the other hand, the Medicaid recipient spends about $1.00 at best for health services. The Social Security recipient spends a good part of his life earning an honest living working on a job. While employed, he paid for an expensive health insurance policy to cover himself and his family and still had an expensive deductible to pay before he received any benefits from his insurance. The Medicaid recipient is eligible for benefits any time he is eligible to receive a welfare check of any kind.

With all of the benefits of welfare, why would a recipient who feels comfortable and satisfied wish such a lifestyle want to prepare to work? For those young people who know no other lifestyle, the traditional classroom will not change their way of thinking. It may add to their ability to be better *street pharmacist.* It is time that we get 'in cinque' and work to change the values that our children are growing up with. Our school curriculums need to be adjusted to accommodate the kind of minds that

41

our inner-city children are taking to the classrooms. They are not exactly what Jean Piaget and Ralph W. Tyler had in mind.

THE INTERNET
First published June 14, 1998

Computers are fast becoming the way of the world, especially with the internet being available for a few dollars a month to everyone who wants to get on-line. One can talk and visit around the world in a matter of seconds. Every business has a computer and most homes have computers. Computers are as plentiful in homes as televisions, VCRs and cars. Every home has at least one car and most have two or three. The same goes for televisions and computers.

Windows are dominant using Microsoft, manufactured by Bill Gates who has admitted that Windows 98 has flaws. There was Windows 3.1and earlier versions; 3.11,95 and now a flawed 98. Some people, including yours truly, are now the owners of their third computer, trying to keep up with the latest changes, hoping that this will be the one that can be upgraded to the point where you really do not need to buy another computer. The most often heard sentence is, "You need more memory." Every best program or latest program, calls for *more* memory.

The more memory you have, the more memory you will need, because programs are made in such a fashion that getting more memory will still have you wishing that your old computer was capable of corresponding with your new computer. You had grown accustomed to the old, but the new will have its day.

There are so many avenues to explore on a computer and so much to learn about the usage of a computer. Students are learning every day and taking classes to learn about all of the options. Young men as well as young women have this opportunity. It is time that older citizens get 'in cinque' and keep up with what the children are learning. This will narrow the generation gap.

INTERNATIONAL BUSINESS
First Published September 2, 1998

There was a time when it was trite to hear someone say, "What has the price of butter in China got to do with me?" It was believed then and still by many that what happens in other countries does not touch our daily lives. For many of us, when this saying was common, it may very well have not touched our lives because so many of us were so poor until it was the kind of situation in which we lived that we were not aware of the existence of the great depression.

Our daily lives were not interrupted. We had experienced economic depression long before it was a fact of life for most Americans. It was our normal, daily lifestyle. We lived on such a low plane until the only way to go was 'up.' The great depression devastated the middle class and the rich, but it made Black America sing a new tune and dance a new dance. Recovery for the masses meant hope and inspiration to Black America. As Maya Angelou put it, we continue *'TO RISE.'*

Will we continue to rise when Russia is in a state of turmoil politically and economically? Wall Street has already taken some unusual dives since the devaluation of the Russian ruble because of the billions of dollars being lost by Americans who have invested in Russian businesses as well as the money that the United States has put into aid to Russia. There is the possibility that our federal government will put more money into the Russian 'sinking fund,' and at the same time attempting to put more depressed, unemployed, homeless welfare recipients off the dole.

The dole is not what most indigent Americans want. They would prefer a job which affords them enough money to live a decent life, unencumbered with the government bureaucracy as a watchdog. It is hard to find a job which has net pay which is more than the welfare check. Why work if the government check is more? Many hard working Americans take home less than the welfare check, while foreigners hoard American dollars, putting the world at economic risk. Too often, the thanks is a bombed embassy. International business is here to stay and is the way of life now in the business world, but it is time that we get 'in cinque' and let laborers in America have something to celebrate.

43

THE MONEY GAME
First published September 24, 1998

The new millennium is fast approaching and many people and industries; especially the money industry is concerned about what effect the inability of the computers to handle the number 2000 will have on society. The current computer set-up will revert to 1900 unless something is done to enable it to show 2000. There just *may be* a message there. A message which says that we need to stop, take inventory and back up.

We need to back up to a time when men were men, husbands and fathers and women were wives and mothers and children acted like children. Unless a change is made, the year 2000 will find us mired deeper in debt, violence, inequality, abject poverty and dire insecurities. This is real. The underlying trend toward these ends is real. If we take inventory we will see how the plan is working.

Less money is being appropriated for educational facilities and more for correctional facilities. Why? Acquiring salable skills is no guarantee for acquiring employment in your field. You may acquire employment however, but that which affords a lot less income than the area in which you are most qualified. Why? The elderly are being turned out of career employment on flukes that cost them some retirement benefits. Why? It all adds up to two things. The ***rich and the poor.*** We are headed toward a two-class society: *the very, very, rich* and the *very, very poor.*

It is a fact now, and not just talk, but the rich is becoming richer every day while the poor is poorer than poor, every way. The bad thing about the poor is that the welfare is being taken from them when they are not prepared to fend for themselves. This leads to violence and crime; a well laid plan. Then, why educate those whom are bound to the correctional facilities? The more serious the crime, the longer the stay, or perhaps, forever. Then too, why waste money on the elderly? Save that money for corporations to grow larger and take over more independently run businesses. **MONEY** is the name of the game. If you do not have any, you are not in the game! It is time that we do something to reverse these trends.

If men begin to stay with and support their families while women keep the home and raise their children, teaching them moral values while de-emphasizing the value of money and helping them to learn how to live within their means, the demand for consumable goods will go down, as well as the price of goods. We must get 'in cinque' and chart our own constructive courses for the new millennium.

Y2K

First published January 25, 1999

What are we going to do when the clock strikes 12:00 o'clock P.M. on December 31, 1999? We will have arrived at the beginning of Y2K or the year 2000. Will cyberspace be in total chaos or will things just roll along as usual? At this juncture, no one knows for sure what will happen, but one thing is for sure, we need to prepare for this event just in case Murphy's Law sets in; that is, that everything that can go wrong, will go wrong.

One kind of preparation which I personally stay on top of is keeping a copy of all of my records, because I am a natural skeptic. The coming of Y2K has not caused me any fright in that respect. I keep a bank book with regular entries whether the clerk wants to make them or not. I am sure that they refer to me as 'that ole nag or hag,' but being morally mature, it does not ruffle me at all, just as long as they make my entries. There have been occasions at drive-in window where I have actually sent my book back and requested an entry because none was made, alluding to the fact that I should receive a quarterly statement.

I am not too keen on the electronic transfer of funds either. I agree that it is quite convenient, especially for the sick and shut-in and the plain ole lazy. I still like to have my check in my hand and decide *how and where* I want to deposit my coins, without having to check on when the funds arrived and how much *etc.*, and then transferring them to some other place that I might want to put them. I feel the same way about those automatic monthly withdrawals to pay monthly bills. If I should get into a really bad financial situation and want to 'rob Peter to pay Paul,' it would be hard to do with those monthly drafts nipping at my bank balance.

Speaking of a bank balance, those ATMs (automatic teller machines) seem to all be located in places where any and everybody can check out *your bank balance!* Aside from watching you and getting your access codes, ATMs are fertile grounds for crime such as robbery and often death. The trip to the ATM may be better served inside the bank. We need to get 'in cinque' and evaluate what is important and what is not important in order that we may cope if Murphy's Law sets in with the advent of Y2K.

TORT REFORM
First published August 31, 2002

Day by day, it becomes more apparent that there is possibly a correlation between the push for tort reform, medical insurance and malpractice, corporate bankruptcy and slavery reparations. It is clear. Let us begin with tort reform for this missive. Let us first define 'tort.'

According to Funk & Wagnalls Standard Desk Dictionary, Vol.2, N-Z, tort, with reference to law is: "Any private or civil wrong by act or omission for which a civil suit can be brought, but not including breach of contract." Most tort cases in the recent past have involved the use and administering of hazardous drugs to medical patients by a medical doctor, who often are said to get 'kickbacks' from pharmaceutical companies for prescribing such drugs. Much too often, the recipients of these prescriptions have been Black. This is not exclusive however, because people of other ethnic backgrounds have been prescribed these same drugs but not on as large a scale so as to be recipients of large tort settlements as have been many persons of color. This upsets some people because they feel that people of color should live simple, frugal, impoverished looking lifestyles and not the flashy, ritzy, lifestyle of the rich and whatever. They feel that they have not done anything to receive millions of dollars. Their lives are not worth a plugged nickel in the eyes of some, so why millions, or even thousands for that matter?

On the other hand, doctors receive thousands for prescribing those high-priced hazardous drugs. Too often, the doctors dispense the samples in one hand and the prescription in the other and have no idea how much poor people will have to pay for them. The doctors complain about how much malpractice insurance costs, while the poor patients want to get well and complain about the high cost of medical services and the superfluous cost of medical drugs. The patient wants to get well or least feel better, so they sacrifice and pay for the doctor over and beyond what Medicare, Medicaid, medical insurance will pay. They do the same for the astronomical cost of medicine.

An example of the high medical costs, picture yourself being seen by a physician for about five minutes after the nurse takes your vitals and your bill is $500.00. A prescription for an allergy medicine is given to you for 30 pills, a month's supply which costs $95-$111.00. That averages out to about $3.45 per pill. This is an ongoing medicine bill even if you do not see the doctor every month. If you have insurance for medicine, you will still have a co-pay of about $75.00 to $84 anyway. This is the scenario when you survive the prescription. All medicines have a side effect and for some people, it is <u>death</u>. Now, who has the right to decide whose life is not worth a dime, doctors, lawyers, legislatures?

Lawyers are writing letters to their clients to lobby the legislatures not to try to reform tort laws. Doctors have signs in their offices asking you to push for tort reform because if you do not, you may not have medical services available to you and your medical insurance costs will go up, as if it is not too high now. Some signs say *"If the doctors leave your state and you get sick, who are you going to call, your lawyer?"* Legislatures will most likely bend to the most powerful lobbyists. It is time that we get 'in cinque' and contact our legislatures. The people need to make this decision, not doctors or lawyers. We put legislatures in office with our votes and they <u>should listen to us</u>. MAKE YOUR VOICE HEARD!!

REPARATIONS
First printed September 2, 2002

There is an ongoing push for tort reform in many states and this has a very high correlation to medical practices and malpractices, medical insurance, corporate bankruptcy and slavery reparations. In my last missive, 'tort reform' as it relates to medical insurance for the patient was discussed, with regards to the underpaid and overworked people of this country.

The underpaid and overworked people of this county are those who work all of their lives barely keeping body and soul together because they have not had an equal opportunity to secure the kind of education which would make possible the ability to obtain skill of the caliber which would lead to a life of happiness and all of its frills. Most of these people are the descendants of slaves and former slaves. To them, freedom has not meant securing 'the blessings of liberty to ourselves and our posterity.' It has not even meant securing the 'forty acres and a mule' which was promised to freed slaves by the Freedman's Bureau in 1865, when it was created to see after the welfare of the freedmen.

Freedmen had twelve years, 1865-1877 to become citizens and use their rights to vote, though they had no education with which to utilize these new rights *which were recorded on paper.* The actual utilization of these rights remained on paper for most freedmen. They continue to remain on paper for most descendants of slaves and former slaves. A limited opportunity, under duress in many instances, to learn to read, write and arithmetic was what the fortunate freedman was able to secure. The opportunity to secure employment at a decent wage was withheld from the freedmen and only a limited opportunity exists today. The ratio of poor Blacks to wealthy Whites has remained steady for the past three hundred years in America. So, why not millions in tort awards to Black? *And,* for that matter, why not slavery reparations?

Unlike the American natives that we call Indians, Freedmen had not treaties with the government; got no pay and for all practical purposes have 'wandered in the wilderness' for not forty, but well over hundreds of years instead of being isolated on a reservation or given an isolated territory in which to live. Some reparations *are due* the descendants of slaves who built this country. They are due from those who have profited. That would be big business and big government.

The Slavery Reparations Movement is in high gear, but there are those who feel that it will fissile just as the 'forty acres and the mule' did, because the reparations cases are being thrown out of court as fast as they go in, but on the other hand, greedy lawyers *are becoming mega-rich* on representing Black and anyone else who they can reel in, to get in on the tort cases. It is time that we get 'in cinque and realize which way the wind is blowing with regards to tort cases and tort reform. Let your legislators know how you feel about the legality of tort reform and slave reparations. They are realities.

Reparations is another word for tort award. It is just a special kind of tort award. The end result is the same; an award to compensate for a wrong. Where does the money for the award come from? It is usually in the form of insurance carried by the business or the doctor. Premiums paid, the insurance company should pay up in case of a tort settlement. Yes, the insurance company made big bucks, too. They have a lawyer, also. Who is underrepresented here? The little ole sufferer! He gets the short end of the buck! So, *why has corporate America been using creative bookkeeping and hiding its real value from the government and its stockholders and going bankrupt when found out?!* It is simple. Can we get water from a rock? If business has no money, where is the reward? If government is juggling funds, where is the money? You cannot award what you cannot find. It is time that we get 'in cinque' and realize that business and government have not capped fees that poor people pay, but their ability to secure funds with which to pay fees.

SOCIAL SECURITY PENALTIES
First published November 4, 2003

At a time when Congress, our senators and representatives have sent our President eighty-seven billion dollars ($87, 000, 000, 000. 00), in addition to the seventy-nine billion ($79, 000, 000,000.00), that it appropriated in April, 2003, poor working Americans are struggling to survive on a modest income of five hundred dollars if they receive SSI (Supplemental Security Income) from the Social Security Administration. This is given to people whom have not met the requirements of forty quarters of work covered deductions for Social Security benefits.

One must work ten (10) years and have forty (40) quarters of covered employment to receive benefits at age 62 or earlier if one is disabled. Disabled, by the Social Security Administration means that you are ***not able* to *do anything***! If you complain and appeal long enough, they may award you the SSI. There are some jobs on which workers received such low covered employment until when they do retire; the benefits are so low that these persons may be eligible for SSI along with their Social Security award, thus making them eligible for Medicaid coverage as well as Medicare. The help given to American citizens is good, but not good enough to really call this kind of living adequate in a society which can literally spend billions of hard-earned American tax dollars on any country which has the kind of resources that are found in Iraq, Iran and Afghanistan, and when brought to this country, is too expensive for citizens to purchase. We can give $87 billion to Iraq who owns the oil that we are not able to purchase without missing a meal here and there. Americans who do not receive SSI are unable to purchase oil and oil products because of the elevated prices whose revenues line the pockets of the rich and infamous corporate leaders and politicians in America and abroad.

Working Americans who pay into Social Security and secure 40 quarters of coverage still have a shocking awakening if they worked as a government employee in a state which does not deduct social security taxes from their paychecks and as a result receive a government pension each month. At retirement, they will find that they will be penalized with the GPO (Government Pension Offset) and/or the WEP (Windfall Elimination Provisions). A worker's social security benefits are cut in half and a surviving spouse cannot receive their spouse's benefits either. It is time that we get 'in cinque' and let our congressmen know that Senate Bill 349 and House of Representatives Bill 594 need to be passed to eliminate the GPO and the WEP.

GOVERNMENT AND BUSINESS
First published January 20, 2004

It has been said that 'politics make strange bedfellows.' It appears that much takes place when some of the politicians are sleeping and really not in bed. They can just take a recess and the things that they have worked on for months get action which will take even more months to reverse.

The irony of some of the actions, especially those taken by our President, put a judge on a bench nominated and approved only by him. This seems to be a drastic move when a judge is confirmed by a *majority of one,* but ironically, it is legal. Section 2 of Article 2 of the *United States Constitution* gives the President the right to fill vacancies: "The President shall have power to fill up all vacancies that may happen during the recess of the Senate, by granting commissions which shall expire at the end of their next session." This is an election year and the judge can serve in his appointed position until a new Congress is in session.

Congress makes all laws and the President's job is to see that the laws are executed or carried out by the proper authorities. He can make suggestions regarding laws, budgets *etc.,* but it is the prerogative of Congress to make them into laws.

Business in America wants new laws to permit foreign immigrants to come into this country whenever they need them to work on low-paying jobs in service areas. Our President is willing to see this happen. In addition, he would like for their temporary stays to be made legal and renewable for three year periods, as though the unemployment rate in the United States is a ground Zero.

There are too many people receiving public assistance who could work in many of the jobs that are given to non-citizen foreigners for minimum wages. Those who want jobs are not hired. What we do not know is how many of these businesses which employ immigrants *really pay minimum wages.* We know that businesses which have moved to foreign countries from the United States, often do not pay minimum wages, but still charge market or above market prices in the United States for foreign made goods. It is time that we get 'in cinque' because our Congressmen need to know that jobs in America need to be made available to unemployed Americans, especially those whom are in a position to leave the welfare rolls and make a positive contribution to the economy of this country. The legalization of workers who will work for less while Americans live in poverty cannot be good for business or America.

III-WAR

WEAPONS OF MASS DESTRUCTION
First published September 25, 2002

The Prime Minister of Great Britain, Tony Blair has been working tirelessly to convince Parliament to side with United States President George W. Bush, to vanquish Iraq's Saddam Hussein. As of this date, he is encountering a tough go of it. The same is true of President Bush's request to Congress for unlimited power in the region. It appears that Congress will go along with him because of the political atmosphere; the exchanging of favors *etc.* which takes place in Congress on a regular basis. The consequences of supporting a war effort is what worries me and most Americans the most. It appears to be an obstacle for the United Nations Security Council as well.

What will be the consequences of an attack on Iraq? If Saddam Hussein **really does have** a stockpile of weapons of mass destruction such as biological, chemical and nuclear warfare agents and **he is attacked** and ready to put these weapons into action in minutes after being attacked, how is such a reaction combated. What kind of neutralization agents does the United States or Great Britain have to use to combat mass destruction? Is there some notion that if Hussein is destroyed that Iraq will roll over and die? Is there peace in Afghanistan? Where is Bin Laden? What is really at stake here? Oil? Control of oil? Middle East peace or World War Ill?

If this conflict does end in a world war, which we pray that it will not, with Hussein being a part of the Islamic world, what reactions de we expect from the rest of the Islamic and Christian worlds, as well as the rest of the world which does not embrace Christianity or Islam? How is this encounter going to affect the Palestinian-Israeli conflict which is still **not**

settled, with massive retaliation campaigns going on presently? In the last Iraqi conflict, *Desert Storm,* Israel was bombarded with missiles from the Islamic world as the United States reined terror on Iraq. Are we prepared to do this again? Is our homeland security up to what can and could happen if this confrontation comes to fruition as our President has already positioned troops strategically near Iraq and according to the <u>Vicksburg</u> **Post**, Sept. 24,2002, a Vicksburg man has leased land for the military to use, on the eastern cost of Africa, near Yemen, which is supposedly an al-Qaida stronghold, to make it possible "...for the military to go to take what it needs."

Why, as a leader of the world in humane treatment to and for the rest of the world, does the United States want to go down in history as the aggressor of a small country which *feels,* with no degree of certainty, that it is a threat to mankind, because it does not want to give the small country a chance to prove itself? There has to be more to this than meets our eyes or our ears. It is still not too late for us to get 'in cinque' and let our senators and representatives <u>*know for certain*</u> how we feel about this matter and encourage them to avoid the ultimate results of a world war, labeled as the *aggressor.*

IRAQ AND ISRAEL
First published January 10, 2003

For most of 2002, we have been in limbo about the status of our country in its involvement in the Middle East. We have gone through the invasion of Afghanistan, interventions in North Korea and fear about the status of homeland security since September, 2001.

It would appear that in spite of the United Nation's inspectors saying that they have not found a 'smoking gun' in Iraq, our country has readied troops near Iraq in preparation for an attack anyway. Our President has stated that Iraq will be attacked in the near future. It seems that there is no way to change the President's mind, regardless to the situation in Iraq. Having found no 'smoking guns' in Iraq, interest has turned to North Korea, now considered another member of the 'axis of evil.' Since no 'smoking gun' has been found in Iraq, it is now believed that Iraq shipped all of its weapons of mass destruction to North Korea.

Anyone born before 1945 knows the history of North Korea and war with its enemies, even if they were blood kin relatives. We know now, in defense of South Korea, how many countries pulled out of Korea without a victory, including the United States. We are also aware that the Soviet Union was an ally of North Korea during the Korean Conflict in which more Americans died than in World War II. It should be speculated, that not much of that situation has changed even though the USSR has been dissolved, because Russia still leans toward North Korea and Iraq with favoritism.

Because of U. S. favoritism toward Israel, an attack on Iraq will trigger an attack on Israel, just as it did in Desert Storm. Whatever it is that the United States wants out of the Middle East would probably be better left alone for the sake of the world. The Middle East and North Korea are hotbeds for World War Ill. We still need to continue to contact our legislators in our states and in the nation, to forge for peace in every applicable way possible. It is time for us to get 'in cinque' and work and pray for peace in our homeland and in the world.

UNITED STATES OR UNITED NATIONS
First published May 14, 2003

After living in Texas for twenty years, with the idea that everything in Texas was the biggest of whatever it was, I find that the state is not really large enough to hold its legislators. The Texas politics have become so great that the great state of Texas cannot hold it all. The legislators had to go to Oklahoma to productively work on issues which affected the citizens of Texas. Their absence from the Capitol put the Texas House at a standstill. Sending state troopers to return them to Texas had no effect either. There is something about Texas law, reminiscence of the days when the Texas Rangers **WERE THE LAW** in Texas. That air seems to prevail not only in Texas, but in the United States and the world. Somehow, the Texas air appears to invade the universe as pluperfect.

We have seen how Congress jumped in and passed legislation to support the President from Texas in his drive to declare war on Iraq. We have seen how billions of dollars were appropriated to destroy Saddam Hussein and Iraq, without the sanctions of the United Nations, the organization which legally held the power to make the decision to attack Iraq. We have also seen how Congress is set to provide the billions of dollars to rebuild Iraq.

Just as the United States invaded, attacked and 'conquered' Iraq, without the sanctions of the United Nations, the only organization legally authorized to set up a new government in Iraq, the United States has already gone ahead and put someone in charge. Prime Minister Blair is doing his best to stay in the game, but he has much opposition in the British Parliament. As a matter of fact, some of the key players in Parliament, during the war, who wanted to opt out during the war, are now resigning from their posts, stating emphatically, that only the United Nations has the right, legally to do what the United States and Britain are trying to do, without that organization.

At the same time, it makes one wonder if the United States' financial obligation to the United Nations, which has not been paid, makes our President feel that the United States is no longer a member and does not need to abide by the laws of that body, whose residence is in New York, in the United States.

On the other hand, why is it so difficult for Congress to pass a tax cut bill for the hard working Americans whose tax dollars, billions of them, too many to count, have paid for a war, now known as 'Mr. Bush's War,' for which too many Americans felt was unnecessary, illegitimate and immoral? The tax cut has passed the House and has been sent to the Senate. **Who** will benefit? It is time to get 'in cinque' and let Congress know where **OUR Priorities are!**

THE INVASION of BAGHDAD
First printed April 11, 2003

It has been a month now since America has been aware that the Coalition forces, led by American military leaders, began their invasion of Iraq in spite of the large protests against it, here in the United States and around the world. That first night, we watched the calm and beauty of Baghdad as well as some of the "bombs bursting at night and the rocket' red glare." This television display took the place of some of the favorite shows watched by Americans nightly. The pre-empted war shows went on daily for the first week of the invasion. I missed all of my favorite soap operas and situation comedies. I tried to stay busy in order not to let myself become depressed.

War is depressing, no matter who is fighting where. As a child, I feared that I would never become an adult because of the daily war reports by news commentators. They spoke of the number wounded and the numbers missing in action; the numbers taken captive as prisoners of war; the places on the 'front' where battle was taking place and the positions of the allies and the enemies. The truth of the matter is that I did not know a single soul on either side of this war, but it literally scared me to tears and fears which I shall never forget. I moan now to think of how it is all affecting our young impressionable children today who already have too many 'knocks' against them in the first place: broken homes which once may have been whole; one-parent homes that were never whole because one parent was ***never*** there; drug-laden homes and neighborhoods; crime-laden neighborhoods; mis-education and under education in our schools; un-employment and under-employment in our municipal entities; greed and graft in all governmental agencies; corporate fraud; natural and national disasters; religious betrayals; racial tensions; medical distress for doctors and patients; financial disasters in the money market. One can see with all of these ails, how soap operas can be so relaxing, enjoyable and educational.

On Wednesday when Saddam's stature was toppled by American military units, I did not see my soap operas. Each major news network showed the statue being toppled and the Kurds dancing in the streets at ***least seven times*** per hour. I counted them when I played the tape on which I thought I had some soap operas to watch. I had watched the U. S. House of Representatives debate on the gun law which was up for passage when the statue was being toppled, but ***that is another story!***

We all realize that national security is important and by now, most American communities have in place, some kind of emergency plan for its inhabitants in cases of disaster. We are also aware that radio and television stations feel the necessity to keep us informed of news that we can use, but it is time that we get 'in cinque' and let them know that we do not need to be continually inundated with the horror of war and terrorists actions.

AFTERMATH OF IRAQ INVASION
First published February 2, 2004

This New Year and the President's message have settled in on us. We have received information from several reliable sources, including the Secretary of State, Colin Powell, that our President **NEVER** had any information that Saddam Hussein had any weapons of mass destruction or WMD as they are currently referred to. There is also the notion that America has less to fear now that Hussein is in captivity. Very little is now mentioned about how President Clinton's administration had nullified the ideas of WMD in Iraq.

The upcoming presidential election may be affected by the final admittance that there never were any weapons of mass destruction in Iraq to cause an alarm in the United States or the world. By now, it should be clear to every voting American who felt that they should have contacted their Congressman requesting them not to vote for passage of that huge budget to send Americans to Iraq to invade that country seeking something which did not exist.

The invasion of Iraq has not looked good for the United States at home or abroad. Our foreign relations have suffered and our moral status is at an all-time low. Aside from that, our economic status is at a seemingly low level standstill, as money needed to take care of homeland duties, have been neglected for military purposes which are serving no purpose. Our income is on the decrease because inflation far surpasses any increase which we might have gained, coupled with all of the losses we suffered when the stock market took a dive behind the Enron/Anderson oil scandals.

Pensioners whose monthly check are derived from investments by pension funds witnessed a ***decrease*** in their monthly benefits; that is, those who continue to get a check. Other retirees saw a decrease in profits from annuities. Overall, the Bush administration has been and still is a drain on the pocketbook of retired Americans living on a fixed income. There is no hope for future 'catch-up' among retirees as it is with the working population. The only possible solution other than voting for government officials who will listen to the electorate is to return to the work force. It is time that we get 'in cinque' and impress upon our government officials that they need to work for the people of this country, not the whims of the President.

IRAQ: OUR HONOR TAINTED
First published November 2, 2004

The election is over and hopefully, the mudslinging will be forgotten since some of the 'mud' included ugly facts. It is regretful that there was dirty fighting during the campaign for President, but some candidates believe that 'all is fair in love and war.' This past campaign was all out war and too much of it was about the 'war;' the one in Iraq, that is, where more soldiers are bring killed every day as others prepare to go to take their places.

Fighting in Iraq has resulted in oil pipelines being set afire on a regular basis, boosting the per barrel price of crude oil from which fuels are made, thus sending the price of gasoline above the $2.00 level in many places. We have voted. What did we vote for? More war and higher fuel prices or a withdrawal of American troops from Iraq.

Since we did not find any weapons of mass destruction in Iraq, we must find the missing ammunition. It should not be difficult to find since American military personnel is being killed by that ammunition every day.

We want to give dishonorable discharges to soldiers who refuse to face certain death when they DO NOT KNOW WHO THE ENEMY IS in a foreign country. It is bad enough when we do not know who the enemy is *in this country.*

As a country, our honor has taken a beating. Many countries look upon the United States with disdain now because of our actions in Iraq. We pulled out of South Korea and Viet Nam just as other countries before us had done and we can pull out of Iraq. A government has been formed and Saddam is in custody. Why must we stay in Iraq? The United Nations should be given the opportunity to do what it was formed to do, without the United States taking the lead.

It matters not how the voting went. Someone had to win and someone had to lose, but something has to be done about our young men being killed every day in Iraq and Afghanistan. Where they are really needed is at home doing homeland security, because this is presently the most vulnerable country in the world. We are divided on too many fronts while our homeland lacks adequate protection. We hear the propaganda in the media and the average one of us, if we chose to be traitors, could upset our own little bailiwicks with ease. It is time for us to get 'in cinque' and influence our government to ***get the troops home.***

IV-HOLIDAYS

THANKSGIVI NG
First published November, 1995

In 1621, the Pilgrims celebrated their first year in America and set aside several days to rejoice and give thanksgiving along with approximately 100 native Indians and about 30 new settlers who were not passengers on the *Mayflower*. There had been about 1102 passengers on the voyage in 1620. Many of these Pilgrims had made the voyage to the New World for different reasons though the underlying reason for many was religion. Some of them wanted adventure and others wanted their children to be raised in an atmosphere of freedom away from the Church of England or in a Dutch community. None-the less, they all wished to find some form of freedom.

Freedom was so important to the Pilgrims until they toiled with relentless determination to erect homes and cultivate the soil to sustain themselves, along with much help from the natives, mainly Squanto, who showed them how to plant corn and secure necessities for life.

Life was loss by half of the pilgrims because of the harsh winter weather through which they had to toil for survival (Todd and Curti, *Rise of the American Nation,* 1977). The Thanksgiving holiday celebrations spread to other New England colonies as a family day of prayer and celebration, being thankful for a bountiful harvest. The day of Thanksgiving has been proclaimed by governors and presidents since 1621, but they chose the last Thursday in November to be set aside for the celebration. President F.D. Roosevelt convinced Congress in 1939 to declare the fourth Thursday as Thanksgiving Day, and as a legal federal holiday. This move added an extra week for Christmas shopping, in order to help business *(World*

Book Encyclopedia). The day after Thanksgiving is considered to be the first 'official' day of Christmas shopping. We need to get 'in cinque' and revisit the original meaning of Thanksgiving; prayer and celebrations for a year of survival in a harsh, cold and dangerous world. HAPPY THANKSGIVING to all.

THE MEDICARE 'SURPLUS' AND THANKSGIVING
First published November 10, 1993

The Thanksgiving holiday season is quickly approaching and in light of recent elections in some state, counties and localities, many Americans are getting set to make some gross adjustments in the economic aspects of their lives.

Economically speaking, our country has spent more money in two years than the previous administration saved in eight years. Three years ago, this country was out of excessive debt and boosted a surplus after meeting national obligations. Much of the *SURPLUS* was Medicare and Social Security funds which were and are still being used by other departments of the government. Today, we are in the 'red' and the flow is like a crimson tide as it continues to go deeper into the billions of dollars for homeland security and foreign military purposes. At the same time, Medicare and Medicaid benefits have been effectively cut, especially in therapy, which is so needed by many senior citizens. These cuts have been made in services which are mostly provided to patients in their homes by home care agencies which provide physical therapy, speech therapy and occupational therapy. Most *Medicare Summary Notices* carry this information as an ALERT on the back of the form.

The Thanksgiving season is also the time of the year when the Social Security Administration begins to make adjustments for a cost of living increase in benefits and an increase in the cost of Medicare benefits which will be effective in the New Year. For so many seniors, the increase in the cost of Medicare benefits are *more* than the raise for the cost of living, causing some seniors to receive *less* benefits in the coming year. The government 'giveth' and the government 'taketh away.' Keep in mind that our Congressmen who make these laws will not be affected by them when they retire. For the rest of their lives, they will be well cared for financially and medically. They need to know how their actions affect those of us who have worked many years to try to reap the benefits of hard labor in a society which is *supposed* to care. It appears that each time the Congressmen give themselves a raise; there is some kind of cut in benefits to the working poor and retired.

The working poor and retired have the same right to a bountiful Thanksgiving as does the rich and famous. We all need to be thankful that we are yet still alive in these times of global turmoil, but at the same time, we need to keep our lawmakers aware of the little things that affect us so greatly. Let us get 'in cinque' in 2003 and make sure that our Congressmen know the pros and cons of their actions as they affect us and our Thanksgiving.

CHRISTMAS SHOPPING
First printed November 30, 1993

Then 'Back to School Sale' signs barely came down and Halloween was not yet on our minds when we saw the first hint that Christmas was coming. We really did not have time to think about Thanksgiving or give any thanks before we were showered with signs, letters for donations, more credit cards and investment opportunities to beat the tax man before year end. With no means of escape, there was the gift list sizzling on the back burner of our minds. The children know what they want before we ask or have ever heard of it. Many adults have no idea what they want until after they have seen it all. So, how do we go about trying to please everyone on our list?

I heard a minister once say that it is hard to tell the men from the boys, except by the price of the toys. Now, let us see. You can get a Barbie doll costing from $5.98 to $200.00 and if all of the accessories are desired, the cost can be untoward. The average toy for girls costs about $20.00, 'and up. Toys for boys are just as ridiculous. The least expensive car or truck is about $9.99. Everything else is 'and up.' Up goes up until you begin to wonder if the toy is for the boys or the 'old boys.'

Once the children ae taken care of, you concentrate on the adults who are nearest and dearest to your heart and expect to spend no less than $25.00 for a half-decent gift. It becomes expensive if you have a few near and dear ones. Then, there is no way to keep a friend under $15.00. Even acquaintances feel that they are worth $5.00 or more, not to mention the 29 cents on the Christmas card that you bought.

Our sentimental feelings cost us a bundle as our credit cards make debtor's history and the merchants' cash registers sing a song of glad tidings.

More and more, we forget the reason for the season; the birth of the Christ child, Jesus. It is time to get 'in cinque' and put less emphasis on the materialistic spirit and more on the Holy Spirit and return Christmas to Christ.

THE SAVIOR'S BIRTH
First printed December 13, 2004

This is the time of the Savior's birth! The time of year that we call Christmas, because it symbolized the time of the birth of Christ. **His** coming was heralded by the Angels as the 'perfect light,' the 'king of kings,' the 'Messiah,' 'Yahweh,' and *Jesus, the Christ*. Today, we just say *Jesus Christ,* as the proper name of the Savior and Lord of all Christendom; that is, those people who call themselves Christians and believe in the teaching of Jesus Christ.

Because we believe in the teaching of Jesus Christ, we celebrate Christmas. The most outward sign that we are celebrating Christmas is the massive decorations which we place on our home in objects and decorative lights. People who do not believe in Jesus Christ also decorate with the lights of Christmas. Too often, our lights do not reflect any of the symbols of the Christian religions, so it is difficult to tell which decorations are not religious and which ones are not in celebration of the Christ child.

Many Christian churches often show some sign of the immaculate birth with a nativity scene or a lighted cross or a lighted star which indicates characteristics of the *Bible* description of the holy birth over two thousand years ago. The greatest and most elaborate decorators for Christmas are done by the retail stores.

As early as October, some retail stores begin to call our attention to the coming of Christmas. Their decorations are mostly geared to stimulating us to getting into the spirit of buying presents for our family and friends. The Thanksgiving and Christmas parades seen on television have some of the most extravagant decorations that we wish to see and their costs in some instances are prohibited. They put us in the spirit to spend money; so often, money which we should not spend or debts which we should not make because we have been programmed to do this.

We can reprogram ourselves to bring back Christ to Christmas by making it a time of the year to reflect upon the good things that we have done all year and celebrate those successes with our family and friends in a manner befitting the birthday of a king; a savior, one who has made our successes possible with unconditional love and happiness a possibility. This is a serious time and there is no time like the present that our young should learn the true meaning of Christmas. We need to get 'in cinque' and have a merry, merry Christmas where ***Jesus Christ*** gets all of the honors

THE NEW YEAR
First published December 23, 1993

As 1993 comes to a close, we look forward to the New Year, and the year holds many meanings for different people. The operative word, however, is *new*. For too many of us, 'new' is gone by the end of January, but we still capitalize on the 'new' on the first.

1993 has meant many things to many of us and some of those things; we want to stay in our pasts. There are precious moments which we wish to see anew in 1994 and eagerly take with us into the New Year. Many of us will see 1993 go and 1994 come in different ways in different places. Some of us will revel in the spirit of champagne and some of us in the Holy Spirit. Nevertheless, most of us will take advantage of the new chance to do many new things that we did not do in 1993.

Some of us will learn to say, "I love you," to our children and mean it. Some of us will learn to say, "NO" to our children when needed and not be afraid that they will love us less. Many of us will come into self-realization and stop living through our children or for our children and live *WITH* our children.

We can use this new chance to displace ignorance with education; hate with love; gangs with families; violence with peace; materialism with spiritualism; prejudice with tolerance and racism with wisdom. An increase in the positive attributes will result in more avenues of employment, a drop in welfare rolls, equal opportunities in higher education and housing, a lower crime rate and an overall healthier nation. We need to get 'in cinque' in 1994 and make this a REALITY.

1995: NEW RESOLVES
First published January, 1995

A new year means many things to many people. It is to many the time to vow to take off those extra fat pounds which we have carted around for a year or more. The desire to lose weight is more often related to how we will look in that smaller wardrobe which we can no longer wear, than to how we feel and how the loss of weight will affect our overall health.

The New Year gives all of us the opportunity to assess our strengths and weaknesses and vow to 'accentuate the positive, eliminate the negative and don't mess with [the] in between." I am positive that we all have done or do some things for which we would like to improve upon. Aside from shedding some pounds, I need more sleep and rest and vow to go to bed earlier and get up earlier in 1995.

The year, 1995 is going to be unlike any year we have EVER known and it offers us an opportunity to come together as a **FAMILY, COMMUNITY, NATION** and **RACE.** We MUST recapture the essence of togetherness if we are to survive. OUR CHURCHES MUST LEAD THE WAY!! Let us get 'in cinque' and 'watch' the New Year unravel as we come together in body and spirit.

THE BANG OF 2003
First published December 30, 2002

We have seen the old year, 2002 pass away and welcomed the New Year, 2003. It has not come in with the same bang that we witnessed a few years ago as we ushered in the new millennium, but we have experienced the evolution of the high tech at a much swifter pace than we did prior to the beginning of the new millennium. In a few years, we have gone from the 8 millimeter movie film, to the videos and now to digital technology on a disc. The same is true for cameras.

Cameras have come a long way from the old Brownie Kodak and black and white Polaroid to instant color Polaroid to digital and computer cameras. Many of us just got used to the regular 35 millimeter camera and some of us have no desire to use the digital kind. There are those of us who are equally comfortable with the regular videos have no need for the DVD. Our VCRs afford all that we need to see and record. If we decide to purchase a DVD player, that will entail throwing out the old VCR and the videos and then purchasing the DVDs to play on the new machine. There are many things that we need to throw out of our lives to begin a New Year, but they do not entail machines. We need to get some of the clutter out of our lives.

For the past year, some of us have been in limbo trying to sort out the things that clutter our lives on a daily basis. We all want to live clean and wholesome lives and do the thing that help to make us better persons. Yet, there are those things, many of them material in nature, but some are not, which we find cluttering up our lives.

Some of us have 'friends' and relatives who seem to set out to make our lives miserable. We need to recognize that anyone who interferes with our health and happiness does not deserve to be a part of our daily activities and need to be on the short list or avoided. We need to keep close to us those persons whom help to life us up and make our lives more meaningful and enjoyable.

Enjoyment should be a large part of our daily lives. Life is to be enjoyed, every day. One does not have to be a millionaire to enjoy life. Often, just being in the company of someone who really lifts your spirit and respects you as a person can be enjoyable. Knowing that you are appreciated can be enjoyable. Positive experiences can make life enjoyable.

Experiences can be enjoyable if they are positive, regardless to whether you are making the experience or on the receiving end of it. It goes both ways. We often find, however, that the experience is more gratifying when we make it positive. It is time for us to get 'in cinque' and make our daily lives more positive.

OUR CELEBRATIONS DURING THE YEAR
First published May 28, 2004

Over the years, holidays have changed to accommodate the working masses and big business. Christmas, Valentine Day and Easter are about the only holidays which are really celebrated on the assigned day now. Everyone wants to celebrate Christmas on the 25th of December regardless to what else is going on. No one wants to work on Christmas Day.

Very few people have a day *off* from work for Valentine Day, but everyone likes to give or be a recipient of something sweet and lovely on Valentine Day, regardless to the day of the week on which it arrives.

Easter always falls on a Sunday because the calendar is set up that way. The problem there is it is difficult to predict which Sunday it will fall on or in which month it will be celebrated. That calculation seems to depend on what the moon is doing, but we do know that it always follows Good Friday.

We have just celebrated Memorial Day. For families, Memorial Day is a time to think of loved ones whom have passed from our midst; collect our thoughts and memories and dedicate ourselves to keeping them in our hearts and memories.

For many other, Memorial Day is barbeque/party time. There is nothing and no one to have a memory about. Memorial Day represents a Monday off from work. It is a good day to picnic, play golf, ride a horse and do many things that you would not have the time to do, ordinarily, because of the job. It will be celebrated on a Monday or a Friday close to May 30. It is difficult to plan when exact dates are not employed, without the use of a calendar.

The 4th of July will arrive on a Sunday, so we know that Monday following the 4th, or Friday before the 4th will not be a work day for many. We must get 'in cinque' and realize that without a calendar, our days can be difficult.

V-TECHNOLOGY

GROWTH IN SCIENCE
First published September 30, 2003

In times like these, fast living, fast food, whirlwind courtships, quick unplanned marriages, long overdue marriages, where the children of the couple bear the rings and strew the flowers; far-flung families and high technologies, it almost seems unreal that too many of us really do not believe in friendship, love, and God. We feel that all of the so-called good things that we have are because **_we_** have caused them to come about. We have accomplished so much due to growth in science, physically and socially.

With so much growth in science, it is amazing that no one has claimed to have seen Heaven and met God there. We claim to have visited the Moon and have placed scientific rovers on Mars. Some of those who do not claim to have seen or heard God, feel that they **_are_** God, and there are too many of them in leadership roles in our country. There are a few of us however, who are thankful for what God has bestowed upon us; feel grateful for all of the scientific progress which has been made and feel the warmth, kinship to the world, love and the presence of God in all of the wonders of the world.

The few of us who appreciate kinship, love and warmth in this present world are indeed lucky. That luck has not been by chance, but by the belief that 'doing the right thing' all the time, is what keeps our world in-sync. Families and friends with discord should survey the wonders of the world, take inventory of one's relationship to the world, and make some positive decisions about the route of action to take to heal and be on one accord with the world: friends, families, neighbors and God.

Too many people believe that 'God is dead.' That belief stems from the fact that too often we fail to see what miracles have taken place in our lives. We take too many things for granted and thus do not give thanks for our blessings. The old saying, 'stop; and smell the roses,' is not a bad idea. We need to think and pray about the problems we have caused others, the willful wrongs that we have done, the people whom we have alienated, the problems we could have solved and did not, the good we can do, and make room for healings to take place in our lives. The thorns may hurt when you are pricked by them, but the scent of the roses can make you forget the pain. We miss a lot of love when we do not see the whole picture. It is time that we get 'in cinque' and take inventory of our lives, values and action and appreciate the growth in science.

GAMBLING: COMPUTERS
First published February 23, 2004

Long ago, in the days of yore, gambling was not the same kind of temptation that it presents in this day and age. True, there were those individuals who bet the farm in an attempt to make a quick buck or in an attempt to get out of debt, while plunging deeper into the mire. There were also professional gambles who bet the big bucks. Because it was their profession, losing was as easy as winning. They studied the odds and were able to make educated guesses about betting.

Most often, the professional gambler played a card game like Poker or Tonk, unless he was skilled in billiards or dominos. These gamblers were also usually *not* family men and I say men because women did not usually gamble. This was a man's thing. Today, it is a different story, especially with the advent of computer technology.

The computer has changed everything in our daily lives, including the number of women who now gamble, including senior citizens on fixed incomes who are lured into the casinos with cheap meals and 'busting out money' several days a week. Retires have more spare time and the lure makes some casinos look like senior citizen hangouts.

Seniors benefit from the computers also. There are some good things which have resulted from computers, and with all new things, there are many, many side effects. The older slot machines were not propelled by electricity and the odds were a bit more realistic. Today, the slot machines are propelled by electricity and controlled by a computer. You can play every slot machine in a casino and the central computer keeps track of everything you win or lose. The computer programs your luck. The computer decides which few machines will pay some money and which ones you can play all day and night and never win a dime.

One does not have to go to the casino to lose money. You can sit down to your computer and play slots and lose your money on the Internet. You can lose money on the Internet just as easy as you pay your bills on the Internet. It is a lucrative business, just as popular as the lottery business. A few people get lucky in both endeavors, but the majority of people, *do not!* If one wins two million dollars, the gambling establishment will make at least four million dollars. Casinos that make fifty billion dollars a year may permit about ten million in winnings to leave their establishment. Compare the profits to the winnings and you know that gambling establishments did not go into business for you and me. Therefore, we need to decide if gambling is fun or a serious business of aggregate loss. We need to get 'in cinque,' and if we must gamble, pay for the rent/house note, utility bills, car note, installment account payments *etc.*, **before** we take off to the casino or sit down to the computer and bet on a machine for which we have no control.

INTERNET CONNECTIONS
First published August 2, 2004

No matter how long you live or where you live, it does not take a lifetime to realize that some things just will never be right, regardless to how hard you work at it. These are the times when you have to go with the flow. At my age, sometimes I feel like making my own flow, especially when it comes to telephone usage and getting connected to the Internet.

I have purchased a certain telephone company's long distance service and Internet service a couple of years ago to find out after changing to a more liberal long distance plan a year later, that if I did not stop using the Internet service, which calls for a long distance dial-up, that my long distance service will be suspended, restricted or cancelled without further notice, as my long distance service is for *voice use only.* I did some scrambling to check out my service agreement, and sure enough in fine print in the last paragraph of the explanations of all of the fine features that my new plan had, there was the words *voice* use only.

It never occurred to me that the use of a fax machine, computer, or TDD machine was <u>*not*</u> voice operation. Since my ability to hear is on the wane, it appears that this time that when I do need the TDD machine, that some other arrangements will have to be made for me to communicate. I found myself in a dilemma.

I had to choose to keep my generous long distance service because I talk to family and friends every day for long periods of time, or find another internet provider that I could contact in my local area, like across the street, not 80 miles away, because I cannot use this long distance carrier's Internet service because they do not have a telephone dial-up number in my town and the nearest one is 80 miles away. Then it all began.

It took me six hours and ten telephone calls to connect to another Internet provider with a local dial-up telephone number. One of the problems lies in the fact that most of the help agents with whom you speak on the telephone, either do not speak English very well and you have to discern which syllables they accent or you can get caught up in the automated loop which does not have the menu option which you need, but carry you through every one of them before they permit you to speak with a <u>*human being,*</u> while being on hold at least 5 minutes on each option. You hope for '*frustration resolution!*' We must get 'in cinque' and read the fine print more than once in our agreements and save a lot of headache and frustration in the long run.

VI-HEALTH AND HAZARDS

AIDS
First published November 17, 1993

Often, as a youngster, I heard my elders say that 'cleanliness is next to Godliness.' It has just been since knowledge of the acquired immunodeficiency syndrome epidemic that this phrase means something to me. I am still not sure what it meant to them, except it was a means to make sure that I kept things clean.

Today, the term 'cleanliness is next to Godliness' means that keeping yourself and things around you clean may play a big role in preventing many diseases, especially the dreaded AIDS disease.

Every medical and educational entity has some well thought-out, well written literature on the how's and whys of AIDS. Many of us read it and take it to heart while some of us, too many of us, think we are not vulnerable. Thus, the disease looms more intensely than ever.

A pamphlet HHS Publication No. (CDC) HHS-88-8404 was mailed to postal customers and should have made it to every household in the United States. It is entitled "Understanding AIDS" AND IS REPRODUCIBLE. There is very useful information on the subject in this pamphlet. Our children need to have this knowledge.

Although the pamphlet is valuable, it does not tell us that ALL of the ways of contracting AIDS are KNOWN. They tell us what they believe they are sure of. Since there is an UNKNOWN, we need to practice cleanliness at all cost. CHILDREN NEED TO KNOW that they need to wash their hands before eating and after using the toilet. They need to avoid getting the blood of others on their bodies, especially if they have an open wound.

Although the Surgeon General has said that there is no risk from saliva, sweat, tears, urine or a bowel movement, we know there is risk in blood, everywhere. That put the toilet at risk in my opinion, so let us get 'in cinque' and make sure we prolong our lives by putting 'cleanliness next to Godliness.'

NEWBORN HEALTH
First published January 21, 1994

While it is of the most utmost importance that mothers-to-be get adequate prenatal care, it is just as important that they get post-natal care and proper care for their newborn babies.

It is especially important that young mothers, who breast-feed their babies, eat only foods which are healthy for their babies. In addition, they should not indulge in social activities which can pollute the milk that their bodies produce for the newborn baby since certain antibodies in the mother's milk provide some immunity to certain diseases for the baby.

Mothers who do not breast feed their babies still need to be careful about their diets as some foods tend to give our bodies offensive odors and can cause a new baby discomfort when being held. The child will cry and be fidgety and may be thought to be sick.

Even though there are antibodies in a new mother's breast milk, all babies need immunization for communicable diseases, beginning at birth. By the time a child is old enough to attend public school, he/she should have had a basic series of immunizations and need only a booster. Let us get 'in cinque' and keep our children healthy. Healthy children have the best stamina for learning in today's society.

LEGALIZATION OF DRUG
First published July 28, 1994

There is a lot of furor in our Congress these days about removing our Surgeon General, Dr. Joycelyn Elders from office because of her outspoken ideas on the legalization of drugs in our country. She has a very strong opinion on this matter which may be due to personal reasons.

I also have a strong opinion on this matter and I support Dr. Elders in the belief that drugs should be legalized. I feel certain that there are as many people who disagree with me on this as there are those who feel that the sale of alcohol should be banned from cities in counties that are 'wet.'

It appears that the sale of alcohol and other drugs are going to be with us indefinitely. It seems that government agencies have won some battles on many fronts against drug trafficking, but the war is far from over. As long as there are 'big bucks' in drug trafficking and no age limitations on dealers and users, the war will continue.

If the government would step in and allow drugs to be sold legally, put a ceiling price on cost, and age limitation on use, a tax to fund rehabilitation centers, laws to require rehabilitation at certain junctures during use, the government would make a profit on sales; the user would not need to steal and kill to get drugs; AIDS statistics would go down among drug users; drug illegal trafficking would be diminished; denial among those in need of help would be reduced; more help for addicts would be available; the illegal attraction would be gone. Finally, drug dealers would need a license to sell drugs and could not demand 'big bucks' for their wares. They would have to get a legitimate job and not have to 'watch their backs.'

Get 'in cinque' and weigh the merits of legalizing drugs in our country. If you support Dr. Elders, let your congressman know it. Fear not. There will always be 'bootleggers,' but the profits will be much smaller and they will be much more vulnerable.

DIABETES
First published April 5, 2004

It appears that my name has been put on a health issues mailing list since the publication of the first article which I wrote concerning diabetes. I have been well armed regarding what various entities are doing to help to eradicate the disease. The last article dealt with the work of the Juvenile Diabetes Research Foundation or JDRF which can be accessed on the internet at (www.JDRF.)

Since that time, I have received information from Medtronic MiniMed which has advised me that one day there will be a cure for diabetes. Until there is a cure, they are counting on the successful development of an artificial pancreas. "That's because an artificial pancreas-an insulin pump and a continuous blood glucose sensor that safely work together to regulate blood sugar levels-means about the end of fingersticks and shots."

This company states that they have devoted 20 years to development of an artificial pancreas and are already in clinical trials. They feel that this is the next best thing to an actual cure. They believe that they have the technology and resources to make the artificial pancreas a reality.

According to Medtronic MiniMed, the fingerstick and regular HbA1c tests are crucial to managing diabetes. The fingerstick tests measures blood glucose at a specific point in time and the HbA1c test gives an average over a period of time, but neither points out the highs and low between tests and can blend into the average.

There is a prescription, registered name, CGMS System Bold test which can give a clearer picture throughout the day of blood sugar levels filling in the gaps between the fingersticks and HbA1c tests.

There is also the insulin pump which controls delivery of insulin in the manner that the pancreas would do it. The insulin pump therapy is touted as being superior to the conventional insulin therapy and daily injections.

The organization is also making contributions to JDRF for each person who contacts them regarding management of diabetes. We need to get 'in cinque' and do all we can to reduce the number of diabetes sufferers, especially children, in this country.

OBESITY
First published March 16, 2004

For years, I have fought fat! The proper name for my affliction is obesity. Yet I choose to call it what it is; fat. We call chickens, cows, and pigs fat when we find a lot of grease in them when we cook them and it is the same thing when we eat them; fat. It helps to make us fat. We, not just me, but our nation has become fat. Surely, we can blame McDonald's for a lot of it because it is a fast food eatery.

Fast food eateries cook food fast. We eat it fast and then we get fat ***fast!*** That may be the reason that a New York mother sued McDonald's. Her son allegedly ate all three of his daily meals there and his weight and health went off the chart. I blame his mother for allowing him to eat there on a regular basis which is an indication that she was **_not_** doing her job. I feel that McDonald's in this case should have counter sued.

Mc Donald's and Kentucky Fried Chicken have nutrition charts available and if you ask for one, they will give you one. These are the only two places which I have asked for one. After checking them out, I decided to make my trips to these places scarce and in emergencies when this is the best I can do for eating.

On the other hand, it is equally important that we know what we are eating and the amount of fat that we consume, but it is also the amount of food we eat. We eat too much! As an observer of people, a social scientist, I have learned that several things seemed to have ushered in American obesity: food stamps, McDonald's and other fast food establishments, pizza parlors, free school lunches and breakfasts, instant foods and the microwave oven coupled with convenience stores.

Personally, I have nothing against any of the above stated items, but I do believe that we need to use more discretion in our selections and better timing. I am going to eat pizza, but I try to omit other high caloric foods when I eat it, usually on Saturday when I prefer not to be caught in the kitchen, yet do not want anyone to tell me that I am obese.

Obesity has become one of the main issues with the U. S. Secretary of Health and Human Services. He is advising us to lose weight as he believes, as I do, that obesity and diabetes have a very high correlation, especially in children. The average fat child has diabetes. If it is not discovered at an early age, he will usually have it as he ages. We have wondered why there is so much diabetes in this country and it seems that it is all because we eat too much and too much of the wrong things, causing obesity and diabetes. It appears that we are in a hurry to get fat, sick and die. Those of us with low metabolism rates, who do not exercise and eat too much, need to get 'in cinque' and go on a reduction diet.

WEIGHT LOSS PROGRAMS
First published April 12, 2004

By Now, most of us who started a diet to shed those holiday pounds which we took on during Christmas and New year discovered at Easter time that we had slipped backward and that Easter frock did not fit as we had hoped. With renewed interest and new focus on shedding that unwanted adipose tissue, we are back on the weight-loss trail.

At the outset of this chronological year, the book stores were and still are crammed with dissertations on how to lose weight. Everyone who has any clout in the medical or quasi-medical field, who had any desire to write about losing weight, has written one, and they all tout theirs as the best way to lose weight. I have read about many of them and even tried some, too often with poor results.

One of the oldest weight-loss programs that I can recall is the patented Weight Watcher's program. It is a group endeavor in which you pay to participate. Richard Simmons' program emphasized exercise and food exchanges to maintain a balanced diet while losing weight. This program also called for some payment of fees if no more than for the plan itself.

Another plan which I have tried is good for a couple of weeks for a quick loss of 5-10 pounds was successful for me in my younger more active days. You eat a boiled egg and a half grapefruit for breakfast and lunch and a steak and spinach for dinner, but it is harmful if done more than two weeks. I was given the Cabbage Soup Diet but found that my patience with making the concoction was too short to try it though I observed a lady who really took off weight and found a new husband who swept her off her feet, out of town, closed her profitable business and to an exciting new life as a result.

Dr. Phil promises an exciting new life in his book on losing weight, just as Dr. Atkins in his book, a program where you can purchase commercial food in stores for this program. The South Beach Diet, also written by a doctor, emphasized control triglycerides as the key to weight loss. The diet devised for diabetics is similar to the South Beach Diet and Richard Simmons diets as they would have count the grams of fat and carbohydrates that you consume daily and make exchanges based on the allowable totals of certain foods, while permitting the consumption of 1800 calories per day.

Calorie counting is what I have found to be the ***most effective*** of any diet. I have found that if I consume 500 less calories per day than I need to maintain my current weight, that I can lose a pound in a week. One must consume 3500 less calories than is needed per week in order to lose a pound. I count calories. When I *do not cheat*, I lose weight. In twelve weeks, I have lost 12 pounds. I eat what I want to eat without concern of the grams of fat, carbohydrates or triglycerides. I eat less. The key to losing weight is to **_eat less!_** We eat too much! When we eat less, we consume fewer calories, thereby we lose weight. It is time to get 'in cinque,' lose weight and be healthier.

VII–MEDICARE AND INSURANCE

COMPETITION FOR MEDICARE DOLLARS
First published November 24, 2003

From the Gulf of Mexico to the Canadian border, one can see Christmas decorations galore. It appears that this year has had so many negative experiences for so many of us until we want the nightmare to end.

Every day, on the television, the radio and in the newspapers and news magazines, we read about the American casualties in foreign lands. No one in this country ever imagined that this would be the case when Congress appropriated funds for the military expeditions at the request of the President. Congressional faith is also reigning as military troops get fifteen day leaves from Iraq, Iran and Bosnia and then are sent back to the front for another campaign and another chance to lose their lives. It appears that there is no end to this fiasco, as more money is pumped into war efforts while Americans, especially senior Americans get the shaft.

It appears that it is not enough that Social Security and Medicare treasurers are being used to pay for other areas of the federal government's budget, but here is a new assault on those funds being demanded of Congress by our President. He wants to fix the Medicare and Medicaid benefits programs to be in direct competition with corporate programs. The passage of this competitive aspect of the bill will be riding on the idea of helping seniors to pay their prescription bills. Hogwash!! The other seemingly weird thing about this effort is the AARP (American Association of Retired Persons) has bought into this fiasco. What is in this for the administrators of AARP? There has to be something other than benefits for senior citizens who have become members of AARP. Is it the fact that AARP sells Medicare supplement insurance which is competitive with other supplements?

If Medicare benefits are made to be competitive with corporate plans, it appears that the cost of Medicare benefits will triple in cost, defeating the purpose of purchasing it in the first place. Most workers paid into Medicare while working and got coverage for a least forty (40) quarters or ten years prior to retirement, at a cost of approximately $5,000. 00 during these ten years. Then, after retirement, the cost of Medicare has not been reduced. A retiree pays each month of retirement and two payments during the first month of retirement. Each year, the cost of Medicare increases, usually wiping out any increase due to the rise in the cost of living. It is time to get 'in cinque' and let our Congressmen and AARP know that we are not in accord with the new Medicare plan being pushed through Congress.

PRESCRIPTION COST AND DISCOUNTS
First published May 3, 2004

Last week, we discussed the option of purchasing a prescription drug discount card from a Medicare-Approve insurance company or keeping a card which you have obtained as a part of your Medicare supplement insurance program with which you already have prescription drug coverage. If you already have a discount card without supplement coverage, with a Medicare-Approved company, there is no need to get another card unless another company provides a greater discount than you already have. The other variable to assess is the monthly or annual cost of the plan you choose now. From observation, these plans will have various prices and even perhaps different discount amounts. A plan which costs $10.00 per month or $120.00 per year, may not offer as much discount as a plan which costs $20.00 per year, so this is what one needs to know to make an educated choice until such time as you may purchase the prescription drug coverage directly from Medicare in 2006.

In 2006, prescription drug benefits will be a part of Medicare and the plans may vary, but the cost will be $35.00 per month with a $250.00 deductible. That is, you will pay the first $250.00 for your prescriptions. From $250.00 and up to $2,250.00, Medicare will pay 75% of your drug costs and you will pay 25% of these costs.

Once your prescription drug costs exceed $2,250.00, YOU will pay 100% of the cost until your costs reaches $3,600.00. Medicare will pay about 95% of the costs of your prescriptions after your cost reaches $$3,600.00

According to the Social Security Administration, extra help will be available to people with low incomes and limited assets. Income limits will be set in 2005 and those persons with income below a certain level will not have to pay the premiums or the deductibles. Those person will only have to pay a small co-payment for their prescriptions.

At $35.00 per month, the Medicare coverage will cost $420.00 per year. If your prescriptions cost $50.00 per month, the cost will be $600.00 per year. After you pay the $250.00 deductible, only $350.00 will be left for you to pay 25% of, which would be $87.00, bringing your total out-of-pocket expenses to $757.50. *Without the Medicare coverage,* it would have been only $600.00 for the year or $157.50 *less.* It would not be worth the premium.

On the other hand, if your prescription drugs cost $1000.00 per month, or $12,000.00 per year, you would spend $420.00 for your premium and your deductible of #250.00 or $670.00. The cost between $250.00 and $2,250 would be $500.00, making the total spent up to that point, $1,170.00. You would pay 100% of the next $1,350.00 until you reach $3,600.00 and you would have spent a total of $$2,500.00 out-of-pocket money. After you have spent $3,600.00, Medicare will pay 95% of the remaining cost and you will pay 5% or $407.50 of the $8,250.00 left totaling $2,927.50. Three-fourths of the total cost would have been paid by the Medicare insurance, making the premium worthwhile. So let us get 'in cinque' and make the right choice.

MEDICARE APPROVED CARDS
First printed August 10, 2004

Finally, the Medicare-approved discount cards are available for purchase to help to reduce the cost of prescription drugs for the elderly. The cards, regardless to the insurance company which issues it, will bear a black oval symbol with 'Medicare' in the oval; the 'R' will extend outside the oval bearing a cross which will make an 'x' or 'Rx,' with 'approved' below the oval. If your card does not carry this seal, it is __*not*__ Medicare-approved.

This discount program which has been put into effect is temporary. It will be phased out when Medicare begins to cover prescription drugs, which they *do not* pay for now. This program will go into effect in January, 2006 at which time the discount cards will no longer be of use.

The discount card can be purchased by any person eligible for Medicare. Persons who have benefits from Medicaid will not be eligible for a discount card. Most cards will cost about $30.00 or less, but one would need to figure out which one gives the greatest discounts for the drugs needed. Various companies will have different prices for their cards and different benefits.

To decide which company to use, one would need to see which company pays the most on the prescription needing to be filled. Of course if you already have a program which gives a discount on prescription drugs, you may not need or want to purchase a Medicare-approved card. However, if the discount card gives better benefits than your supplement, you may want the card.

One needs to be aware of the offers in the mail to seniors, especially from insurance companies offering a 'senior security plan,' as though it is a state or government plan. Do not be confused by such offers as they are pitches to have you purchase life insurance. There will be a statement in such fine print that you will need a magnifying glass along with bifocals to read, stating that it is not affiliated with Social Security Administration or any other government agency.

To find out more about the Medicare-approved discount cards you may log on to www.medicare.gov, selecting "Prescription Drugs" or call 1-800-MEDICARE (1-800-6334227). Though not perfect, let us get 'in cinque' and erase fear, frustration and doubt about the new program designed to help us save money on prescription drugs.

GENERAL FUNDS vs SOCIAL SECURITY AND MEDICARE
First published December 23, 2004

Some of us are still celebrating the festive holiday season and we find ourselves in yet another quandary about Social Security and Medicare funds. And, we wonder why, when we get a five dollar raise on our Social Security check for a new year, we find that our Medicare fees have been increased five dollars, consequently our cost of living raise went to pay for the rising cost of our medical care.

President Bush feels and has felt ever since he has been President, that young Americans should be able to divert some of their Social Security taxes to private accounts. Taxes are currently put in the General Fund and are used for everything from the paper clips in the oval office to the expensive Hummers used in Iraq.

Privatizing Social Security taxes would mean less money in the General Funds. That is understandable, but what is not understandable *is why* the trustees of the Social Security Board have not seen to it that the Social Security monies and Medicare monies are not put in a separate fund for those purposes. It would help if the monies used for other things are repaid, but that does not happen either. The Social Security deficit is caused by other departments of the government using Social Security and Medicare monies.

It should be common knowledge now to ***all Americans*** *that the taxes paid by the workers of America for Social Security and Medicare are used whenever and wherever the federal government sees fit to use it!* It appears that we are lucky that there is anything available for what it is intended.

We work hard, pay income taxes, Social Security and Medicare taxes and quite often have to jump through hoops to begin receiving the benefits which we think we are entitled. If you become disabled during your employment years, you must not be able to ***do anything*** in order to be eligible for Social Security Disability benefits. It is easier to become a recipient of SSI or Supplemental Security Income, which is also administered by the Social Security Administration. Many people, who have never been employed, are recipients of SSI, having never contributed anything to the funds. They are protected under the 'equal protection of the law; amendment and have the same rights as any other American citizen, and even some non-citizen immigrants.

It is time for our President and any other government official to stop trying to put the fear of the future in our hearts and get busy trying to do the right thing when it comes to the government benefits in which we have a stake. It is time for us to get 'in cinque' and let our Congressmen know what and how we feel about the administration of Social Security and Medicare benefits.

VIII-FAMILY

FAMILY RESTORATION
First published September 13, 1994

Confucius said, "An orderly family is the key to a peaceful society and a well-run government." If this is true, our society has a multiplicity of disorders. It also would mean that we need to get our disorderly families in order.

The word 'family' has been 're-defined' by modern sociologists. There was a time when a family was defined as a mother, a father and some children. If there were no children, a married man and his wife were defined as a household and called a couple. A single parent with children was defined as a 'broken' family. Of course, we have always had the extended family of grandparents, parents, grandchildren, aunts, uncles, cousins, sisters and brothers.

Minority sociologists have known for years that any living arrangement which involved an denomination of 'blood kin,' was **FAMILY.** Family members knew their 'place' in the family. He/she or whoever earned the 'bread' in the family was generally the head of the family and was respected by the rest of the family. Everyone in the family had daily chores and were expected to get them done without too much prodding.

Families were generally large and living quarters were usually small, which meant that everyone had to respect the other members' space. Consequently, the family harmony reigned. When peace was disturbed, the head of the family restored order as all members generally supported the family head's decisions. Family order contributed to a peaceful society.

We MUST get 'in cinque' and restore order to our families. Our families need 'heads.' They need working heads. They need sober heads and drug-free heads; caring and loving heads; thoughtful heads; heads with the ability to put young people of all ages on the RIGHT TRACK before they are school age.

FAMILY STANDARDS
First published January 18, 1995

The family is the basic social unit in any society. Our communities all over our country have experienced a breakdown in our basic unit which has had a domino effect on the rest of society. Being progressive as we are, we have changed the definition of 'family.' Sociologically speaking, this may be good and desirable. In reality, this new sociology has not been all that it is cracked-up to be.

Normally, families consists of parents, (a mother and a father, grandparents or aunts and uncles, even cousins and older siblings sometime) children and in many instances other relatives of the immediate persuasion. Regardless of denomination, the 'parents' set the standards for the family and enforce as well. The children of the family follow the directions of the parents and as a rule, the children are well behaved and experience success in school and other social organizations. Their concept of appropriate behavior is much different from that of children who grow up in a re-defined family situation.

Children from one-parent homes especially those without a father, have the concept that a father is in no way a necessary variable in a family. It is this concept which also gives rise to the birth of babies by teenagers. Girls have babies fathered by boys who have no interest in family or fatherhood, but in sex. They make naive girls equate sex with love and so the problem grows. Parents, get 'in cinque' and pull your family together and put our children on the road to acceptable social behavior.

FAMILY TOGETHERNESS
First published March 29, 1995

There was a time when families sat around the radios, in the days before television, and when they sat in front of a twelve inch television screen to hear and/or see a musical concert. The music was often classical or baroque, jazz, folk songs, the 'standards' or popular songs. The music was wholesome and easy on the ear.

Families had preferences about the category of music which their family members enjoyed as there was usually only one radio or one television set in the home. Everyone had to listen or watch the same program. The families developed togetherness.

The family togetherness was reflected in the school curriculums. Before prayer was taken out of the public schools, many children learned the songs which they sang at church on Sunday, in the school on the next Monday.

Learning to sing was not the only music taught in public schools. Music appreciation was an important part of the music course. Listening to the great works of the 'master' and learning about their backgrounds was important and required learning.

It gives me great pain when I hear students commenting that 'classical' music gives them a headache or causes them great discomfort. It is time that some of the sounds passing for music be buried in the past. We need to get 'in cinque' and expose our children to MUSIC.

There may be some wholesome, non-deafening, understandable rap music to be heard and hopefully there is, but our children need to be aware of the wholesome alternatives to 'bump and grind,' the 'be-boxing,' and the 'Tootsie Roll.'

SOCIAL GRACES AND THE FAMILY
First published April 2, 1995

Much is said about the shortcomings of single-parent homes in regards to the upbringing of young children. Yet, many fail to realize that many of America's most outstanding citizens have and still come from single-parent homes, but homes where they were loved and nurtured and felt compelled to excel.

On the other hand, one often hears about the merits of homes where both parents reside and bring up their children. It is seldom that you hear about the children from homes with both parents where the children are growing up like weeds without any discipline, proper nourishment, adequate clothing or love.

This is often referred to as a dysfunctional family. I prefer to call it a non-functional family. Both parents are caught up in the 'rat race' trying to make a dollar in order to keep body and soul together in most instances and consequently have no time for their off-springs. They barely have time to feed their children and more often than not, the children are not fed properly. Many of these children do not know how to sit down at a table and eat properly using the silverware instead of eating with two fists instead of a fork. They are not taught how to keep themselves and their belongings clean; how to pick up after themselves and keep their home fairly orderly. They have no respect for each other or anyone else. These are the children whose parents are first to go to school to find out or 'tell off' teachers whom they think are mistreating their children. These are the children who tell the teacher all of their problems because there is no one at home who will listen to them.

We need to get 'in cinque' and realize that many children are sensitive to what goes on around them. In addition, they observe closely what goes on around them and what is said around them. Parents of all denominations and household classifications should be aware of the social graces of their children and teach them how to act. This is a skill which children should have WHEN THEY ARRIVE AT SCHOOL, not learn after arrival.

TAKING BACK THE NEIGHBORHOOD OF FAMILY?
First published May 11, 1995

On a regular basis now, you can pick up a newspaper or magazine and read about communities and their actions to *take back their neighborhoods.* It sounds good on paper and makes good reading. Certainly, there are some techniques and positive points to be acquired from reading a bout, seeing or even being involved in such activities. It just sounds like putting the 'cart before the horse' to me.

I have this very strong opinion that in order to take back the neighborhood, you must first take back families and homes. After all, we learned in the early years of our education that families lived in homes which made up the neighborhood. Further, the neighborhood usually had within it, a school where the neighborhood children left their homes five of the seven days of a week to attend. Then, there was usually a church or several, depending on the size of the neighborhood.

The families in the homes have changed drastically. They have transcended patriarchal (father headed or ruled), and matriarchal (mother headed or ruled), to child-centered or juvenile-ruled. I am still trying to process what is taking place when adults place this type of burden on children.

Carving out a living or a meager existence can be a burden to many parents but there is still no need to relinquish parental responsibility and put a child in complete control of his destiny. When this happens, all too often, 'there goes the neighborhood!' It is time for parents to get 'in cinque' and 'TAKE BACK THEIR FAMILIES.!' When families are again controlled by responsible parents, the neighborhoods will again belong to families.

FAMILIES AND SOCIAL DISTANCE
First published October 17, 2003

Every year, especially since Alex Haley's *Roots,* families have gotten together annually and semi-annually to have a family reunion. It has become so popular until some individuals attend three to four a year to be involved in their maternal and fraternal family get-togethers.

People who are descendants from a common ancestor come together, talk, plan, eat, play and socialize with relatives who have surnames in common, or a parent who has the same surname as an ancestor *root.*

Family members see each other and most only hear from each other when it is time for a family reunion. This one annual meeting is often all that they have in common other than their surnames. Some even send each other Christmas cards and invite them to special affairs from time to time. Once in a while, a friendship is formed and that is good.

Once upon a time before televisions, computers and cellular telephones, people had time to know their family members and care for them as relatives and friends. Everyone is in a hurry now and barely remember the names of their family members unless they see them regularly and talk to them on the cellular telephone sometime between doing the e-mail and watching television.

Because of this social distance between relatives, it is no wonder that there is a great demand for nursing homes and retirement homes instead of just being sick or simply retiring *at home!* We are widening the cultural lag chasm. We have lost the real meaning of loving and caring. We see loving and caring now as the ability to pay for the services of a retirement home or nursing home for our loved ones; our family members who have the same surname. We depend on someone else to do what families used to do. That includes raising our children in nurseries and daycares. Some of us even depend on the schools to feed our children.

When we are at home and sick, there are *for hire* agencies which will take care of us at home because our family does not have time. We are on a fast track to where? We live a little bit longer, but where, doing what? It is time that we get 'in cinque' and get acquainted with our family and make it possible to depend on family in times of need because we love each other unconditionally, not as a social situation or obligation.

MARRIAGE: FIXING THE FAMILY
First published September 13, 2004

With crime blatantly on the rise and neighborhoods making proposals on a daily basis to 'take back' their neighborhoods, it would appear that they would give some thought to 'taking back families.' The breakdown of the family is one of and perhaps the basis for so many of things in our society today which is wrong, or going wrong. It is broke and it needs fixing.

In an attempt to 'fix' the family, we are very busy working on all of the symptoms. We spend our wheels on teenage pregnancy, lost morals, drug use and sales, low or lack of income, unemployment, inadequate educational systems, homosexuality, promiscuity, deadbeat dads and mothers, atheism, politics, taxes, inadequate health insurance services, inequalities of all kinds and the list goes on and on.

It would be very difficult to decide which of these factors should be worked on first to fix the family, but there has to be one that begins with a mother and a father. It is from these two variables, that the child is added, making the couple become a family. A man and a woman without children are *__a couple, not a family,__* whether they are legally married or not. If there is a child or children born of the couple, *__it is a family,__* legal or not.

Different societies have different ideas about what the goals of a marriage or family should be. These goals are based on what the local society considers how families should originate and how they should be organized. Matches are made by parents in some societies with the couple having no say in the choice. The choice must be made within certain groups in some societies and in the United States, most matches are based on *love* and less frequently others are based on financial independence and stability.

The *love* marriage is about the *__least__* stable of all marriages in the world. If the love is lost, everything goes down the drain: home, children, possessions, companionship, security and social and economic status. *Institutional families,* the kind still predominantly found in Europe and other countries, possess all the characteristics that exist in the *love* marriage, but the family stays together. The *love* couple leaves the institutional family or the extended family and lives alone. They want children for fulfillment, not to be a part of a working institution, but something to adore and love *(Sociology, Paul H. Landis.)* Because America is considered a 'land of plenty,' young couples venture out to get their share of the 'American pie.' Too often, there is not a healthy slice within their reach and love dies. Divorce enters and another family has 'bit the dust!' It is time that we get 'in cinque' and pass a law to require 'couples in love' who are potential parents, to take and pass a course on *__Foundations of Love, Marriage and Family__*. It can lead to better choices in mates, more stable marriages and families. This could be a required high school class.

IX-MOTHERS AND FATHERS

DEADBEAT PARENTS: PART I
First published April 26, 1993

We hear a lot today about *'deadbeat dads'* and wonder why they exist. The answer is simple. Most 'deadbeat dads' have or had 'deadbeat dads.' It is with them, a way of life. There is however, another variable in this scenario which we will discuss in Part II.

Deadbeat dads teach their sons what they know about life and how to live it. They want to conquer the nicest girls for their wives and teach their son the same values. These men usually idolize their own dads even after they have deserted their moms who are left behind to rear them.

Some of the 'deadbeat dads' BELIEVE that women are strong and will survive along with the children that they leave behind because "My mama did it. She took care of us after my dad left us. My wife (or girlfriend) can do it too."

The problem with this reasoning is that the 'deadbeat dad' has no idea in many instances HOW his mom did it. He further has no idea how his kids' mom will do it, nor does he care. His own mom had either been too busy trying to do it and did not have time to let him know how, OR she really did not WANT him to KNOW HOW she did it. In either case, a 'deadbeat dad' was responsible.

We need to get 'in cinque' and start requiring by law, parenting classes for 'deadbeat parents who leave their children's welfare to others.

DEADBEAT PARENTS: PART II
First published May 3, 1995

Deadbeat parents come in two varieties; male and female or dads and moms. We discussed the first variety last week, dads. It is mom's turn now.

Being a mom, I have observed moms throughout my lifetime. Some were moms of my friends; some were my friends, some were the moms of my daughter's friends; some were social service clients, while others were moms of my students and some of their friends. Though some children are not sure who their fathers are, most know who their moms are. Ironically, moms are TOO OFTEN, the reason we have a double standard in the social activities expected and permitted in boys and girls and men and women.

Girls are expected to be feminine, dainty and innocent and pure. Yet, they are expected to marry boys who have grown up like 'alley cats.' It is not unusual for 'alley cats' to remain 'alley cats.' No mother in her right minds wants her daughter to marry an 'alley cat' but she fails to see her son as one! This is an example of what I mean.

I was visiting a close friend one day while her teenaged son was entertaining his girlfriend in their basement recreation room. I inquired about their presence down there without her and her reply was that she did not care what they did. I was terribly upset as I knew that she was very concerned about what her daughter did. I suggested that she should think of her own daughter and want other mothers to be protective of her in their home. Her argument was that she would not permit her daughter to visit a young man in his home and if she did, she deserved whatever happened to her.

Needless to say, I thought long and prayed hard that all mothers would realize that their sons need guidance just as their daughters do and they also need to learn to be protective of girls rather than exploitive, regardless to whose daughter the girl happens to be. Mothers, get 'in cinque' and protect every mother's daughter and teach every mother's son that if the girl is not good enough to be his wife then he should not get involved with her.

'BEING LIKE DAD'
First published June 13, 1995

This time of the year, around Father's Day, many thought come to mind. Because of holiday commercialism, one would get the impression that all fathers are 'in cinque' and worthy of 'fatherly praise.' Be that as it may, I came across a poem, author unknown, which I feel says more about Dad than anything else I have read recently:

> "Well, what are you going to be, my boy, when you've reached your manhood's years;
> a Doctor, a lawyer, or orator great, moving throngs to laughter and tears?"
> But he shook his head, as he gave reply in the serious way that he had;
> "I don't think I'd care to be any of them; I just want to be like My Dad?"
> He wants to be like his 'Dad.' You men, did you ever think as you pause,
> That the boy who watches your every move is building a set of laws?
> He's molding a life you're the model for, and whether it's good or bad
> Depends on the kind of example you set for the boy who'd be like Dad.
> Would you have him go everywhere you go? Have him do everything you do
> And see everything that your eyes behold. And woo all the gods you woo?
> When you see the worship that smiles in the eyes of your lovable little lad,
> Could you rest content if he gets his wish and grows up to be like his Dad?
> It's a joy that none but yourself can fill; it's a charge you must answer for;
> It's a duty to show him the road to tread ere he reaches his manhood's door.

It's a debt you owe the Almighty God; a great joy on this earth
    to be had;
This pleasure of having a boy to raise who wants to be like his Dad!

WHAT'S A DAD?
First published June 3, 1996

I read an article a few days ago about a young man who called his father-in-law 'Dad.' He started out by mentioning that "Dad" was a man whom he competed with in vying for his wife's affection. He also described how this man gave him advice which he looked upon with suspicion because he had not had the benefit of knowing his *own* dad. He described the relationship of this man to his mother-in-law and soon began to see some merit in the things that he gave him advice on. He discussed the outing that he and his father-in-law took together such as hunting, fishing, ball games and his private little jokes and 'secrets' which they shared. It became obvious to him that his father-in-law was perhaps everything that he would or could have had in a father of his own. He ended by saying that he simply called him 'Dad.'

It is a beautiful story in which a fatherless child, especially a boy, found a 'dad' he could call his own, even as an adult. This kind of relationship, full of *respect, love, trust and camaraderie* is the benchmark of a father-child relationship. It is what it should all be about. Father-daughter relationships should not be an exception. As a matter of fact, these are often stronger than father-son relationships. Boys often bond stronger with their mothers, it appears, from observation, but families in which there are two loving parents, the ties usually bind.

No matter what type of family a child belongs to, there is still a good reason to uphold and promote the natural order of things; a home with a 'Dad.' It is time to get 'in cinque' and put the *"Million Man March"* into ACTION! All good men MUST come to the aid of the *family!!*

MOTHER EXTRAORDINARE
First published December 10, 1996

I am behind in my reading and just got around to reading my August, '96 magazines. I was touched to tears as I read the August 19, 1996 article in the JET magazine concerning the quadriplegic mother whose daughter was recently married in a beautiful ceremony in which this handicapped mother played an organ solo.

Just to make certain anyone who has not read the article or have a vague idea as to what quadriplegic mean, the definition according to <u>The New American Dictionary and Health Manual</u> by Robert E. Rothenberg, M.D., is one who..." has paralysis of all four limbs, as in certain spinal cord injuries. When the Department of Public Welfare attempted to take custody of this lad's child, she demonstrated to the courts that she had the ability to care for her infant daughter by using her mouth and tongue to change the baby's diaper. Afterwards, she was granted full custody. She later learned to play an organ with her tongue and make a living to support her family by playing on the Boardwalk. She refused to accept public welfare.

In addition to *not* accepting public welfare, this quadriplegic lady *literally adopted* a six year old boy who is now twelve years old. She also has a seventeen year old daughter, but was a single mom for a long time.

This article, to me says a lot. If a single mom without the use of any of her limbs can diaper a baby and financially support herself by learning a skill which she can do and showcase, it makes one think that too many 'parents' are non-productive because they are apparently suffering from quadriplegia of the brain. Surely, able-bodied adults should and could do a better job of caring for the adults of the future than is currently taking place in our society. Black boys and girls have just <u>*got to have* *more and better*</u> <u>***role models.***</u> It is time that we get 'in cinque' and lay a better foundation for our children. Whether celebrating Christmas and/or Kwanza, it will be a good time to dedicate and commit to a better future and New Year for our children. Have a *MERRY MERRY HOLIDAY!*

X: SEX

THE LITTLE THREE-LETTER WORD
First published September 25, 1993

One little three letter word has been a source of curiosity for young people for a very long time and apparently an area of exploration and continuous education for many adults. It is SEX.

Tons of books have been written on the subject and lately, many are in graphic detail. Schools 'teach' sex education. Parents teach sex education and so does a child's peers. Who is he going to believe?

As a child, I read every book that I could get my hands on, from the Birds and The Bees to The Stork Didn't Bring You. Fortunately I learned that kissing did not produce fertility.

Books at the disposal of children today teach that the body undergoes changes at puberty and that boys and girls are different. Now that AIDS (Acquired Immunodeficiency Syndrome) is an epidemic, children learn that clean needles should be used to 'do drugs' and that sex can kill you.

Parents find it difficult to talk to their children and some like my parents, put books at their disposal and entertain questions based on the readings. Some parents really do not know what to say. *Some have not learned enough to say.*

Schools carefully teach whatever no reasonable parent would object to; anatomy and the way various germs travel throughout the bloodstream and affect one's health. How the germ gets into the body is not an area of education *unless it does not involve sex.*

Peers are the greatest educators of all. They know everything first-handed and are willing to share all they know with their friends. The sad thing is, they do. Children get a misdirected and unreliable sex education from their peers which results in fertility and diseases.

Parents: talk to your children. Get 'in cinque.' Tell them the truth. Do not rely on others to give your children a reliable sex education. It will not happen. Schools give useful information, but parents need to reinforce it with the missing links. When you talk to your children, they will not need to talk to their friends. Better yet, they will not believe what they are told by others if you give it to them straight in the first place. 'Get in cinque.' Do it.

TEENAGE PREGANCIES
First published October 11, 1993

It was not too long ago when I was asked to become a part of a community organization which focused on teen pregnancy, representing another organization in which I am an officer.

I turned down the opportunity to be a part of this group for several reasons. The first reason is that I am interested in preventing teen pregnancy. The second reason is that once a girl is pregnant, she ceases to be a girl and becomes a woman. My third reason is that proper education at an early age for boys and girls is not readily available.

Preventing teen pregnancy will automatically eradicate the problem. Steps to do this are necessary and it requires community effort, but not from formally organized groups. It has to come from the concerted efforts of parents teaching sons and daughters the old Puritan standards upon which this country was founded. SEXUAL ACTIVITY OUTSIDE OF MARRIAGE IS NOT AN ACCEPTABLE ACT. The purpose of sexual activity is to procreate and the institution of marriage is the proper place for it. It forms the basis of a FAMILY.

This is the knowledge which needs to be driven home to young men and women who are physically able to procreate, but not legally eligible for marriage and parenthood. (Reason two will be discussed at a later date). Responsible adults need to get 'in cinque' and teach their children how to acquire self-control and refrain from adult activities until they are able to take responsibility for their acts.

TEENAGE PREGNANCIES: II
First published October 25, 1993

I promised to discuss my second reason as to why I declined membership of an organization to work on teen pregnancy because a girl ceases to be a girl but becomes a woman when she becomes a mother. This is what I was taught as a young girl, and in addition, I was no longer permitted to be in the company of such friends.

Not too long ago, in the distance past, when a girl became pregnant, the young father was sought out to declare his willful intention to marry the mother-to-be or to reluctantly participate in a 'shot-gun wedding.' There were few instances when these were not the choices, 'and they lived happily or unhappily ever after.' The birth certificates of the babies had both parents' names on them.

Today, young girls become pregnant and immediately they are transferred to an alternative school for young mothers-to-be while their cohorts continue to attend the regular schools and keep on procreating. This course of action follows the traditional double standards of our culture. It needs to change. Young men need to be accountable, willingly or unwillingly.

The latest trends in computerized technology, DNA (deoxyribonucleic acid) testing, sonograms and blood testing, along with paternity leaves, demand a change in the way we treat teen pregnancy. The word mentor sounds good, but is not the answer. TEEN FATHERS BEARING RESPONSIBILITY IS THE ANSWER.

Teen fathers need to be in school along with the expectant mother. They need to attend at least half of each day in a parenting class which is set up like a home with real babies and real problems to handle. They should work together and take responsibility for their actions. They should be encouraged by their own parents, cooperatively, to establish a home of their own as soon as possible even if it means parental dependency. Parents should be supportive until their children are independent.

In other words, get 'in cinque' and help your children to become responsible parents, not the perpetuators of birth certificates where the father's name is 'legally omitted' because EVERY child has ***two parents!***

SEXUAL EDUCATION IN PUBLIC SCHOOLS
First published January 2, 1994

It is the common belief in most communities that schools are in existence and designed to educate the students who attend. Because of this belief, the local communities, county and state governments tax citizens in order to pay for the education of its youth, especially those who fall into the category of the ages four through sixteen years.

For years, as long as anyone can remember, most emphasis has been placed on the 'three r's.' This was the main emphasis when families took responsibilities of teaching social skill and insuring that their children had proper nutrition, clothing and transportation to and from school.

As time has gone by, the family has given up much too much of its responsibilities to the government, via the schools. Many children get all of their meals at schools, purchased or free. They learn all of their social skills at school and many other necessities, or referrals for such at school, BUT they cannot get an adequate education because one very important subject is *not allowed* in the curriculum in many schools: SEXUAL EDUCATION!

Schools teach health and acquaint students with their anatomy. They teach them what they already know; where their sex organs are and the proper name by which to call them, but fail to explain how they should be taken care of or used in regards to the opposite sex. There is no mention of birth control because abstinence is all that students are taught about, which is noble.

Is there any wonder that teenage pregnancy and childbirth are on the rise? When we teach our children where the babies come from, they need to know how they got there in the first place. They need to know how to prevent unwanted births as well. Is there any wonder why so many children are abused?

As a community, we need to get 'in cinque' and start teaching our young people some real sex education in school, as the average family is not really equipped to speak candidly and intelligently with its children. Since the government has taken on other family responsibilities, it should not hinder progress.

HOMOSEXUALITY - ETC.
First published June 3, 1995

There is a sticky subject which I feel we are not giving enough attention to and consequently it is wreaking havoc for many of our teenagers. The subject is homo-sexuality. It is often difficult to detect in girls but most often too obvious in boys. It is our boys who are having the most problems coping and therefore are increasing the statistics in teenaged suicides and attempted suicides.

Teenaged suicide is and has been a serious problem for the past two decades. Parents and many friends of these victims are appalled when the suicide occurs and rack their brains endlessly trying to figure out what drove a child to this end.

The driving factor is often friends and parents who 'do not understand' and refuse to try to understand the often confused and frightened child. The child is frightened because his family and friends expect him to be 'normal' and he knows that he is NOT what they expect or call normal. He is confused because he fears that he will no longer be loved or respected by his family and friends if they find out that he is not normal. He will carry this self-secret within himself and try to hide it from those whom he loves and whom he wants to love him. This makes it difficult for the child to talk with someone who can help him to resolve his problem with himself and his family and friends. If he cannot make this transition, attempts at suicide usually follow. It is the only way they know to cry out for help. All too often, the cry is fatal.

Parents, get 'in cinque' and observe and talk to your children. Let them know that your love for them is unconditional. We know that some homosexual activity is learned and some is due to hormonal imbalances. Survey the situation and secure proper professional counseling for your son or daughter who has tendencies toward homosexuality. The gay rights movement is in full swing, but until society accepts it as 'right,' our young people are still in danger.

TELEVISION AND SEXUAL EDUCATION
First published October 15, 1998

Today, a young lady of the ripe old age of 13 years asked me if my daughter had come to me and asked me for permission to use birth control pills. I simply replied, "No." She then told me that her aunt had told her that she could come to her when she was ready to or wanted to use them. Before I could ask a question, she immediately said that she was not ready yet, of course, but that she would be able to go to her aunt when the time came. The day prior to this a young man of the ripe old age of 11 years old, had 'accidently' dropped a condom on the floor next to his desk. He and his property were referred to the counselor.

Teachers are not at liberty to discuss sex education with children at school without the written permission of their parents in many districts. Teachers may not have the same viewpoint, ideals and moral values as a child's parents, therefore, it is best that parents discuss sexual education with their very own children and not leave it to teachers, other children and according to what I hear the children say, **_Cinemax._** One boy told me, "Cinemax gets it on!" I said, "Well, perhaps I need to let your parents know that you are watching Cinemax." He said, "They will say that you are telling a story, because we don't have Cinemax at my house." I said, "Then, what I need to tell your parents is that you are watching Cinemax at someone else's house."

It is important that children are monitored at home to learn what parents desire them to learn, and they need to be monitored away from home. I personally learned that the standards you set in your home for your children sets limits for them, helping them to know when they have gone past the limits, but it does not keep them from going if they feel that you will not find out about their trespasses. I put my foot down on party records in my home, to find out later that my daughter could recite a certain one, word for word without missing a verb or object when I inquired of her about words or statement that my students found funny in class. She learned it as her friend's house; a friend whose mother did not mind or did not know what they were listening to. The televisions get the same treatments as tapes and CD's.

Personally, I feel that parents should not subscribe to shows that can vastly influence their children's actions negatively. It is time that we get 'in cinque' and know what our children are watching and decide upon the wholesomeness of it all.

XI-MORALITY

PEACEFUL EXISTENCE
First published January 3, 1995

Churches witness their greatest attendance for religious services during the Christmas holidays and Easter according to some ministers. Mother's Day is another great attendance getter in some denominations. These particular holidays for Christians are held during the same time as similar holidays for other religious groups. All of these holidays are centered on religious events in the life of *a 'messiah'* or some ceremony related to the harvest.

Large attendance rates during these holidays only, are indications that a large part of our population look upon these times as special, with some kind of blessing to be gained if one participates. It further appears that the believers also feel that their attendance on these special days at worship will be enough to carry them throughout the rest of the year. With this kind of religious participation, it is clear that the importance of the holiday is what our children are learning about. There is a serious omission of the principles of how to live a holy life and treat others as you would be treated.

Children need to know that being holy does not entail being what they call a 'nerd' or 'geek.' They need to know that our religious beliefs form the basis for our daily peace full existence. They need to know that regular religious ceremonial participation helps to build character and an individual who can cope positively with the ills of today's society. Parents and ministers need to get 'in cinque' and show our children the way.

REVAMPING RELIGIOUS CENTERS AND LEADERS
First published January 11, 1995

Religious beliefs, as a rule are a part of the average family's heritage, passed down from one generation to another. Whole families usually are of the same faith and often worship in the same religious center or a similar one if not residing in the same locale. Many families are re-evaluating their religious beliefs all over the United States these days as religious leaders have rocked religious organizations with scandal after scandal in the past few years.

Ministers who have taken the oath of celibacy have broken their vows and engaged in secret weddings and fathered children. Ministers who have taken the oath of poverty have been accused of stealing money and services from congregations which provide them with homes and table comfort. Ministers who vowed to live holy have been accused of mistreating their mates while engaging in illicit love affairs with members of their congregations and communities.

It is time that faith in religious leaders is restored to the position of real leadership in the community because in some communities, the church or religious center is the only vestige of ethnic identity left. Therefore, we need to get 'in cinque' and revive our religious centers and our religious leaders in order that families may have a nucleus.

COMMUNICATION: THE KEY TO MORALITY
First published February 3, 1996

Too many of our young people are leaving home these days for some reason or another, when they are really too young and innocent to cope with all of the evils of a fast-paced society. Time was, eons ago, young men especially, left home at an early age; some as young as thirteen years of age, to find gainful employment with which they could support themselves and in some instances send money back home to "Dear Ole Mom,' if the exodus had been a pleasant one.

Many of the young men had a minimum amount of education but a lot of 'mother wit' and common sense which enabled them to survive in a rugged society which required men to be ___**men.**___ Do not be mistaken, there was a lot of evil around in the 'good ole days,' also. The reality was, however, that the average person with all his wits about him could readily see and avoid much of the evil. *Good Samaritans were not as rare* in those days as they are now. Today, a *Good Samaritan* is suspect of having a hidden agenda. Everyone is suspect of having a hidden agenda. Do not mis-understand, *there are **devils*** out there masquerading as Good Samaritans, so it pays to be careful.

The complex world today makes it imperative that parents ***talk to children*** about what they will find outside their homes that might make life 'out in the world' not that great bowl of cherries that they think it is. If parents find it difficult to get their children to open up and talk to them, they should leave the door open so they can talk when they decide to do so. Communication is of utmost importance.

Lack of communication is one of the things which cause many young people to run away from home. A lack of understanding on the part of parent and child too often leads to a lack of communication. The child does not talk to his parent because he feels that his parent *'does not understand; him or his situation.'* It is time that we get 'in cinque' and pay more attention to our children and *all* of their needs. They need to stay at home with adult parental supervision until they have the world of work skills to survive in a fast-moving complex world.

"THE TRUTH SHALL SET YOU FREE"
First published August 8, 1996

It is normal for parents to love their children and stand by and stand up for them any time that they are needed. Parental love should be unconditional. By unconditional, we do not mean that parents believe everything that their children tell them about their activities and their relationships without question, as some of our children are prone to twist the truth a bit about many things.

The truth can untangle many webs and 'can set you free.' Our children need to be taught to TELL THE TRUTH regardless of the outcome. Arriving at a point in life where you can tell the truth and be ready to accept the consequences is ***called moral maturity.*** Children need help to grow and become morally mature, as when they lie, 'one lie calls for another.' Furthermore, a lie remains on the conscience, in constant fear of being revealed. The truth on the other hand, once told, frees the conscience and the sub-conscience. A wholesome thereafter is possible.

A wholesome life is what we all want for our children. Such a life would eliminate the possibility of the kinds of tragedy that children can cause for parents who trust and believe them, and for themselves. When children know that their parents will engage in fracases based on lies that they tell them, the children often grow up to be bullies and often end up dead at the hand of someone who could care less about their parents' attitudes or dispositions. The same tragedy could befall a parent who fails to inquire about the merits of a situation involving his/her child. For that reason, we need to get 'in cinque' and teach our loved, adored and admired children to tell the truth in ALL cases.

DAMNATION IN A HANDBASKET
First published December 11, 1996

The more I look at the state of our culture, our morals or *lack of morals;* it appears that we are now defeating the purpose for which this great *God-fearing* country was established. The people who came here to settle came to have freedom to worship as they pleased, the god and denomination or their choice; to gain wealth and political freedom. However, when the Supreme Court of the United States of America decided that Mrs. O'Hair and her, who is now a protestant minister now, had a right to be atheists and therefore also decided that her son did not have to be subjected to prayer in public schools, that is when America started down the road to damnation in a 'handbasket!' The good of the nation was sacrificed for the benefit of one individual who no longer appreciates it or who never did.

One does not have to be a historian, highly educated or above average in intelligence to realize that a grave mistake of which the ramifications are far-reaching, has been made. **A country without morals is a decaying country**. Without religion, we have no morals. Complete separation of the state and church is *impossible*. Our government manufactures all of the legal tender in our country. If we cannot have prayer in school, why does our money say, "**In God We Trust**?" Why does government want to trust a god whom our children, who spend most of their day, trying to learn to be good citizens, cannot practice learning to trust in school? All children need to begin their school day with more than bread. We can give them free breakfast and lunch but not the ingredient which will help them to be decent human beings and good citizens. This is the crux of the decay of the United States of America; *no prayer, no morals.* It is time that we get 'in cinque' and ***PETITION*** (One of the rights in the First Amendment to the *U.S. CONSTITUTION,* along with freedom of religion) the courts to reverse the Madalyn O'Hair decision: *Murray v. Curlett, 1963* which was combined with *Abbington School District V. Schempp* when it was heard by the Supreme Court.

Every public school district in America could combine its efforts and the O'Hair decision reversed instead of trying to do it as a single district or school in a district. A union of this sort would tell the courts something and get a worthwhile job accomplished. This needs to be a petition from across America. We need to get the ball rolling fast or the courts are going to learn a new word for 'criminal case backlog.' All children do not attend church or mosque or synagogue, ***but they all attend school!***

MORAL POLLUTION
First published January 26, 1998

There is pollution in America and then there is POLLUTION! Every time one turns on the television or the radio, the airwaves are polluted with the ins and outs of the most private activities of any human being. Is one led to believe that certain groups of people in this country will do ***anything,*** including keeping track of the sexual activities of the highest elected official in order to find a way to remove him from office?

Before the days of the *Scarlet Letter,* man has tried to legislate morality. By now, as a civilized country, we should know that this cannot successfully be done. "Thou shalt not commit adultery," one of the Ten Commandments of the *Bible,* was ignored before the ink was cold. That was over two thousand years ago. Jesus even told those who wished to stone the woman in the square, "He who is *without* sin, cast the first stone." Yet, we are still casting stones and not keeping the Ten Commandments.

In this the kind of pollution that we want our children to see on television, hear on the radio and read in the newspapers? This is a period of time when I hope they care more about that noise set to music that they call 'rap.' Maybe they will listen to it instead of all of the 'he say, she say' about big time political ramblings of the famous and infamous for whatever the reasons may be. It is bad enough when scandal strikes our homes and towns and get into the wind, but it is downright disgraceful when the world knows about it. It would seem that, when a man is married and his wife is not concerned about his meandering, that others would let them be.

On the other hand, what type of female is willing to air her personal, private, and intimate affairs with the world, unless there is a great deal of financial gain in it for her? Why would anyone risk their self-respect and credibility about something for which the ultimate goal is a haunting of generations to come? It is time that we, American citizens get 'in cinque' and get a grip on the real issues facing America and help our children to know the difference between 'fact' and opinion,' wherever it appears.

LIFE AS AN OPENED BOOK
First published December 21, 1998

This is by all means, the end of the worse political year in the history of the United States, ending with the impeachment of a President of the United States, whose only harm has been to himself and his loved ones because of his concept of morality.

Morality is a characteristic which we are not born with, but must learn and work to become morally mature. That includes being truthful about whatever you feel that you are morally mature to do. It is rather inherent of living the kind of life where there are no skeletons in your closets. On other words, your life and lifestyle should be an 'opened book.'

Whether your life is an 'opened book' or not, there are still limitations to your personal life that you do not want others poking around in, and questioning you about. This does not have to involve your sexual activities either. As an example, I applied to purchase a piece of real estate from a certain governmental unit and I was asked the question, "Where did you get your money to make this purchase?" I did become indignant and cancelled the application in a resentful manner because I felt that my personal affairs were being intruded upon, especially since I was going to pay cash. Had I borrowed the money, I felt there may have been some need for such a question, but using cash, I felt insulted, degraded and angry.

No matter how morally mature we are, there are certain personal matters that we just do not want to discuss with other people, no matter how close they are to us or how pertinent the information we have is to someone else. When we are put in a situation to be contrary, this is what often happens. It can happen to any human being no matter how many god-like characteristics they have. No human is infallible and that is not one of the characteristics of a President of the United States as described by the *U. S. Constitution*.

As 1998 comes to a close, we find ourselves involved in a combat crisis in Iraq, a political, partisan impeachment of the President, inflation, rising personal debts, quality education declining, rising crime rates under-recorded, control substance use still out of control, increase in homelessness, decrease in employment and decrease in faith in God. It is time that we get 'in cinque' and get 'our heads on straight,' because with all of these problems, 1999 needs the right start. May we all have a ***Happy New Year!***

MORAL MATURATION AND THE HOME
First published October 11, 2002

Too often we wonder 'what is wrong with our young people today.' We think and ponder and too often come up short of a logical answer. Our young people do not appear to have learned all of the social graces that we expect that they should have. We find them ungrateful, insolent, rude, irresponsible, not trustworthy, unreliable and irrational. These are a few of the adjectives often used to describe our young people. We fail to realize that they were ***not born*** this way. We are very slow to attribute their character to their home upbringing. In the past, this was the perfect answer to the question. Why not now?

There are so many more variables to be considered in this time and age than in earlier years. Yet, we cannot dismiss the home upbringing as the most significant variable. It is still the home which provides the basic skills of life for all children. This means that the home is really more important in the lives of children today than in the past. It should be the home which introduces the child to all other areas of life, beginning with the religious aspect. The belief which one holds should and most often does originate in the home. It is upon the basis of one's beliefs that one usually chooses the path that life will take.

Life's path begins at birth. The mental, physical and social growth begins at home with parents. When biological parents are unable to raise their children, they usually turn them over to someone who can help them to develop into responsible adults. Sometimes, that other person is a loving grandmother, an aunt or older sibling. For the most part, many grow up successful. We seldom hear much about the children who are described as wonderful, trustworthy, reliable, law abiding, courteous, respectful, initiative and loving. These children became all of those pleasant characteristics in their home.

Life temptations that take young people into unpleasant, unwholesome, and often illegal situations do so because of home upbringing or the lack of it. Years ago, children knew 'which side the bread was buttered on.' They knew what was expected of them and what their limits consisted of. Today, too many children are alone too long and must use their own poor judgment in complicated situations. When they make the wrong decision they are chastised based on how they got the $125.00 to pay for the last pair of tennis shoes, or their PlayStation, name brand jersey, video game, live hip hop concert tickets or latest DCD. Seldom do we hear reminders of the right choices to make. It is time for us to get 'in cinque' and teach our children how to make the right choices in order that we might use wholesome adjectives to describe them, because they are *wholesome and respectful.*

XII-ABUSE

NEGLECT
First published July 27, 1993

The other day, I went to see a man about repairing a door. As I left the resident, I could hear crying and moaning. Inquisitive as I am, I sought out the sound and discovered that it was coming from a child who was sitting on the cub of the street along with two other children.

Upon seeing the children, I immediately went to find out why there was sadness. I soon learned that the oldest child, age 8 was crying because her mom had left home and gone 'across the bridge' according to the 4 year old cousin.

The old children's protective service worker in me rose up and inquired about the caretaker in the absence of mother. The 6 year old said that 'Big Mama' was seeing after them. I asked them where did they live and they pointed to a group of apartments nearby. Then I asked for an address and neither child could tell me his address. I asked the brothers where their mother was they told me that she was at work. "Good," I said to myself.

Again, I asked the children who was home to see about them and they finally agreed that they were ALONE and had not eaten. It was now afternoon. The 6 year old told me that he was going to cook some hot links when he got back home. The 8 years old advised that her mom had told her to stay at home so no one would call the welfare. I suggested that they return home as they could have a heat stroke sitting on the curb in 90 plus degree weather, hoping in the back of my mind that "Big Mama" was at home. The little 8 year old told me that they were going to the park and they started in that direction. There were supervised children in the park who were having lunch. I wondered if they expected to have a share somehow.

The crying had ceased and like all good citizens, I notified Human Services of the situation. What else could I do? I started to buy them some food, but would mother curse me out because "We don't need your charity! You think you high and mighty and my children need your handouts. I take good care of my children! You just mind your own business, woman!"

I thought of taking the children to Human Services but would I, an honest citizen be arrested for abducting children? The neighbors who saw me talking to them and who were not concerned about the crying and moaning would surely call the police.

I did not dare to ask the neighbors to see after the children as they were talking loud, smoking and drinking and did not appear at all concerned. I did not know any of them and they seemed to be unfamiliar to the children as well.

What is the lesson to be learned from this experience? There are many. We should all be concerned about the welfare of OUR CHILDREN. THEY ARE OUR FUTURE! Child neglect often leads to outward physical abuse. Hunger for food, love and attention IS ABUSE. Research has shown that children abused often have multiple problems in school. Children with problems are called 'problem children.' Learning is often a problem of the 'problem child.'

Parents, friends, neighbors and Christians, we MUST raise our children. Bring back the neighborhood concern and CARE. Install it like cable TV in every home and get 'in cinque.'

VIOLENCE IS ABUSE
First published September 3, 1993

Turn on your radio, your television or pick up a newspaper or selected news magazine and you see or read about violence. Much of the violence, much too much of the violence has been perpetuated by youthful offenders whose ages range from two to twenty-two. Much too much of the violence takes place in the home and at school. Sophisticated weapons are used to do violence. Where does a minor secure a weapon? That is one question.

What makes a minor decide that he or she needs a weapon? That is another question.

There are many people who say that rap music and the media are responsible for youthful violence. There may be some truth to some of this, but the bulk of the responsibility falls on parents who have the responsibility to teach children the difference between right and wrong and reality and fantasy. If they learn the difference between right and wrong, that will be a step in the right direction.

Many children daily witness violence in their homes and in their neighborhoods and feel that this is the 'American way.' Then these same children go to school, to the malls, to church and around the neighborhood offending others and feel that there is nothing wrong with their actions. Their parents defend them often saying that their children are defending themselves from others and have that 'right.' They fail to realize *that their rights end where the next person's rights begin.*

Too many parents put weapons in the hands of their children by leaving them where they are accessible or by making them feel that they need to have them for protection.

Parents need to stop their acts of violence against family members and friends and set limits for their children explaining the difference between right and wrong; reality and fantasy. It is time to get 'in cinque' and stop the needless violence in our home, schools and neighborhoods.

PARENT ABUSE
First published December 3, 1993

While a lot of attention is paid to child abuse, there is another abuse which has a much more significant and permeating effect on families. It is parent abuse.

Many loving, well-meaning and attentive parents are abused every day in our society. These parents do all they can to care for their children and put them in the best case scenarios on a daily basis. They put their best foot forward in caring for their children, but they walk lightly because they are not sure where the thin line lies which if they cross over it will make them a bad parent, or a child abuser.

The reason for their fear lies in family codes and state laws which set limits for how families and family members care for and discipline THEIR children. Good parents are afraid to discipline their children for fear the children will call 911 or the welfare agency that investigates child abuse cases. Consequently, children are NOT disciplined and have taken control of their homes and schools and other places ordinarily run by adults. They organize into groups and gangs and then they set the rules.

Frightened parents stand by waiting and hoping that the police or some benevolent organization will do what they wished they had the power to do; make their kid mind!

Parents, get together, get 'in cinque' and utilize your 'God-given' rights and discipline your children. Do it now and the police will be left out later. Fail to discipline now and watch your child be disciplined by youth officers and police later. Get 'in cinque' and take control of your children.

SPOUSAL ABUSE
First published January 12, 1994

There is one question about spousal abuse which always comes up: "Why does she or why does he continue to live with him/her when they are treated so badly?" There are at least two very good answers to that question. In some instances there are three good answers.

First, women especially, will continue to live with and depend on an abusive spouse out of *fear*. At this point in their lives, she is more afraid of the outside world and all that it holds than she is of her spouse. After all, she loves him and he 'loves' her. He will constantly tell her that he cares for her and that there is no one else in the world, outside their home that will look after her and take care of her the way he does. Some of these women have professional jobs and earn enough money to support themselves, but they are afraid to trust another man or themselves on a social level. They continue to be abused by their spouses.

The second reason why women stay in an abusive relationship is *hope*. Hope was one of ingredients of the prenuptial relationship and it continues to play a great role after the nuptials. Women know the capabilities of their spouses as well as their limitations and they pray and have hope that their dreams will come true. Their spouses will wake up, see the light and appreciate them and then the abuse will stop. They will live happily ever after. These occasions rarely come to pass, but women continue to hope. They ignore the statistics and keep on hoping. They will listen to advice from friend, relatives and professionals, but continue to remain in the relationship. If they leave, they always go back to the abusive spouse who may get on his knees and swear that the abuse is over. If she still has hope, she will return.

A third, but not nearly as important reason why women stay in an abusive relationship is *shame*. Many women are ashamed if anyone knows about their abusive relationship and will do most anything to keep it hidden from neighbors, friends and family members. They harbor a feeling of failure and loss of self-esteem. These are the kind of abused spouses who are subject to deep depression, violence to the abuser or self-destruction from controlled substances or other forms of bodily harm.

It is time for abused spouses, especially women, to take a close hard look at their relationship and get 'in cinque' and out of the nerve-wrecking situation. As Denise LaSalle sings, "Drop That Zero and Get Yourself A hero!"

PEDOPHILES
First published July 21, 2003

The midst of summer is here and it is the time of the year wherein we must be extra careful and watchful of our children with regards to the dangers that lurk. We most often think of keeping them safe from the hot sun and it consequences, the various bugs and other critters which can inflict danger upon us, children and adults as well. Somehow, we forget about the one danger which can inflict life-long agony upon young girls and boys, the pedophiles of this world.

Too often, we pick up the newspaper; hear the news on the radio and television only to hear that some child has been molested. Years ago, this was almost unheard of. In yonder years, parents taught their children to be seen and not heard. That also meant that they were not to hear about anything untoward that they had done and were to always be under the watchful eye of some adult. As a result, very few unpleasant, immoral things happened to our children. Many mamas were of the "Ma'dea' disposition, that is 'pistol packing mamas' and the average person in his 'right mind' was not going to 'mess with 'Ma'dea's child.' On the contrary, with drugs on the rampart, too many people in this day and age are *not in the 'right mind.'* This means that it is crucial that our children, the future generation be protected from the dangers of molestation

As a social worker, I have learned more about molestation that I care to remember. It was difficult for me to have to take a four-year old child to the doctor to verify that she had a venereal disease and see that treatments were followed through upon. You can only imagine the tears and screaming of a mother whose child is being taken away from her because of sexual abuse, by a relative in the home, no less. You wonder how these things could happen.

A young child is most often abused by someone he or she trusts and feels will not harm them. Once that trust is thoroughly secured, the secrets begin. The child is made to feel that the relationship between him and this trustful adult is something that *only they share;* therefore no one else needs to or should know about it. Even when the child doubts the relationship and feel that something is wrong, he will be assured that this is right and gifts are given, or some special treat to cement the relationship. There are some secrets that are kept through fear and intimidation. These are the kind wherein the abused often end up committing a heinous crime if not being placed in an institution for the mentally and/or emotionally disturbed. It is time that we get 'in cinque and be watchful of the summer activities which can be dangerous to us and our children.

XIII-BROTHERLY LOVE

REAL LOVE
First published May 26, 1998

If you in any way observe youth today and happen to discern anything about their values, you readily learn that love of humanity is *not* one of their strong traits. Love ends with ***family*** whether it is biological or gang related. Everyone else is the ***enemy.*** When they venture outside the family, love has one meaning only; **<u>SEX.</u>**

Sex is the one and only thing which occupies the mind of a large number of youth about age 11 and upward. They want to emulate the singers, rappers and movie stars whom they watch on television daily. They portray the sexiest sayings, clothing, dances and actions to them. They want to be like them; say what they say, sing what they sing, dance their dances and do what they do. The sparkling, glittering, backdrops and costumes will be there when they *arrive.* They know that if they can get everything just right, that they will ***arrive.***

Every song, movement, words and rhythm give some overture to love and sex as the very same thing. Listen to the words and hear, "*Sex me up;*" "*Make passionate love to me;*" "*Can't nobody love me like you do.*" "*Let your love come down.*" "*Freak me with your love.*" "*Don't gimme no lip if you can't gimme no hip.*" The videos make these words even more explicit. What is heard is seen and makes an even deeper impression in the mind of young people. These impressions on young minds make it almost impossible for them to learn anything of value which will help them in the future years as adults.

Young people live and long for a time when they can legitimately engage in the visions of ***love*** that they harbor in their minds and souls. Too often, too many of them cannot get beyond these visions and consequently choose a path of destruction at a very early age. Frustrations encountered with failures lead many to turn to drugs and other illegal activities as a means of survival. Those with an aptitude to rise above their nonproductive status may eventually do so if the opportunity comes their way. Many will be lost in the mire. We need to get 'in cinque' and put more effort into rescuing our youth and giving them more positive alternatives as they grow into adulthood. They need to know **real love;** unconditionally, from the heart, not the head.

LOVE ONE ANOTHER!
First published December 7, 2003

There is still room on this planet for a reason and a time to pray. This is the season of joy and giving; the time to make life worth living, because this is the time of year that the birth of the Christ child is said to have taken place, in a lowly manger, signifying the humble state of his birth.

This is the time to rejoice but there is so much illness, physically, mentally and emotionally among us until the most peaceful thing to do is to pray for our loved one and those persons who are far away from home on hostile battlefields. We need to pray for bereaved families everywhere.

Bereavement is something that most of us go through at some point in our lives. Far too many families face bereavement at this time of the year when they want to be happy and concentrate on the purchase or handcraft of certain presents for their family and friends. Sometimes, the vision of the almighty dollar clouds the memories of some family members and they forget about the love that they had or should have for each other.

When a family member dies, regardless of the season or the reason, will or no will, there are those who are unhappy, evil-minded and set out to make other members of the family unhappy and uncomfortable when they should be showing and feeling love for those whom are left behind and still able to return their love. They are especially upset when a loved one leaves an item of value to someone other than themselves. They forget that people have a right to give their belongings to whomever they choose, dead or alive. There is no need to be resentful of the beneficiary, especially to the point of destroying the property or causing bodily harm to the beneficiary.

When a person feels the urge to destroy what he cannot have, it is time for him to see a psychiatrist or a psychologist. Responsible family members should make it a point to see that such a family member receives the care that they need. What better time than the advent season to have this done! It is time for us to get 'in cinque' and realize that "What is For Us is For Us" and violence has no place in the scheme of family things! If Uncle Joe liked Brother John well enough to give him his Rolls Royce, be happy for him, he may give you a free ride. "Let us make love instead of War!

DONATIONS THAT SHOW LOVE
First published June 23, 2004

If you are in a habit of contributing to every worthwhile cause that solicits donations from you, then you find yourself being the recipient of that organization's house organs if they have one. I receive *"Habitat World"* and enjoy the various transformations that Habitat for Humanity makes around the world, in the United States and foreign countries.

Even before I knew that former President Jimmy Carter was involved with Habitat for Humanity, I felt strongly that this was an organization worth supporting, because everyone deserves a decent home. Years of going into substandard housing, as a social caseworker in large urban areas, makes you aware of the dire need for decent adequate housing. Too often, the outside façade gives no indication of what is behind the closed door.

The people who are living in substandard housing are not living there because they want to, but because a circumstance, too often beyond their control, is the reason for their being there. The main reason is most likely an inadequate or lack of income. Many residents are not unemployed, but *underemployed*. Employment is one of the criteria for being eligible for a Habitat home as well as the physical activity of actually building the house. Since many of us only know that Habitat builds houses, low income houses, we often think that they too, are substandard and object to Habitat homes being built in our neighborhood.

Habitat for Humanity, not only works to help people have decent homes, it also works to help people live as Christians through breaking down barriers among neighbors by showing *love*. The founder and president of Habitat, Millard Fuller believes in the **Bible** quote: *"Love*

your enemies, bless those who curse you, do good to those who hate you, and pray for those who spitefully use you and persecute you." – **Matthew 5:44**

One, who can truly live by that scripture, can be called a pure Christian. We can see why former President Jimmy Carter won the Nobel Peace Prize and works to dispel the NIMBY ('Not –In-My-Back-Yard') fears of Habitat home locations. There is a variety of acronyms used to describe how people feel about Habitat home. They range from BANANA: "Build absolutely nothing anywhere near anyone," to CAVEs: "Citizens against virtually everything," and NOPE: "Not on planet earth."

There are many ways to become involved in organizations that help mankind through volunteer services. It is time that we get 'in cinque' and help to make this world a better place instead of putting rocks and stones in the pathway of goodness.

XIV-VOTE

VOTING IS IMPORTANT
First published October 21 2002

For weeks now, and months in some instances, we have seen the billboards on the highways and streets of the states, and posted in private yards, filled with signs urging us to vote for various candidates for governmental offices, along with their mottoes or basic beliefs as to why they are best for the particular office for which they are running. Much of what we see is politics at its best. We often choose one political party over the other. Even when we vote for independent candidates we are still being political. We are telling the other parties that we do not like what they are standing for.

Regardless to what we believe, or do not believe, we **NEED TO VOTE.** Voting is the only way some of us have to make our desires known as to who we want to hold public offices in our governing bodies. This is also true for legislative propositions which are put before us for which we need to vote for acceptance or rejection. Failure to vote often results in that which we wish had not taken place. Too often, we feel that our vote will not count, but we must begin to feel that every vote counts.

True, the Florida fiasco of the last presidential election is not an ideal example of reasons to vote, but rather a ***good reason to make sure*** that ***YOU DO VOTE.*** There have been some voting irregularities in many states as long as Americans have been voting, but ***<u>we must still get out and vote!</u>*** Another good way to insure accuracy in voting is to get involved in the process by attending voter registration and polling seminars and participating in the polling procedures and watching for irregularities.

Some of us, who complain about the results of an election, fail to take that most vital step to voting because we have not registered to vote. It takes only a few minutes of the day whether you are employed or not, to register and become a qualified, genuine voter; to have our say about who and how our government runs. Having no say leaves little room to complain later. If you vote, you did your part. Just reflect on the trials, tribulations, constitutional amendments, civil rights laws and lives lost to secure the right to vote for all eligible Americans, and this alone is enough to make one feel compelled to go out and vote, or if not able to get out to secure the proper forms for absentee voting. It is time that we realize how important voting is in this country and get 'in cinque' and VOTE!

VOTING FOR OUR COLLECTIVE WELFARE
First published November 14, 2002

The national elections are over and counted. The Republican Party swept the nation with the majority of the votes for governors, senators and representatives giving the Republican Party a majority in the Senate and the House of representatives. Many people who voted for Democrats are disappointed. In fact, some were disappointed before the elections as in one of the big cities of Texas; it was discovered during the early voting that Democratic votes were registering as Republican votes on some voting machines. The matter was taken to court, but to the dismay of the voters and their representatives, those voted did not count in any way. It leaves a lot to be thought about with regards to the other votes, for some skeptical Americans.

Regardless to how we voted and the end product, the important thing is that we did vote. In every race, someone loses and someone wins. But we must look at the bigger picture. This is America and it does have in existence a living _Constitution._ This document, the _United States Constitution_ is the framework by which our government is supposed to work, making it possible that every citizen in the United States is guaranteed the rights embedded with it.

With the Democrats losing control in Congress, many minority members feel that there is no hope for progress anymore; that civil rights will take a backseat and setback during this Republican administration. This is not the first Republican administration where there was control in Congress and the Executive branches of the government and probably will not be the last. Many things did not go well in some Democratic administrations. Just as the Republicans have gridlocked Democratic endeavors, the Democrats will gridlock Republican endeavors. Both parties must work for the betterment of all the people and as quiet as it may be kept, minorities make up the majority of the American population.

It is true that the majority of American's population is white, but they are a combination of European descent rather than the so-called WASP, or White Anglo-Saxon Protestants which are spoken of in sociology books of the past. We are beyond the melting pot and the ethnic ploys of days gone by must be revised. The majority has as much to lose these days as minority members of this country, and with terrorism as it is today, no one is exempt. There will be some wrongdoers among us as long as we exist, but we all must get 'in cinque' and do our part to promote justice and goodwill in our midst. We cannot afford to look the other way when we see that something is wrong. Be a Democrat, Republican or Independent, our collective welfare is our goal.

APATHY
First published July 28, 2003

It is election time in many places during this time of the year for county governments. There are many offices to be fill and plenty of candidates who feel that they are the correct person for the job. Some of them may be right for the job which they pursue and may the force be with them?

Too often, the electorate is not as informed about political party activity or the qualifications of the candidates running for office. People are concerned about, "Do I know him? Do I like him? What church does he belong to? Whose child is he?" rather than being concerned about what the individual has to offer to positively help the community; what qualifications make this individual the right person for this job; and if his experiential background is conducive to this job. These are the kinds of questions one should ask if one is truly concerned about the progress of the community.

Our motives for electing a person to a government office too often is closely related to what that person, in office can do for you, personally.

We look for connections that will help us to 'get over' when we come to a 'bump in the road.' We look for the 'spoils' that are possible to be had in a governmental office, without a thought of the good for the average citizen and taxpayer. We follow a trail of greed and in the long run it is a costly decision made at the taxpayer's expense.

Some elected candidates, as political officers, in an attempt to help those who elected them, in their pursuit of the spoils end up in uncompromising positions which can be hazardous to their social as well as their economic well-being. There have been cases of loss of life due to winning a hot contested position. It is sad to say, but things do happen, especially when the social contract between the governed and the governor is made without a forum wherein those who would govern find out what those to be governed desire. It is similar to a marriage. If both parties are not on one accord, a divorce or something worst could be the end of the relationship. It is time that we get 'in cinque' and become knowledgeable about what we vote for. Regardless to what decisions we choose, the ultimate decision should be not to fall prey to APATHY and **VOTE!**

PART II - SUBJECT CONTENTS

I-EDUCATION

SAVING LIVES WITH EDUCATION
First published January 14, 2005

For some time, I have had the idea that building more prisons instead of more funding for education is one of the worse ideas that Americans can envision and follow through with. Each year, there is more money appropriated for prisons and prison upkeep than is put into education. Further, it is rare when the money spent on prisons and prison upkeep profits the public.

Prisoners get three meals per day, a bed to sleep in and many material things which they might not have outside the prison walls. They have an opportunity to work and play with close supervision. They have the opportunity to learn how to be a good citizen and to get an education if they desire. The only problem is that few take advantage of the positive aspects for rehabilitation, and as a result, government funds are spent for naught; the best result being that of keeping the wrongdoer off the streets and not among upright citizens for a while.

Upright citizens, firefighters and law enforcement officers used the help of prisoners in La Conchita, California a few days ago to help to rescue victims in the mudslides that were occurring there. If prisoners can be trusted to help save lives in life-threatening disastrous situations, why is it that they are not sent to Iraq to help save lives?

Saving lives is saving lives, regardless to whose life it is. The argument against prisoners serving in the armed forces has been that they are a security risk. If they can risk their lives to save lives by helping to rescue victims in a mudslide, they can risk their lives in the same way that young bright men and women are doing in Iraq today. Since the enlisted men and women do not always know who the enemy is, prisoners from the United States *would at least not look like the enemy and may be lifesavers.* Prisoners do not have duties where they use weapons to be useful in the military service. They do not have to be security risks.

If prisoners are enlisted to be sent to Iraq to risk their lives and help saves lives over there, it will lighten the burden on taxpayers for prison funds and free up money for education. In that way, our country could solve three problems with one idea, or as the old saying goes, we could 'kill three birds with one stone.' It is time for us to get 'in cinque' and re-evaluate our military resources and enlist able-bodied prisoners to serve in the armed services. Military time served could cut their sentences and help them to return to society with fewer stigmas.

SCHOOL ATHELETICS AND FEAR
First published September 28, 2005

Many students attending college are able to attend because they have received athletic scholarships because of their demonstration of prowess in high school. When they enroll in college, they expect to continue that prowess throughout their college days. To have come through high school with a degree of security in their playing ability, it will depend on the coach as to how much they will progress or fail to progress in college.

Progress in college for some coaches is the ability to see that their players do well in the subject matter of the academic courses that their players are enrolled, as the chances of them becoming professional in their endeavors is next to nil. They make certain that the main reason for these students being in college is to secure an academic degree and help them to focus on that. That kind of coach instills into his/her players a sense of worth; that they are a worthwhile individual and worthy of praise in their endeavors. This kind of coach works from a positive angle with the students, encouraging them to strive to do their best at all times and to keep a healthy attitude when they love as well as when they win. They are taught to be wholesome, clean-hearted and clean-spirited in their play, and to respect the rights of other players. The students know that they are playing a game. *It is not the game of life.* This kind of coach draws respect to himself as he/she gives, shows and teaches respect to his/her students. Students find playing under the leadership of such a coach rewarding.

On the other hand, when a coach goes about demanding respect from his players because he/she wants them to look up to him/her; to feel perched on some pedestal, to make the players feel that no matter how much they know about the game or how skillful they may be, *'None is greater than me!'* This kind of coach feels that punishment is the ultimate way to teach a player what he should or should not do in his relationship with others. Students receiving scholarships are constantly reminded that they can be kicked off the team and lose their scholarship if their actions are not exactly as the coach demands, whether possible or impossible. When classes or physical illness or discomfort conflicts with practice, the coach insists on the player's presence on the field even if he should be in bed or in class, or he is threatened with some kind of punishment. The end result of this type of coaching is ***sheer fear.*** No student should be subjected to this type of treatment.

Athletics are wonderful for helping to make a well-rounded individual in any school setting, but it is time that we get 'in cinque' and take a closer look at coaches and evaluate them like we do classroom teachers. Some of them are ruining the lives of young men and women in colleges today. Fear should not be a part of a college career.

BLACK CHURCHES AND COLLEGES
First published September 22, 2005

Long before Black students in the South were allowed to attend public school, home school by a generous member of a reading family was the way Black children learned to read, write, spell and do arithmetic. In states where Negroes were free, they were attending public schools and college ***before*** the Civil War. John Russwurm is recorded as the first Black man to graduate from a college. He graduated from Bowdoin in 1826. As time went on, during the era of Reconstruction, religious groups or missionary societies established schools in Southern states for minority students. As early as 1861 The American Missionary Association, often referred to as "Aunt Mary,' was in the forefront of the establishment of many of the historically Black colleges as well as The New England Freedman's Aid

Society (*From Slavery to Freedom: A History of* Negro *Americans,* by John Hope Franklin).

Churches are responsible for two historically Black colleges which are still functioning today; Lincoln University in Pennsylvania and Wilberforce University in Ohio (*(Black History: A Reappraisal,* Edited by Melvin Drimmer). Lincoln University was founded by the Presbyterian Church and Wilberforce University by the African Methodist Episcopal Church.

Land Grant Colleges were established by the states under the 1862 Morrill Land Grant Act. Alcorn University of Mississippi was the first such college for Black students in Mississippi when Hiram Revels, an A.M.E. minister and one of the first two men of color to serve in the United States Senate, was appointed its first president in 1871. By 1878, it was renamed Alcorn Agricultural and Mechanical College with emphasis in those two areas. By 1974, it was renamed Alcorn State University (*Alcorn State University Mini Catalog, 2002-2004).*

As churches and church organizations played a great role in the establishment of minority schools in the South, it would appear that churches have lost their touch. There is something in the way which is keeping the churches from supporting some of the schools that they had a hand in establishing. Most historically Black colleges are now integrated and accepting students of all races. Why are the churches *not supporting* their own? Every year, many of the well-known historically Black schools are closing their doors because the churches are not supporting them. It is time for our churches to get 'in cinque' and re-evaluate their programs. We sing the songs and pray the prayers but we are not 'walking the walk' when it comes to supporting youth education, and wonder why they do not attend church.

SPANISH ACCOMMODATIONS
First printed May 2, 2006

About forty years ago, school systems in the United States across America in places where there were large concentrations of non-English speaking people, adopted a program called "Teaching English as a Second Language.' The program did not last long, but some ten years later, when local calls on a public telephone cost ten cents and the telephone companies wanted to increase the cost to twenty-five cents, the particular telephone had to display directions for use in Spanish as well as English. Once that was accomplished, the fee could be raised to twenty-five cents.

Spanish is the language that the Native Americans learned from the Europeans who came to this country exploring the land and looking for riches to take back to Europe while introducing Christianity in the form of Catholicism to the natives. As a result, most Spanish speaking American are members of the Catholic Church, but most of *the litany was spoken in Italian*, but they learned the rituals!

Every government has rituals. The United States of America has rituals. It has tried to unite all of the people of different tongues from different countries into 'One Nation Under God; and some ethnic groups seem to just *not want that.* They want to be *'one nation within a nation.'* The most dominant group appears to be those of Hispanic descent. The word descent refers to the many Hispanics who do not speak Spanish, but they still want to sing the *'Star Spangled Banner'* in Spanish. The Black Americans sing *'Lift Ev'ry Voice and Sing'* in English, no Swahili or Congolese, or any other African language because they descended from Africans, so why a Spanish national anthem in Spanish. We are not in Spain!

It stands to reason that the concessions made to Hispanic regarding the Spanish language would lead them to feel that they should sing the country's national anthem in Spanish. It also appears that they do not want to be citizens of the United States, but citizens of whichever Spanish province or country from whence they came, or where they plan to build a new nation. Before the English as a second language was introduced, every person entering this country was encouraged to speak ENGLISH. English is the official language of this country and all vital records and statistics are recorded in English. The birth certificates of those persons of Spanish origin, who are born in this country, are written in English. English as a subject is **_required_** of **_all students_** who graduate from American public schools. Spanish is offered in most, but is **still an elective course!** Americans need to get 'in cinque' and eliminate the divisive tactics taking place in this country, as it weakens the nation causing it to be vulnerable from without. Katrina has shown us what is possible and she did not sing Spanish!

SOCIAL STUDIES IN THE CURRICULUM
First published July 5, 2006

It appears than many Boards of Education have decided that the Social Studies curriculum has become an unnecessary element of the educational adventure. This leads one to believe that many of the people whom have been selected to see to the fostering of education especially public education are in need of some serious counseling from experts in the field of curriculum building or shall we say *education*.

It is no surprise that we just celebrated the Fourth of July or Independence Day here in the United States, and a good number of loyal and patriotic Americans do not really have any idea as to what the holiday is about. This is because in many elementary schools, the students are only taught to celebrate. Many of the holidays are simply a time to celebrate; a time to get together and have fun. That is all. There is no serious celebration to the celebration. When all that the students learns in elementary school is to celebrate and have a good time; food, drink, dance and be merry, his mind is not very open to what it means when he encounters this date in high school or college for that matter, unless he is a serious student of the Social Studies.

Social Studies is all about life. It is about what we do as human beings on this planet and how we either do get along with each other, or we do not manage to get along and why. Social Studies not only helps us to know what we have done and why and to figure out how to avoid some problems and solve others. As quiet as it is kept, so many of the physical science discoveries that have been made in the last century, have been quite dependent on advancements in Social Studies.

Social scientists have observed and made scientific classifications of human behavior and it has been on this basis that physical scientists have made advancements to solve many problems that plague humans. Social scientists do not limit their observations to the social activities of humans, but to other animals on the planet as well.

Psychology is the study of humans which is a 'marriage' of social and physical science for which there are prerequisite studies in both the social and physical sciences. One needs a solid foundation in History to truly understand the physical and social world. Geography is important to help us find our way to new places and know what to expect when we get there, unlike Columbus who did not know where he was going or where he was when he got there or where he had been when he returned; but advancements in Social Studies has helped us to avoid that dilemma with new knowledge. We must get 'in cinque' and keep Social Studies in our school curriculums as requirements.

PRESIDENT BUSH'S 'STATE OF THE UNION'
First published January 24, 2007

We have been told what the 'state of the union' is. Congressmen listened with poise and dignity and were on the whole very respectful of what President Bush had to say on last Tuesday. There seems to be unanimous approval of the need for improvement in health care in the United States as well as the need to use less gasoline, but there is still overwhelming dissent regarding the build-up of more troops in Iraq. There are citizens who feel that NO CHILD LEFT BEHIND also needs fixing.

There has been a need for some type of national health program for years. Mrs. Clinton tried to work with a committee to initiate a national health care program when her husband, Bill Clinton was president. Her efforts failed then. The Medicaid program, the health program for the indigent has suffered in the past six years, providing less service for more money. The rise in cost of Medicare, the health program for the elderly is really in a confused state and also need fixing. Congress needs to take along hard look at Medicaid and Medicare and rework them to provide maximum benefits to the recipients. At the same time, Congress needs to lay a foundation for health care for every person in this country as there are still too many working individuals who cannot afford health insurance and earn too much to be eligible for Medicaid or they are not old enough or sick enough to qualify for Medicare. Proper health coverage alone could reduce the use of gasoline.

It sounds plausible that car manufacturers should make vehicles that are more economical in the use of gasoline, thus reducing the need for the substance. Using bio-diesel sounds good, but how many people with cars that are not eligible to use bio-diesel will be ready to make the switch? Will auto mechanics be qualified to change older cars to use bio-diesel? Will bio-diesel be produced in the needed quantity? We need to know.

It is nothing new that the majority of citizens do not want to see a build-up of more troops in Iraq. This is a no-brainer, but NO CHILD LEFT BEHIND is a failure and as a result, *more students are being LEFT BEHIND.* Attempts to raise test scores is what NO CHILD LEFT BEHIND is really about. Teachers are teaching what is on the test in hopes that their classes will raise their scores. It is time for us to get 'in cinque' and let Congressmen and women know that we do not agree with some of the President's programs, especially those pertaining to education.

NO CHILD LEFT BEHIND
First published September 2, 2007

The **No Child Left Behind Act** was passed in 2001 to insure that no child is trapped in a failing school. The NCLB Act supposedly gives more flexibility of choices for students and parents, especially if they are attending a low performing school. It also gives (LEAs) local educational agencies more flexibility in the use of federal dollars, especially those used for the reading programs in the lower grades. Schools are supposed to improve each year and students are tested in grades 3-8 each year to insure that they are not being left behind. Awards are given to schools that meet or exceed the (AYP) or adequate yearly progress or close achievement gaps. Parents and students can choose a better performing public school when the one they are attending fails to achieve adequate yearly progress. If the school fails for three or more years, students may choose to attend a private school where in school district must allocate 20% of Title I funds to provide for supplemental education. After five years of failure, a school runs the risk of reconstitution under a restructuring plan.

The NCLB Act attempts to insure that every child can read by the completion of grade 3. This may very well be what is happening at most schools, but what progress is being made at the 4th, 5th, 6th and 7th grade levels? What has happened to the 16-18 year olds that they no longer are able to read on grade level, especially the 8th grade level? Why are children ages 16 through 18 years of age unable to pass an 8th grade test and enter high school?

Of course, schools offer options for these students; they can remain in 8th grade for three years, that is until they are 16 years of age and if they still have not passed the test, they can take Option 3, Pre-GED where there is no opportunity to secure Carnegie Units which will progress them to a high school diploma. Instead of Option 3, Option 2 should have provisions for remediation to help the student pass the test in the areas where he is failing, in a high school setting along with his peers rather that in a skill program with adults with whom he is not emotionally, socially or physically able to compete.

If after a period of remediation a student is still not able to master the 8th grade test, then Option 3 should be considered, but not before. Entering Option 3 too often is ***not completed***, leading to a dropout situation and a child *being left behind*. When a child does not have the opportunity to enter a high school where he can earn Carnegie Units, ***he has been left behind!*** We need to get 'in cinque' and make some positive changes to handling this situation.

THE VARIABLES OF EDUCATION
First published September 16, 2007

School districts have been posturing for many years now attempting to attain a level 5 to be recognized as an excellent school. With the last report of standing, too many schools in our country are moving down the scale instead of up the scale. The Irony is that many of the same teachers who struggled to get the better rating are still working when the less than better rating was attained. If the teaching variable is the same and the rating drops, there is some other variable that is responsible for the change. When that variable is identified, then some progress can be made in our school ratings. There are at least four other variables to ponder: students, parents, administrators and school boards.

Just recently, Dr. Julia Hare stated on Tavis Smiley's "State of Black America Conference,"... *"That the teachers are afraid of the principals, the principals are afraid of the superintendents and superintendents are afraid of the school boards and the school boards are afraid of the parents and the parents are afraid of their children and the children are not afraid anyone!"* If this is true, we know who is in control of learning and test results.

The powers that be have almost made it impossible for parents to *really discipline* their children effectively for fear of being pointed out as a bad parent when they do not take the reins in their own hands and then deny that right to anyone else who will. That is, the denial comes until the child ends up in a home for children in need of supervision, under the auspices of a human resource unit run by some state agency. The education of the child is interrupted and his test result will reflect the lack of continuity. This would not happen if parents took a more positive look at where their children are and where they want them to go. A positive look means taking inventory of what is good and what is bad and accentuating the positive for better result at school. ***The bottom line rests with parents.*** The MUST help formulate the kind of attitude in their children that will help to increase their aptitude for learning in any school, public or private. Parents do not have to make their children fear them, but it is imperative they make them respect them so they will not have to be afraid of them. It is time for parents to get 'in cinque' and bring their children up in the way they would have them go and test scores and school ratings will soar.

STRESS AND EDUCATION
First published January 6, 2008

Each New Year, many people make resolutions to do or not to do something during the year. I have never been much at making resolutions because I feel that I like many other people, will break it before the thought get cold or the ink dries. Consequently, I set goals for myself for things that I want to accomplish during the year. As the year moves on and I accomplish a goal, I scratch it off my list. I usually write them all down in the first few pages of my diary, usually, just before I go to be each night.

This year, I have had some experiences during the first few days of this year, 2008, which have caused me to add a new goal, after the fact, or ex-post-facto, to my established list. I have learned that STRESS KILLS. I have been stressed out over the ignorance of some people who attempt to do simple business but lack the knowledge of how to do something and feel that they have all the knowledge that they need and will not take advice from someone who can help them because of knowledge learned from experience. Frustration sets in when an ignorant person refuses to be taught something by someone who ***can and is willing to teach them.*** This is a dilemma too often encountered by teachers. Usually a child who reacts this way has a parent who is not willing to take advice and causes the child to act the same way. This goes back to "why Johnny can't read." The real truth all along has been due to the fact that "Johnny's Mama can't read!" Whether we want to accept it or not, a child has more respect for what his parents say or tell him than he will ever have for a teacher, regardless to how shallow or caring that parents are. I recall once attempting to teach a first grader manuscript writing and his parent had been teaching him box print at home and there was no way to get him in the mode of manuscript until I discovered what was happening and had a conference with the parent and encouraged him to teach the manuscript.

Until Johnny's Mama learns to read, there will be many children "left behind." It is my prayer and hope that today's teachers will understand the underlying cause of so much failure and do all they can to get parents into the mode of learning as this type of stress kills the ones who try to help. God knows that the young teachers entering the world of work today have mountains to climb to work with children produced by the drug and rap culture and when ignorance is blended with those two items, a resolution will not solve the problem. Too often teachers burnout and develop the attitude that payday is the most important day in a school year. Dedication goes out of the window along with enthusiasm. Self-serving administrators are no help either. We must get 'in cinque' and get parents in a ***real learning/ working mode*** with schools and eliminate a gross amount of STRESS.

EDUCATION OR INDOCTRINATION
First published May 23, 2010

It is no secret that the state of Texas is revising its Social Studies curriculum this year, to be effective in 2011. Every ten years, Texas updates it standards for curriculums. The State Board of Education makes these updates. Along with the updates, they select textbooks which reflect what they want taught in the schools. The Social Studies updates are unrealistic to learned individuals who are students of the discipline.

A certificate in History is a basic requirement to teach Social Studies in the state of Texas, but for many years all one needed to teach Social

Studies in Texas was the ability to land a coaching job in one of the schools. Coaches were assigned to teach Social Studies, often a subject they knew very little about, while qualified teachers with degrees in a Social Science discipline were denied the positions because they did not, would not or could not coach some athletic sport. Sports were more important than Social Studies and apparently it still is.

An individual with a degree in a Social Science discipline will have a very difficult time, academically and morally, attempting to teach the new standards in the Texas Social Studies Curriculum Guide. The irony in this is the fact that the textbooks which the Texas Board of Education has approved, will be sent to bookstores and schools throughout the United States for use in public schools.

The new standards call for the omitting of many truths, the exaggeration of others, and the camouflaging of some truths; ethnocentrism, inert propaganda and outright indoctrination. With a degree in Social Science, this new curriculum will be a hard pill to swallow for true scholars of History. *It will be a 'no brainer' for teachers whose main objective is to receive a paycheck at the end of the month. This is the kind of society that the new curriculum will foster.*

It takes passion to be a genuine teacher. Passion will be hard to fine for Social Studies teachers in Texas and any other state which chooses to use the textbooks which are being approved by the Texas Board of Education. Hopefully, other state Boards of Education will take a cautious look at what is being done in Texas and avoid an attempt to rewrite history to suit the present company as it has not been a very long time ago when textbooks had begun to attempt to print the history of the United States as it actually occurred, rather than leaving out vital ethnic information which put the majority group in a shameful light. It is time for citizens to get 'in cinque' and put pressure on the Boards of Education to be about education rather than indoctrination.

TEXT AND TESTING
First published March 17, 2013

Having been out of the teaching profession and the school system for several years now, I have not been keeping in touch with school seasons, holidays and vacations. However, I did notice on last week that each time I went to a busy store, there were no shopping baskets available inside and I usually had to either wait until some were brought inside or go back to the parking to get one. Being someone not anxious for the extra exercise, I usually waited on a cart.

The other thing which I had noticed was that I would see school aged children during the middle of the day when I thought they should have been in school. Little did I know that it was spring break. Once you have retired, every week is spring break or some break and every day is a holiday, unless you have children or grandchildren who are school age. Fortunately, my youngest is in college and I am looking forward to graduation day.

School on any level is not today what it used to be. Most recently, *schools are teaching* **to the test.** Today, the TEST is everything, whether it is the one that one needs to get a passing grade in a subject or the one needed to be promoted to the next level, or the one needed to enter a particular school. There is always the test needed to enter a particular school. There is always the test needed to graduate, but some colleges have a test one must pass in order to major in a particular course of study.

Once an individual completes a course of study, many states have a requirement that one must pass a test for licensing or permission to ply one's trade. Once the permit is granted to enter a profession, whether it is plumbing, carpentering, practicing medicine, law or teaching some course of study, one is expected to pass certain tests or criterion to maintain that profession. Too often the yardstick by which one is measured may not be created equal. One has to be aware of cliques, favoritism and nepotism in the workplace. Having morals and scruples are a necessary part of an individual' persona, but one must always remember that too often it is the **'attitude which determines the altitude.'**

Many inept workers have endured a long lasting career because they knew how to utilize a productive attitude in spite of their inability to perform as needed. They were often promoted to a level wherein they were able to delegate their responsibilities and still come out 'smelling like a rose.'

So much technological knowledge is necessary to maintain employment these days and hopefully schools will continue to teach Reading, Writing and Arithmetic as they will be needed in instances when technology fails and it does. Let us get 'in cinque' and make certain that our schools maintain a basic curriculum in elementary schools wherein the 'text language' is not the only one our young people know because many of them will have a difficult time passing any test written in English or any other language except 'text.'

MUSIC AND ART
First published September 8, 2013

I may be pushing my limits, but I just had to get out today to "Rhapsody in Blue" the pop symphony featuring the musical talent of George Gershwin and his brother Ira. This is the first symphony that I have attended in many years due to the location of my living arrangements. Many small rural urban communities do not have symphonies and very few who do have symphonies, do not have opera.

I was blessed to live in Chicago where all art forms were immediately accessible. In Lubbock, Texas, the symphony was quite good and once in a while, there would be an opera which featured someone from the Metropolitan Opera along with a cast of musicians from Texas Tech University. This was all enjoyable.

In the sovereign state of Mississippi, this form of musical culture was basically found in the state capital. Attending such performances usually meant traveling a hundred miles, more or less and perhaps spending the night in the city. The trip would usually be worth the while but because of obstacles, few and far apart.

Fort Worth, Texas on the other hand, presents access to musical endeavors and finds support for them through a variety of businesses in the city, especially the newspaper and certain airlines. Art is encouraged and supported in the city. A new School of the Arts has recently been built in southwest Fort Worth. It is encouraging to see when many school curriculums are eliminating all forms of art.

Music, especially, does not need to be eliminated at any cost. Most often in elementary schools, students are taught to sing a song. When they enter high school, music is usually participating in a school choir, chorus or glee club. This is good but students need to be taught about the great composers and the influence that they had on society of their day and the things that motivated them. Music can best be appreciated by our youth if they actually know something about the composers. You can check out what our youth knows about the Hip Hop artists. They know the words to every lyric and can tell you when the artist was born, where and why. They have an ever loving relationship with lyricist. I have a difficult time with this because it does not really follow the pattern of music with which I am familiar.

I was taught the history of classical musicians in high school and maybe because I attended a private school, but this is a privilege which all students should have, regardless to the school attended. Music is a part of the American way, and great artists like the Gershwin brothers, Ira and George should be a part of any school music curriculum. In my opinion, George Gershwin is America's most outstanding composer. His brother Ira was the lyricist. George Gershwin was Jewish and I am certain that my daughter and I should *not* have been the only individuals of color sitting in that large music hall today. It seems that certain ethnic groups are not being exposed to fundamental music appreciation. We need to get 'in cinque' and revamp our public school music departments to expose all students to the various avenues of music and art in its history of America.

THE COMMON CORE
First published September 22, 2014

"No Child Left Behind" seemingly has seen many public school children 'left behind.' In an attempt to make it possible for all children to be on the same playing field when it comes to what they should and need to learn by certain grade levels, 'THE COMMON CORE' made its entrance. Many of us are still puzzled and really do not understand *what* the Common Core is.

Last year, *"The Kaplan,'* the educational magazine which is published by the International Fraternity of Phi Delta Kappa, attempted to include a sample lesson on teaching Mathematics, which according to the magazine, was a much simpler way to have students understand the mechanics of numbers. Talk shows have also attempted to *'explain'* what the Common Core State Standards are. There is also an explanation about the standards on the website which can be accessed by anyone with a computer.

The Governor of Louisiana, Bobby Jindal filed a suit in the federal court in Baton Rouge in August, 2014 to sue the Obama Administration over Common Core. He states that "The federal government has hijacked and destroyed the Common Core initiative...Common Core is the latest effort by big government disciples to strip away state rights and put Washington, D.C. in control of everything."

In 2009, a group of state school chiefs and governors who collaborated among teachers, administrators and experts attempted to provide a consistent framework for educators in the Language Arts and Mathematics. The goal was to insure that students in all states who graduated from high school would have all the skills and knowledge to successfully go to college, a career or workforce training programs in order to live a useful life. The Standards:

1. Research and evidence based
2. Clear, understandable, and consistent
3. Aligned with college and career expectations
4. Based on rigorous content and application of knowledge through higher order thinking skills
5. Built upon the strengths and lessons of current state standards
6. Informed by other top performing countries in order to prepare all students for success in our global economy and society (http://www.corestandards.org/about)

The Language Arts Standards are broken down into five parts: reading, Writing, Speaking and Listening, Language and Media and Technology. The Mathematics Standards are Mathematical practice and Mathematical content. Examples of content are included for elementary and high school. Domains for each grade level are included in the content.

Katie Couric has stated on her show that The Common Core Standards Initiative either gets a gold star or a big fat "F." Implementation of the Common Core is encouraged by the Obama Administration's Race to the Top grant program which allows funds to participating states from $330 million to develop standardized testing material tied to the Common Core. Louisiana has already received $17 million. Most states should get 'in cinque' and participate in the program in order to bring the education in America on par with other countries. Testing is slated for this academic year.

EDUCATION: A SCIENCE?
First published May 31, 2015

This year of public school is quickly coming to a close. One might think, another year of academia completed. The schedule is coming to an end and quite happily for many students and even more joyous for some teachers, especially new, first year teachers. For many of the new teachers, "Confusion has made it masterpiece!"

Through the years, education as a field of study and application has gone through so many changes in an attempt to make it a '*science.*' Currently, there is gross focus on the results of test scores for students' achievement and relatively on teacher performance. These two categories alone have many young capable and resourceful teachers thinking of targeting other areas of interest in which to apply their skills. Many have not felt that their skills were aptly utilized because of the interpretations of testing and evaluations and the methods of teaching which they feel have been forced upon them by educational administrators who have supposedly 'helped' them.

One of the first mistakes made by some administrators have been in human relations wherein they assign values to various teachers as having the best way to teach certain subjects and insisting that other teachers follow their models. They attempt to establish their '*scientific*' model for teaching and expect every teacher to be a follower.

Next, new, first year teachers bring enthusiasm to the job. However, that enthusiasm does not last long when one of the worst things an administrator does is to assign a teacher a mentor who works in another school in the district, rather than the one in which the new teacher is assigned and then when the new teacher attempts to model his/her mentor, the administrator objects to what the new teacher does and reprimands him/her. When the new teacher takes a problem to the administrator, instead of helping them with some fresh or new ideas, they end up being reprimanded. Sometimes valuable suggestions from new teachers get them rewarded with a reprimand. Then there are instances when a new teacher tries to keep themselves out of disagreements and situations which would warrant a reprimand, they are often reprimanded for not reporting things that their co-workers have done to make their day a little worst. They refuse to be a 'tattler' and are labeled as engaging in deceptive practices. With this kind of situation which seems to occur much too often in our public schools, we can get some idea as to why young teachers are scurrying to find a better place to work. Consequently, when there is a teacher job fair the lines for interviews are out of sight regardless to the weather. Teacher turnover is hugh. How can schools maintain continuity and rapport with students when some schools have almost all new staff every year? This is an indication that..." Something is wrong in Denmark!"

There is objection from all corners of education about the student testing and teacher evaluation in regard to making public school teaching and education a science. Do we wonder why progress and results were more noticeable back in the day when teachers and students were human beings and teachers taught and students learned? All students, not just a few, came out of school with a certain degree of humanness and respect for themselves and others. Is that the main goal of education that we are able to get along with each other in whatever we do? Is education as a science simply about achievements which will make us the most money or achievements which will make us more loving human beings? Our framers of our educational systems need to get 'in cinque' and weigh their options of what really matters in education. Maybe they need to ask the students what they want.

CIVIL RIGHTS VIOLATIONS
First published October 4, 2015

Finally, the federal government is taking a look at civil rights violations in public schools. How successful they will be in their final outcome is going to be interesting. By now, it seems to be common knowledge that most public schools in the United States are populated by predominantly Black or African American students or in some instances schools may be populated by predominantly Latino students. Regardless to which ethnic group it is, in most instances it is a minority ethnic group. In neighborhoods where the residents are mostly in the upper middle class, you will find a majority of White Anglo-Saxon Protestants and or other groups with high incomes.

Everyone in this country who is over fifty years of age is well aware that when *Brown vs. The Board of Education* was ruled on that it did not eradicate racial prejudices and reactions in public schools. What it did do, is cause the WASP to withdraw their students from public schools and become a part of already established private, often Christian, school or establish a private school for their children where the funds were available. Parents who could not afford to pay for a private school, borrowed funds for the cause if they felt that their children would be able to benefit from the sacrifice. Parents who feared that it would be a waste of time and money left their children in public schools along with the WASP teachers who were ready to retire. After a year or so, the public school was all Afro-American except for a few WASP administrators who did not want to relinquish control.

As soon as the bussing began, a measure to insure that public schools were integrated, I have seen whole classrooms bussed to a Black school, sometimes with their teacher wherein they were kept together the entire day until their return to their home school. This was the way they followed the law; no integration was taking place; separation in the same place is what it was.

Gradually, some students were intermingled with the Black population, but WASP parents were and in some instances they are still always looking for a way to make certain that no Black teacher ever makes any important decisions where their children are concerned. There are a few WASP parents who are humane. They are in sync with reality and life and work to make things better rather than harboring negative attitudes.

Public schools with administrators and teachers who have negative attitudes and cannot rise above racism are the roots of civil rights violations in public schools. Many students who attend school are ready to give any teacher or administrator a difficult time especially if they are of a different ethnic group and *seek to display what they have learned at home.* For this reason, all teachers and administrators should be required to take a course in Multi-ethnic Relations before they assume their duties in a public school. Such a course would put some leverage into action. It could also allay some of the fear of working with people who are not a member of one's own ethnic group. Let us get 'in cinque' and eliminate the reasons for civil rights violations in public school.

LEARNING AND TEACHING SYTLES
First published August 10, 2007

The first week of school has just passed in most schools in the United States, but a few states and/or cities are returning to the traditional opening of school, following Labor Day, when every new student entering first grade for the first time should have had his sixth birthday.

Birthdays have an important role in school entrance, attendance and graduation. Children are expected to make certain accomplishments at certain ages in their growth and development. In addition to thinking and acting a certain way for a certain age, their scores on norm referenced and criterion referenced tests are expected to normally fall within a certain range for their ages. If students fall below the expected ranges, the teaching which they have received gets the blame, though there are many other variables responsible.

Teachers are **_told_** to teach to a child's learning style in order that he may have maximum accomplishments of the subject matter. This is ideal, but the only problem lies in the fact that the average administrator who enters a classroom and find students learning and teachers teaching to the various learning styles, expect to find students in their seats, reading, writing or listening to a teacher who is lecturing. When they find instead, a couple of students lying on a rug reading or writing or listening to music with an earphone while reading or writing, and the learning style concept goes out of the window. The teacher's evaluation goes downhill because the evaluator has not seen a traditional classroom setting. How can a child be on task listening to a radio? How can a child be on task lying on a rug on the floor or with his foot propped up on a desk? When a teacher practices what the experts preach, they are thought of and looked at as an oddball and evaluated as such.

When students feel comfortable in a classroom setting and have confidence that they are viewed as important individuals, they learn more and make better scores on mandated tests. In schools where the learning mode is geared to the students, a private, small school is usually the setting. School boards are busy mandating that schools raise their test scores by doing a better job of teaching children. School administrators are requesting that teachers do a better job of teaching and sponsor all kinds of workshops and highly paid motivational speakers to get teachers in gear for the new trends in teaching and addressing the learning styles of children. Yet, they must address the fact that public schools have not been set up to accommodate the learning styles of the students, but *the mandated teaching styles of the teachers.*

Many public schools are not equipped architecturally, physically, including electrically and technically to accommodate new technology, let alone a different kind of furniture or classroom that would be conducive to learning styles. The current discipline problems in most public schools are a deterrent to anything new which permits a degree of any kind of freedom in school. Most campuses have adopted what is called the *closed campus* in order to curtail discipline problems.

On closed campuses, students are not permitted to leave the campus for any reason except to be checked out for the day by a parent. They ***must*** eat their lunch on campus. They cannot go out send out or bring in lunch to the cafeterias. This is also why many students get a free lunch, whether they need it or not. The school day is often shorter because of no break or recess during the day. This is hard on students and teachers and often lead to a breakdown in morale which leads to a lowering of teacher effort and a lowering of mandated tests scores. We ***MUST*** get 'in cinque' and figure out how to solve this problem as parents, teachers, administrators and school boards, locally and on the state levels.

II-POLITICS

The Hatch Act
First published December 9, 2007

During this season, the yuletide, political elections have abounded along with the commercial holiday shopping. Sometimes the season is not happy as it can be because of partisan campaigning, elections and aftermaths. Some communities have more unrest than peacefulness and rest. In the spirit of Christmas, the birth of the Christ child, we would do ourselves a favor by seeing things as they really are and calling a spade a spade, accepting the fact that it is a spade, and moving on.

In our apathy, that is, with regards to voting and participating in partisan campaigning and elections, we sometimes do not take a good look at what we see. There are many violations which take place with regards to politics that we do not pay any attention to. We always try to look on the bright side. This is good. Seeing the bright side has a dark cloud hovering in the background. That dark cloud can and often is called the "Hatch Act."

*"The Hatch Act (5 U.S.C. 1501-1508) restricts the political activity of individuals principally employed by **state, county or municipal** executive agencies in connection with programs financed in whole or in part by loans or grants made by the United States or a federal agency. An employee covered by the Act may not be a candidate for public office in a partisan election, i.e., an election in which any candidate represents, for example, the Republican or Democratic Party. Principal employment is that employment to which an individual devotes the most time, and from which he derives the most income. ....[No] means exist for an employee who is covered by the Hatch Act to be granted an exception to run in a partisan election"*

The federal government is currently doing a nationwide investigation of violations of the Hatch Act. If we open our eyes around us, we may see some violations in our own little corner of the elective and voting elements. Ignorance is not bliss and neither is apathy. We need to get 'in cinque' with our political and governmental surroundings, make evaluations and take action accordingly, and prepare for a **Merry Christmas.**

POLITICAL FEAR
First published August 15, 2008

It has been forty years since the death of Dr. Martin Luther King, Jr., whom many suspected could have been elected President of the United States because of his peaceful display of civil disobedience and desire to see this country united spiritually, economically, and politically. At that time, Dr. King had a following of peaceful, civil individuals who wanted the same thing that he preached about and attempted to live his life accordingly. Before Dr. King was killed, there had been an attempt on his life by a knife wielding female at a book signing a few years earlier, which he survived and continued to go about the mission at hand. It appears that the current presumptive nominee of the Democratic Party has many of the characteristics of Dr. Martin Luther King, Jr. if we examine the characteristics closely. The difference being that Barack H. Obama is not a preacher, but a politician, but as much as his former pastor, Rev. Jeremiah Wright, is derided, he has said that, "If God wants Obama to be President, he will be President."

If the powers that be, spiritual or human, want Barack H. Obama to be President of the United States, HE WILL BE PRESIDENT! There are a number of incidences which have taken place during the Democratic presidential campaigns wherein Barack Obama's life has been placed in jeopardy. One highly publicized incident with regards to the presidential election is the attack on a Democratic headquarters in Arkansas wherein a party leader was shot and later died. One television news station has reportedly stated that it has been said that the bullet was meant for Barack Obama, though he was stated to have been in Hawaii on a vacation.

Throughout the primary campaign there has been a high key atmosphere concerning the safety of Barack Obama. There has been the talk of numerous threats on his life and that of his family. The Secret

Service Agency has spent millions on protection for Obama and John McCain on the campaign trail, as well as Hillary Clinton, because all three of them are United States Senators. Politically, there are those who for reasons of their own, do not wish to see either of these individuals become President of the United States. For reasons that this country does not now or ever need negative publicity surrounding the election of a President, lies in the roots and founding of this country.

To kill Barack Obama because he is a man of color and the presumptive nominee for President of the Democratic Party at this time is tantamount to asking for riots and /or outright war. Consider the riots in the various cities when Dr. Martin Luther King, Jr. was killed in 1968 by the so called peaceful followers and considers the bolder, less fearful; more informed and more passionate young people of today and then consider the options. It is time for us to get 'in cinque,' grow up racially and act like Christians that we are supposed to be as the world has its eye on us as we proclaimed ourselves "***The world leader.***'

LAST STAGE DEMOCRATIC CAMPAIGNS
First published March 16, 2008

As the days drag on and the political primaries become fewer, the campaigns become a little bit more 'touchy.' Campaign members on both the Clinton and Obama camp have been guilty of saying some not-so-nice things about the other candidate for whom they apologized and withdrew from the campaign because they feel embarrassed or ashamed for what they have said. Of course, once they are no longer a member of the team they feel free to voice their opinions as their own which one withdrawn member, a former Vice-Presidential candidate has expressed that she will do.

At this juncture, there is a tendency to play the 'race card' with regards to Barack Obama's heritage, an African father. Because of his name, he is often alienated because of the belief that he is a Muslim. This country is old enough now, though it is one of the world's youngest cultures, made from the various countries around the world; a variety of ethnic groups, religious groups, cultural differences which together makes this a very rich country offering areas of interest to just about anything anyone wants or needs to know; we should not be so small minded.

With the world situation as it is today with warmongering in the Arab, Muslim and Israeli worlds, and the United States is involved in the mix, one would think that the United States would welcome a President, born in the United States who can identify with other nations and lay a firmer foundation for brotherhood in the world. A Black President would indeed give the rest of the world the notion that this country had finally arrived at a station in life where all men are looked up as equal not only in the sight of God, but in the sight of man.

A female President will have an almost equal advantage in the world, proving that the United States is not a country where powerful men dominate and force their ideas and ideals on weaker nations. Regardless, the Democratic Party would do well to see to the ugliness that is possible, being kept out of the campaign and at best, encourage each candidate to look at the possibility of a single ticket with both their names on it. This will be the only surefire way to win the election in November against John McCain. It is most likely, that the Super delegates will decide who will be the Democratic Nominee. It is making it more important than ever before to press Congress to devise a system which uses the popular vote to elect a President. If they had done this years ago, we would not have suffered eight years of George Bush and the current recession/depression. Let us get 'in cinque' and make our wishes known to Congress.

POLITICAL STORM
First published September 15, 2008

We are experiencing storms of all kinds these days. The Fays, Gustavs, Hannas, and Ikes or tropical storms which have attacked our southern and eastern coasts and continue to rampage and devastate our inlands and have caused crop damage and a slowdown in production of everything which is grown in the regions affected are natural and occur every year at a certain time though some are more dangerous than others. No matter how weak these storms are, they always cause some physical damage even when no lives are lost. These are not the only storm brewing in the United States and their damages will affect the whole country.

The storm of concern is the political bro-ha-has being made by the presidential candidates' ad campaigns wherein they are making up scenarios and projecting them as truth in an attempt to ridicule and discredit each other. It makes one wonder about some of these advertisements and how their existence coincides with the kind of government they will lead once elected into office. If the campaign trail gets any hotter some burning will take place, especially in Alaska, that cold state. There are too many things there to be investigated that concern the Republican Vic-Presidential candidate from Alaska, because she is the one who has added zest to the Republican ticket as John McCain had already lost the race long ago. McCain's age has been against him from day one, as well as his constant agreements with the soon to be 'lame duck,' President George W. Bush. Thank God for the 22nd Amendment to the _Constitution._ The Supreme Court cannot give him another appointment!

If by some chance, Sarah Palin does become President of the United States of America, we may just be in for a 'Bridge to Nowhere!' We need to get 'in cinque' and take a really close look at Alaska and what it produces beside oil and salmon. Does our country need the kind of leadership or lack of it, which Alaska has? Do we need a fashion plate or model in the White House or someone who is able to make decisions based on what is good for the country rather than their own private family? We need to get our priorities in order before we VOTE on November 4, 2008, fifty days from today.

ELECTION FALLOUT
First published November 9, 2008

When the history books of the future are printed, they will certainly mark the election of 2008 as a turning point in the evolution of the United States of America. The campaign in itself was historical because it was the first time in the history of this country that a member of the Afro-American ethnic group had won a major national party primary election. The primary election alone gave many members of minority groups the opportunity to have 'The Audacity of Hope.'

That hope lifted apathy and made the average American feel "Yes We Can." Yes it did, and as a result, America has elected its 44th President, a

Black man, Barack Hussein Obama, the second Black person to occupy a Senate seat since the era of Reconstruction, and first en route to the White House. Americans who elected this man are not the only people who are proud of him. Countries around the world rejoice with America in this history making election and look forward to better days ahead. This election was printed on the front page of newspapers in many countries around the world as well as many states in the United States. Sadly, there are those states and their occupants who refuse to acknowledge the present history.

It is sad because the world is moving onward and so many people with 'issues' or baggage refuse to see the light when majority rules. For the first time, these people who are most miserable know now, how it feels to feel helpless within the limits of the law. It is very frustrating to feel that your thoughts, words and even deeds are not important.

There is hope now, of being heard and being helped. President-Elect Obama has a plan to help everyone, but we must realize that we ***must help ourselves!*** We must also realize that no one man has all the power and that the President must work with Congress to have the laws he want implemented. Mr. Obama is busy and has been since day one following the election putting his transition team in place to occupy the White House following the inauguration on January 20, 2009. Prosperity is not coming overnight and we must know this, but spirits are uplifted to the point where individuals with bare essentials of life are saying that they are happy.

On the other hand, it is rumored that the very unhappy are attempting to make life a little uneasy for supporters of the President-Elect. The ACLU (American Civil Liberties Union) is gearing up for the coming events wherein civil liberties are violated. We must get 'in cinque' and broaden our minds and our horizons as life happens.

PRESIDENT TRUMP
First published, May 9, 2011

It appears that politics is in the air. The 2012 election cannot get here fast enough. Just today, Mother's Day, 2011, I received a card with a portrait of Sarah Palin standing behind the podium with the U. S. Presidential seal on the front of it, smiling from ear to ear. The caption said "Sarah Palin could be our next President of the United States." When I opened it up, the message inside said, "Guess there are scarier things than raising kids. Happy Mother's Day."

Last night as I was browsing on the internet, I came across a Newsmax. com article which headlined in red ink, "Donald Trump Going to New Hampshire. You Can Join Him Online. Click Here Now." The poll urges one to vote to repeal President Obama's healthcare plan and other policies, and also asking if he should be re-elected in 2012.

The poll consisted of 6 questions asking you to support a full repeal of President Obama's healthcare plan; if Congress should restore Medicare benefits for seniors; should illegal aliens be given amnesty; what should be Congress' top priority in 2011; do you plan to vote to re-elect President Obama in 2012 and who did you vote for in 2008. The results of the poll will be e-mailed to you. Following that a smiling face in the box says, "President Trump?"

No matter what President Obama does or how he does it, there is resentment in the air. Ever since the 9/11 incident, The United States has been looking for Osama Bin Laden. Former President Bush is supposed to have said that Bin Laden's rear end was grass and he was the lawnmower. From all of the reliable sources, President Obama has brought finding Bin Laden and his demise to fruition, but many Americans either doubt it or fear that something else terrible will take place as a result of the action taken. Seemingly, there is regret that Bin Laden has been found. The news media also reported that former President Bush was angry about President Obama's activities at Ground Zero following the incident.

George Washington was right to warm against partisanship in government. This country is already polarized and at this juncture in the history of this country, party politics are adding to the polarization, rather than helping to bridge the gaps of health, the economy, socialization, ethics, education, security and citizenship. The America that we love is slowing becoming the America that we never envisioned and one which we are not sure of what we see, hear or become involved in. Propaganda tee shirts saying, "Pray for Obama," quotes <u>Bible</u> verses that wish him and his family destruction. We must get 'in cinque,' keep an open mind and not let the politicians decide our future for our country without input from "We the People."

JOHN BOEHNER
First published October 6, 2013

In this day of high definition digital technology, it should be amazing to see how differences in political differences can come through as racial differences. It is amazing to watch the United States Speaker of the House of Representatives seem to think or feel that he was elected President of the United States.

From the outset of the last inauguration and the nitpicking of President Barack Obama, the Speaker of the House, John Boehner has persistently opposed the Affordable Health Care Act which was an act mentored by President Obama and rendered constitutional by the U. S. Supreme Court. John Boehner and members of the Tea Party, who are members of the Republican Party, have acted in bad faith to hold the President and the citizens of this country hostage in order to get what they desire, rather than working for the good of the country.

Taking a look into the future, it is going to be amusing as to what will be said in the American History books about this time in our lives. It should mention that we are now very vulnerable for attack from any angle because of the government's shutdown. Who knows how vulnerable we were *before* the shutdown? Civilian military workers are being called back to work perhaps because someone with insight saw the imminent need. A law has also been passed to insure laid off workers that they will be paid when they return to work.

The one thing which bothers too many Americans and find the large number of petitions to government ignored, to have changed, in the way the congressmen have established themselves with extraordinarily huge annual salaries and lifetime health benefits and retirement benefits and the American people who are uninsured, especially those in most of the Southern states, will not be eligible for the subsidies provided for in the Affordable Care Act, because they, the Republicans in Congress have no respect for the poor.

The general stereotype is that people of color are poor and that is true, but people who think that way are thinking down racial lines and forget about the *number* of people who are poor. What they fail to understand is that *there are way more poor White people than there are of people*

of color because there are more White people in the population. They are "cutting off their noses to spite their faces."

Poor people are suffering while the Congressmen are dallying with law and order and the economy. John Boehner could very well call for votes to end the shutdown and leave the Affordable Care Act alone; better yet, encourage the governors of the Southern states to expand Medicaid so large numbers of individuals who are otherwise eligible can obtain benefits, especially Texas, where only children in a family which meets the criteria are eligible. Let us get 'in cinque' and e-mail our Congressmen to DO the right thing and maybe censure John Boehner.

III-WAR

IRAQ
First Published January 13, 2005

The Iraq tours of duty which were to last a few weeks, have lasted almost two years. Every week, young, talented, bright men with a possible positive future are sent over to Iraq and Iran to fight unknown enemies. Too many of them lose their lives and leave an empty space in the hearts of those whom they love and left behind. They felt that they were doing a service for their country. Many family members are now wearing the magnetic ribbons saying "God Bless America" and "Support Our Troops."

It is noble that we support our troops, especially in worthy causes. The war in Iraq ceases to be a worthy cause. The main thing is that most Americans have not yet learned the cause. Some of us have great ideas about the cause and do not truly know because we have yet to be told. We know for sure that the reason behind the cause which we were told from the outset is not now, nor has it ever been the **real cause!** Consequently, we have continued to follow the original path set before us for the reasoning behind American involvement in Iraq. There are thinking people in America and it would seem that someone in Congress thinks about what they have been a party to regarding this war.

Aside from there being thinking people in Congress, there are thinking people in the populace. It would appear that some thinking people would contact their Congressmen and attempt to make an impact on them to put a halt to the assault in Iraq. Some e-mail groups have an idea which they believe will make an impact. This ideas has also spread in other means of communication

The latest bright idea is to boycott businesses on inauguration day by

157

not spending a dime for anything for that twenty-four hour period. It is hoped that the impact on business will call attention to the need to stop the war in Iraq. This may cause an impact, but the degree that it will cause some reaction to stopping the war will probably be of no significance. Congressman <u>MUST</u> realize the damage that the war is doing to the moral of the average American and put the wheels into motion to withdraw funding for the war. Without funding, it will be difficult to continue to pursue this endeavor. We need to get 'in cinque' and bombard our Congressmen with our desire to ***stop the war in Iraq!*** The addresses of Senators and Representatives are available on the internet and in the public library for anyone who desires to have them.

HOMELAND SECURITY
First published May 12, 2005

On yesterday, there was an eminent threat to our homeland security when a small aircraft came too close to the White House. There was a 'red alert' in the federal government which went off very well, but they failed to alert the city government about what was happening. Now, what does that tell us about the Homeland Security that the taxpayers, citizen, are paying for?

Our government has allocated an enormous amount of money for Homeland Security and for military purposes at home and abroad. The people of Iraq were not an eminent threat to the United States and we are fighting there. Americans are being killed every day by friendly fire and enemy fire. The end result, regardless of the fire, is that a soldier is dead. Who was he protecting?

Protection under homeland security is for whom? The people in the White House, Congress and other federal offices were evacuated when the small private Cessna plan entered the no-fly zone near the White House. They were all scrambled to a safe place. That safe place is somewhere in Washington, perhaps the underground safe place which was built during a previous Republican administration, wherein the President could continue to run the country if attacked.

All of this is well and good, but what about the average American Joe who does not happen to be a part of the federal government of Washington,

D. C.? What about the Mayor and members of the city government and the other cities of the United States? Where is homeland security for them, for us, who inhabit cities? What kind of government **does not** protect its constituents? How secure are we anywhere in the United States? The citizens of this country **need to know.**

Too often, our governments operate on a **Need to Know** basis. They decide what ***we, the people*** need to know. We may not need to know about every red alert that the Homeland Security staff goes through, but we need to know that ***there is a staff,*** present, willing, able and working on our behalf. We need to know at all times, the level of our danger and the capability of our Homeland Security handling the situation.

Thanks to God that no disaster occurred in the preceding situation, but unless there is a lot of improvements made to our Homeland Security, we need to get 'in cinque' and find out more about what we as citizens can do to improve homeland security where we are, or we are going to be 'up the creek without a paddle!"

THE JOB TO BE DONE: BRING TROOPS HOME
First published July 1, 2005

After listening to President Bush's speech on our involvement in Iraq the other night, it came as no surprise that he does not have immediate plans to being our troops home from that country. He so much as intimated that our enemies agree that U. S. Troops should stay In Iraq until the job to be done, is done.

The job to be done is to bring American troops home, not a year or so from now, but *now.* To add insult to injury, it has now been said that the newly elected President of Iran was involved in the detention and gross treatment U. S. Soldiers in 1979. Of course he denies the allegations. What do they expect him to do? He could be telling the truth as so often it is said that members of certain ethnic **groups *all look alike.*** He may be a look alike, but if any of those persons who lived to see him again say that he was the one, ***true or not, he is the one!*** It is going to be interesting to see how this plays out.

It should be clear to the United State and the rest of the world that the people of Iraq want to be left alone. They show us every day, by killing as many Americans, soldiers and civilians, as possible. Then we send some more to take the place of the dead ones. We should realize that if the people of Iran elected a president whom has oppressed Americans, there must be something on their agenda that our President and Congress do not know, or they have decided that we do not need to know.

We do have a need to know, however, why Congress can put so much of the taxpayer's money in fight effort and does not have money to feed and house the American poor, or educate our youth, especially since Iraq was not a threat to the world, let along America and the Middle East. We still live in one of the greatest countries in the world, but we must realize how much greater it would be if we took proper care of us and then, them. **Charity begins at home.**

Charity should not involve the daily risks of the lives of citizens in this country. We should be able to help others without giving all of ourselves to the cause. After all, some things in life should be about **us, the United States.**

It is heartbreaking when a man, any man in these United States, neglects his family, wife and children to help another lady and her family across town, while his family is ragged, hungry and miserable. Any child protective services in any state in the United States would label him a neglectful parent and take him to court on those charges. In the case of our country, it would be called abuse and neglect because the neglected subjects' hard –earned money is being used to finance the efforts across the sea, while the family at home suffers. We need to get 'in cinque' and pound the messages to our Congressmen that this war needs to end. Limiting the funding will do a lot of talking.

WAR AND THE STATE OF THE UNION
First published February 1, 2006

It was very clear to many Americans that President Bush's State of the Union Address gave a clear picture of a state of *'disunion.'* The only thing positive about the union is that the President plans to continue doing whatever it is that he is doing for the next year. He positively has no plan to discontinue his actions which have us in an uncomfortable situation now.

He positively laid out things that are not favorable in the union, most of which became that way because of his leadership or lack of it.

The war in Iraq is one of his mainstays. He stated that there is 'no peace in retreat,' but there certainly would be some peace in the United States if all of the military personnel in Iraq were home with their families and not dodging bullets and bombs over there. We retreated from Viet Nam and we can retreat from Iraq. The people of Iraq would have more peace, too. They could continue their civil war without our interference and perhaps arrive at *their peace*. The money used for Iraq would keep Americans out of the poor house and boost the American economy.

Our economic outlook is bleak with motor industries laying off over 30,000 employees and closing some production plants; coal mines being shut down in some states; airlines going bankrupt; oil industries still 'cooking books'; unemployment up across the nation with those whom have exhausted unemployment benefits ***not being counted*** as unemployed anymore. Inflation has grown faster than income and the price of everything is grossly high. The Federal Reserve Bank has a new chairman, Ben Bernanke, who is already, after one day in office, speaking of a hike in interest rates.

A hike in interest rates will not help our energy situation. This is the one thing that is disastrous to everyone's budget. As a matter of fact, it seems impossible. Why should a gallon of gasoline costs more than a gallon of milk or a loaf of bread? Why should the heating or electric bill for a house cost more that the house note? Will alternative fuels solve our problems? No. Every farmer in America would need to grow grains to make alternative fuels just for vehicles. Alternative fuels will cost more and the cars which use them, the hybrids, cost more as well. We do a lot with batteries now, perhaps therein lies the answer to our future energy needs.

The Social Security, Medicare and health issues are ongoing, and will apparently be ongoing issues until enough citizens demand corrective measures be taken to benefit us all. We see where our President is headed; we need to get 'in cinque' and let our Senators and Representative know where we ***want to go!***

WAR CONFUSION
First published April 19, 2006

It appears that 'Mr. Bush's War' in Iraq is now a 'dead horse.' We may talk about how wrong it has been to get into it in the first place and how much we need to do to help to bring our troops home in the second place, especially since we now know for certain that there never were any weapons of mass destruction in Iraq. Mr. Bush has repeatedly told us how he was misled with inaccurate information causing him to invade Iraq. It sounds similar to the United States' entry into World War I and World War II; U-boats attacked and Pearl Harbor bombed. Wrong messages and late message cause war.

Are we getting the message that President Bush has his eye on attacking Iran now? They have elected a president and his name is not Mr. Bush, but one could get that idea if you did not know any better. Mr. Bush feels that the Iranians are preparing to make nuclear weapons and he seemingly has no confidence in the United Nations and their ability to deal with Iran.

That leads one to believe that the ongoing shakeup in the White House may just have something to do with the political arena surrounding Mr. Bush's next steps in dealing with the Middle Eastern nations. If Vice President Chaney shoots another friend while Mr. Bush's friends keep leaving the White House, or are being relieved of some of their duties and Mr. Bush continues to staunchly support Secretary of Defense, Mr. Rumsfeld wile at least six generals call for his dismissal due to poor management of the Iraq War and ignoring the advice of field commanders, what does that leave us to believe?

It would appear that the individuals in the field would know more about their conditions, their needs and what they *do not need* while dodging bullets and roadside bombs in Iraq, a lot better than someone sitting comfortably in a lavish office in Washington, D. C. No matter how many stars the generals calling for Mr. Rumsfeld's resignation have, they are apparently more knowledgeable about war in general than he or the President or Vice President. Is there merit in the voices calling for the impeachment of President Bush? It seems that it would be difficult to just impeach the President without impeaching the Vice President as well, as he supports and agrees with the President on everything. If this happened, then the Speaker of the House would become President, The President Pro Tempore of the Senate, the Vice President and the Secretary of State, Condoleezza Rice in line to be the first Female President. We must get 'in cinque' and find out what our President has on his mind.

NEW OUTLOOK ON IRAQ
First published January 10, 2007

The new Secretary of Defense in the President's Cabinet, Mr. Gates, has been to Iraq and given the President his take on the situation in Iraq. Contrary to the beliefs of others, especially retired generals, no more troops should be sent to Iraq and those there should be gradually pulled out. The Secretary of Defense and Mr. Bush have decided that approximately 20,000 more troops are needed to end the war in Iraq. As of this date, the media has reported that 3000 American troops have died in Iraq. That averages about 1000 per year of the war activity. The civil war between the people of Iraq continues, as well as the bloodshed.

It would seem that a decision ***not to send more troops to Iraq,*** especially when one looks at the past results, that such a thought would be a 'no brainer.' Saddam's death has not caused any calm to fall over Iraq, but may have incensed his supporters. The neighbors of Iraq have already declared which side of the civil war they will support if and when the American troops leave and so be it. These people have been fighting among themselves for centuries; during the time of mentioned in the ***Bible*** and before, and the presence of American troops, any troops, other than their own, is **not going to change** anything. These people are Muslims, members of Islam and Islam is a fighting religion. Unlike Christians who are not supposed to fight, Muslims fight for submission. More American troops will not make the Muslims think or act Christian.

Troops from other countries, and especially the United States, have been in Iraq long enough to train one side or the other and leave the fighting to them under their government and leadership, as the United States cannot, and as things stand and America stands in the eyes of the world, will not make Iraq what America wants it to be. The United States cannot be the keeper of nations. We have too many problems of our own.

If 20,000 more troops go to Iraq, we will have 20,000 less troops to

163

defend the United States. We are vulnerable and did not just get that way. We have been the victim of enemy assault for a long time but it was not until the bombing of the federal building in Oklahoma City that we really took a close look at the death toll. The destruction of the Twin Towers was the affirmation of repeated assaults. We need 20,000 troops here in the United States to protect citizens at home. We need to get 'in cinque' and let our Congressmen know how we feel about the issue at hand.

TOO MANY BATTLEFRONTS!
First published February 20, 2007

Soon, it will be spring and our hearts and minds will begin to focus on the lighter side of life, frolicking in the sun, playing and doing whatever it is that suits our fancy. Come as it may, spring will not take us away from the daily reminders that we are a country at war; a situation which weighs on our hearts and minds because of the daily toll of lives being lost and to some of us, for naught.

Life, human life is valued above all else in America. This is what we are taught. This is what the average Christian American believes. If we truly believe that life is valuable, the 'powers that be' should consider this and immediately begin to withdraw American troops from Iraq. There is *no way that a Christian country can persuade a Moslem country to see things their way.* If the Moslems cannot get along with each other, what gives anyone else the belief that they have a quick fix?

Iran, Iraq and Syria are neighbors and their religious beliefs are basically the same. They plan now to have a conference to discuss their problems. The United States is invited to the conference, but they are not the main players. The leaders of these three countries are the ones who must come to some agreements about how they will live side by side.

It appears that if United States troops are withdrawn from Iraq, maybe the car bombings which are being blamed on Iran will stop. If he United States is sure that Iran is placing bombs in places to kill U.S. troops and denying it, and Iraq is ready to sit down with Iran and Syria, it is time for the United States, like Great Britain, to make an exit and ***save American lives and dollars*** in order that they may be put to good use here in this country.

The United States is fighting too many wars in too many different places. If our manpower is spread around the globe, there is **no one left for homeland security!** We are vulnerable to attack from without because it seems that we have been vulnerable to attack from within for quite some time now (Oklahoma City and the Twin Towers). It is time to '*bring the boys home*' and we need to get 'in cinque' and let our Congressmen and Congresswomen know that this is how we feel by writing to them and telling them so. Let Iraq, Iran, Afghanistan, Syria and Saudi Arabia and Turkey, too, if they want to, do their own thing, with each other, without the United States.

PATIENCE UNTIL THE END
First published March 20, 2007

The newly elected Congress of the United States and especially the House of Representatives, led by Congresswoman, Nancy Pelosi, appears to be set on trying to perform the job for which they were elected; to end the war in Iraq.

The House of Representatives is not getting the cooperation which it hoped for from the Senate, but it is pushing onward anyway. President Bush's latest request for more funding to send 3,000+ troops to Iraq to stabilize Baghdad has met with resistance from the House with a resounding "NO!" The President is calling for patience to show that his program works. It does not come as any surprise that Congress and the American people, after four years and the loss of nearly 4000 American lives, not to mention the amount of money spent fighting the endless battles and the destruction to Iraq, have no more room for patience.

After four years of patience and no return on the investment, President Bush's rating has dropped to a dismal low. Yet it appears that only a few people are concerned about impeaching him. Only one man of note has scaled the fence at the White House unlawfully and we still are exhibiting patience until 2008 when the end of the Bush Era comes.

On the other hand, President Clinton did not carry the United States into a war and lowered the national debt. As a matter of fact the word 'surplus' was heard more than anything else, though we know that the 'surplus' included our Social Security and Medicare funds. But, because he chose to have an affair considered immoral, for which there did not seem to be any complaint from his spouse, he was impeached. Not one American soldier died because of what he did and no extra money was spent which could have been used to help the American people. We need to get 'in cinque' as a country and set our priorities straight.

IV-HOLIDAYS

THANKSGIVING PREPARATION
First published November 20, 2011

Time has moved swiftly and the year 2011 is quickly coming to an end. Long before Halloween, the hustle and bustle was on in the preparation for Christmas. It seems that we are a Holiday 'thing' oriented people and we put a lot of energy into getting our 'thing' like we want it so we can enjoy it.

On the other hand, businesses are capitalizing on our need for 'things,' whatever the thing is. In August, they were preparing for the school 'thing.' In September, it was the Halloween 'thing,' and in October it was a double whammy, Thanksgiving and Christmas. The Salvation Army joined the push for Christmas at Halloween. Thanksgiving cannot get here soon enough for the so called "Black Friday" sales, the day after Thanksgiving. It seems that each big store is trying to one-up the other.

Wal-Mart originally started their Black Friday at midnight of Thanksgiving and a few other stores did the same thing. This year, Sears and a few other stores decided to move the opening sales back to the weekend before Thanksgiving. The businesses are making the big bucks, but many employees do not want to put in the extra hours at unusual times, but with the economy in the state that it is in, most are going to push themselves on out to work and just be thankful that they have work.

We often hear the ***"Jesus is the reason for the season,"*** but it is going to take a massive amount of changing the mind-set of a lot of people and businesses to get to that fundamental concept in this computerized digital world. Our children think digitally and we know that adds up to numbers. We must find a way to make the concept of Jesus' birth, digital. The material is available, but processing it will be the issue.

Ironically, Thanksgiving comes at a marvelous time, just weeks before Christmas, and if we can focus on giving thanks, we may be able to appreciate Christmas just a wee bit more. We, the people of the United State of America have so much to be thankful for, even in hard times like the present. We have been experiencing a recession for most of us and a depression for a great number of us, for over ten years which have also spanned several wars where American lives have been lost, guerilla warfare right here in this country and ongoing terror, but we can still be thankful!

American is a compassionate country and helps other nations around the world on an ongoing basis. We should be grateful that we can do this and still hold the status of the number one country in the world. We complain a great deal about our economic situations, but we need to get 'in cinque,' on our knees and give thanks for what we have because in so many parts of the world, there are people who would be thankful if their only needs were what we complain about. Have a ***THANKFUL THANKSGIVING!***

THANKSGIVING IN PEACE
First published November 17, 2013

Today, we are about ten days away from celebrating the national holiday of Thanksgiving. I almost got confused until I checked my calendar as I was wondering if I were getting the old dreaded old age disease of not remembering or being able to distinguish one day from another. It was the television commercial on a program which I had not recorded, so I did not have the option of fast forwarding it, when all I could see were advertisements for Christmas. The newspapers have been at it ever since Veterans' Day passed, but I was not ready for television. To top that off, all one has to do is walk into some of the many stores that have the Christmas trees on display.

Once upon a time when I was a teacher, holidays were very important to children. It was also important that they knew when these days occurred. I now wonder if children really have any idea when or why certain holidays take place. There is so much commercialism about Christmas and from the latest news, it appears that the so called "Black Fridays" will take place earlier than in past years.

We realize that merchants make their most profit at Christmas time and naturally want to boost their sales, but it should be against the law to pre-empt Halloween, Veterans' Day and Thanksgiving to make us aware of all of the 'good' things that they have available for us to purchase to celebrate Christmas.

I enjoy Christmas. It is still one of the best holidays in the year and gives us a big send off into the New Year, but I also want to enjoy the holidays which proceed it just as well, excluding Halloween. My family never celebrated that one; old Southern tradition. This was the time to put up everything in the yard, turn out the lights and go to sleep early to avoid vandalism. I had to indulge at school as a teacher and allow my child to pass out candy, but never to go out and collect it.

This year, I would like to enjoy Thanksgiving without listening to Christmas carols!! It is my hope that all of us could enjoy the day in that same way. This is a day which was set aside by a President of the United States to give sanction to the togetherness of the first immigrant Americans who survived and the Native Americans; the people **who were already here** and knew how to survive and taught the immigrants how to do it. Successfully, they were able to share a harvest meal together, IN PEACE! This is not a tradition which continued to follow in this country as the immigrants became more aggressive and attempted to _take what was not theirs._ Somewhere along the way, we have come to know, understand and attempt to right some of those wrongs which took place. It is in this spirit, that I hope that we will get 'in cinque' and let the deeper meaning of the Thanksgiving holiday be one which we can celebrate in PEACE.

CHRISTMAS AND CRIME
First published December 7, 2006

Christmas carols of all kinds can be heard on the radio, the television, in shopping areas, dining areas and anywhere something is sold or solicited. Christmas decorations abound on every street in every town. Christians and non-Christians are preparing for the great day, December 25, 2006.

For this one day in December, the last month of the year, we spend a lot of money. We buy presents for our family, friends and children. We culminate a year of hard work and some play. We go all out to make certain that we have a bang of a ball at Christmas with our presence and our presents.

One great thing about celebrating the Christmas day is the presence of close family and friends coming together in a warm and loving way. All of the bad thoughts and deed of the year are put aside to make merry and give thanks for the birth of the Christ child at this time of the year. The people who say that they do not believe in Jesus are just as happy as those who do.

On the other hand, the Christmas season has the highest crime rate of any time of the year. While most of us are preparing to make merry, there are droves of unscrupulous individuals just waiting to ruin our spirit by robbing us of our purchases. They take advantage because they know how happy we are and how **careless we are.** On the streets and getting into our vehicles is not the only place we may encounter criminals. Some of them are found in places of business. Keep your eyes on the credit cards and make sure there is no camera to take a picture of it. Make sure that the card that you get back is **yours.** You may receive one that looks just like yours with an expired date on it.

There are nice people out there who do not mind helping you and then there are nice helpers who turn out not to be so nice. On Christmas Eve, an acquaintance stepped off the electric train with several large packages, and knowing that she was an attractive lady, she only had a positive response when two good-looking well-dressed men offered to help her to her car with her packages. She carried on a lively conversation with them on the way and when they arrived at her Lincoln Continental vehicle they put her packages in her car for her, took the mink coat she was wearing and drove off in her car without her. That was not a merry Christmas. Of course, she was thankful that she was not hurt. This is a time of the year to get 'in cinque,' be careful, be thankful, be prayerful and have a very *MERRY CHRISTMAS!*

JESUS THE REASON FOR THE SEASON?
First published December 12, 2010

It is approximately two weeks before we celebrate the Christmas Day. The season got started just after Halloween. The real hustle and bustle began the day after Thanksgiving. And, a hustle and bustle it is.

Somehow, the word 'recession' does not ring a bell with the various businesses, or the customers. Every store in town has a *special sale.* The advertisements tell you that the special prices that they offer today will not be the regular but higher prices by January 1, 2011, so buy now.

I have witnessed many Christmases during times of prosperity when there was not as many 'sales' and consequently, not as many people making the kind of purchases that are being made now. It appears that we are surrounded by a feeling of *'do or die;'* the feeling that this may be the last Christmas that we can do this. We must have this and that or whatever, because this is the last chance to try to be happy. It may feel that way to many Americans because of the constant turnover and job lost prospective.

A dim future is causing many individuals to hope this will be a Christmas that they will never forget, by making it the most joyful one that they have ever witnessed. The downside to this feeling is causing many people to only think of themselves. They are so busy trying to please themselves until they are not using common courtesy or respecting others during this season of love, blessings, beliefs, gift giving and celebrations of the birth of the Christ Child, Jesus.

'Jesus is the reason for the season,' for Christians, though this holiday is celebrated by other religions simply because it is an American tradition. The secular aspect is celebrated and financed by big businesses in order to capitalize on the purchases made by consumers during the holiday season, in their effort to give gifts to family and friends.

It was so simple when we made our gifts that we gave to family and friends, and got together and laughed, talked, ate, sang and danced the day away after having a soulful time worshiping earlier in the day. One would think that with money scarce, we would discover those times again; when the *birth of Jesus Christ was truly considered a blessing to celebrate!* We need to get 'in cinque' and rediscover ***Christmas and Christ.***

CHRISTMAS AND THE 'GOOD OLE DAYS'
First published November 27, 2011

Somehow, some people and some businesses have the concept that the Christmas holidays are all about money. Presents cost money and people spend money to get them. Someone has said that the only difference between men and boys is the price of the toys. To the businesses the day after Thanksgiving is designated "Black Friday" because the money that we spend on that day will bring businesses out of 'the red' on their sales records and into solvent black numbers.

Any way you cut it, businesses prosper during their holiday sales and that is the only way some of them can remain in business. Many proprietors only sell merchandise during the holidays. They are aware that people buy things once they have the 'Christmas spirit.' They will buy things that are not on their Christmas list because they see it and 'the devil made them do it.'

It is one thing to stay up late at night to rush into a store and be the first in line to get the hot commodities which are advertised for purchase on 'Black Friday,' and yet another to either inflict pain on others in the process or become a victim of pain. Last year, at least one person was killed and many others hurt in the process of rushing into a store once the doors were opened to the public for hot sales. This year a pepper sprayer made the flash news and eventually surrendered to the police once the coveted merchandise had been secured and purchased; an electronic game.

Is this what the Christmas spirit and Christmas holidays has come to? Have we completely forgotten the reason for season? Christians around the world celebrate Christmas and there is no doubt that in many instances purchases for presents to exchange plays a great part in the event. Yet many families enjoy a sober holiday with a family dinner, church attendance sharing the joy with friends singing Christmas carols and just being jolly and happy; being thankful for the birth of the Christ Child. I can remember that kind of Christmas.

I used to think that Christmas was really all about being a child. Only the children in our home got presents or gave presents at Christmas. Everyone in our home or visiting with us had an unending choice of fruit, nut and candy the week before Christmas and into the New Year. Cake and pie accompanied the Christmas family dinner which took place after attending church. In the evening, our family attended the Christmas play at church in which the children participated. We had practices for weeks before Christmas learning our speaking parts and words to the song which we sang. Parents enjoyed the presentations which were shared by friends in the community. People were not afraid to go out at night to church as many are now. Caroling went on until the New Year. Groups of people actually got out into the weather and caroled throughout the neighborhood in the evenings during the holidays. Anyone could join in and sing. There were no 'Black Fridays,' 'Blue Mondays' or 'Hot Saturdays.' Christmas was about celebrating the birth of Jesus, the Christ child and we need to get 'in cinque' and find our way back to the 'good ole days!'

THE WAY IT WAS: CHRISTMAS
First published December 26, 2010

Christmas Day has passed and it seems that Sunday, the day after the holiday is just as busy as the day before Christmas. The stores could not open soon enough for the rush to exchange items purchased and received as gifts for Christmas. Some of us, however, do not have the 'after Christmas sale' money as we spent what we had for Christmas.

Spending for Christmas seems to be the main thing to celebrate the holiday, and I have not been convinced that our children are learning that this is what Christmas is all about. Small children expect toys and other goodies for Christmas while being held hostage by their parents that these items will not be forthcoming if they have not been 'good' during the year. In contrast, as a child, I hoped for 'A' toy and perhaps a new dress or pair of shoes; some clothing item. I really hit the jackpot on the Christmases that I received not only a dress, but shoes, knee-high socks, a new coat with a matching hat and muff. Because money was scarce, my cousin and I made Christmas presents for our family.

Our grandmother, who was a public school teacher, subscribed to the educational magazine *The Instructor* and we used the directions in it to make Christmas gifts for our family members. I recalled making some felt house slippers for my great grandmother her last Christmas. I was proud of my finished article and she was proud of me. There was the love and the warmth that made the season glow. We gathered around the piano on Christmas day and sang Christmas carols and that felt good; family feeling the spirit of love and the spirit of the season without the overbearing atmosphere of commercialism. We did not have a lot of Christmas decorations either.

We went into the woods and chopped down a live Christmas tree wherever we were permitted to get one. No one sold Christmas trees. If you wanted one, you could usually get it for asking for it. Stores sold shredded tinsel which we purchased for a nickel or dime and we made colorful chains to put on our tree from construction paper by gluing the strips together. We made ornaments from paper as well, but we could purchase a few glass ones to give our tree some pizzazz. We were allowed to have two regular sized electric lights on our tree; one red and one green. Anyone passing along the street did not know that we did not a string of lights, because those two bubs gave the same impression as a string of lights. We rejoiced!

This was a holiday wherein our time had been spent making gifts and decorations, licking cake batter, cracking nuts, roasting sweet potatoes and finally waiting for Santa Claus and our holiday firecrackers. We had firecrackers for Christmas, not the fourth of July. That was picnic time; no fireworks. Our bang came for Christmas and then we listened as the adults shot off their guns to welcome the New Year after Christmas. This was the signal that our Christmas holiday had come to an end and it was time to go back to school. Those were the Christmases that I will always cherish and hope that our young people can learn to enjoy a Christmas of love, warmth and caring rather than the commercial affairs that we encounter now. Let us get 'in cinque; and work toward the love, hope and peace that we should find in our Christmases.

EASTER!
First published April 1, 2012

Palm Sunday is our clue that Easter Sunday is near. This is the Sunday which celebrates the entry of Jesus into Jerusalem at the time of the Passover. The Passover is a Jewish holiday which is tied to the commemorations of the slaying of the first born just before the Israelites were freed from Egyptian slavery. It also entails the Feast of Unleavened Bread celebrating the actual Exodus flight from Egypt. According to Paul, Jesus was the Paschal Lamb or the sacrificial lamb of the Passover.

We know the story of the Passover, Jesus' trial before the Sanhedrin, the supreme court of the Jewish people. Because of the Passover, they could not order his death and participate wholeheartedly in the festival, so they delivered him to Pontius Pilate, the Roman governor of Judea, who was the judge in the trial and execution of Jesus.

Jesus had warned his disciples that after two days of the Passover, he would be betrayed to be crucified. It was Judas Iscariot who went to the high priest and offered to deliver Jesus unto them for thirty pieces of silver. They sat to have supper together, *The Last Supper,* when Jesus told them that one of them would betray him and they all wondered "Lord is it I?"

Soon afterwards, Jesus went into the Garden of Gethsemane to pray. He asked Peter to go with him and told him how he would deny him three times that night. He went to pray three times and three times he found his disciples asleep instead of praying and watching him. Early in the morning Judas came with a multitude of men armed with swords and identified Jesus with a kiss, so they would know who to deliver to the court to be put to death.

The Sanhedrin was a council made up of seventy-one Jewish sages who constituted the legislative body and the supreme court of Judea during the Roman period. The word Sanhedrin means "sitting together" as a legislative assembly in a semi-circle. The U. S. Senate derived its seating arrangement from the Jewish Sanhedrin.

After the Sanhedrin convicted Jesus with false witnesses, Judas repented and threw down the thirty pieces of silver and went away and committed suicide as he saw that the blood of Jesus was upon him. Pilate's wife warned him not to condemn Jesus because of the visions she had that day and this prompted Pilate to release a renowned prisoner or Jesus. The multitude chose the prisoner, Barabbas and said to crucify Jesus after Pilate could find no fault with Jesus. He released Barabbas, washed his hands and said that he was innocent of the blood of Jesus, a just man. Jesus was crucified and rose on the third day and ascended into Heaven. Hence, Christians around the world, celebrate Easter, the celebration of the Risen Lord.

When we celebrate this holiday, the beginning of the Passover on April 6 at sundown, through April 12, 2012, we should get 'in cinque' and ask ourselves at every opportunity that we have to pray about our joys, love, misfortunes and life as a whole, "Is it I, Lord?" "Am I giving my all to this cause or am I sleeping on the job?"

V-TECHNOLOGY

DANGERS OF SOME TECHNOLOGY
First published October 12, 2006

Technological advances in the world have played a very important role in how countries and nations in the world get along with each other. As the *Bible* states, there are wars and rumors of wars and it has been this way since the beginning of time. The advances in technology have made life in many areas more comfortable and satisfactory and on the other hand, more dangerous.

The danger lies in the misuse of technology. We get electrical power from nuclear sources and that is good. We can do a variety of things with electricity and put to use many appliances and some gratifying inventions that bring us fun and relaxation. Even good uses of nuclear power can pose dangers in the processing of the resources that make the energy. According to some scientists, nuclear power is not as costly as some conventional resources, and that is definitely a plus for consumers. We also have nuclear medicine which has proved to be important in health care.

Another convenient form of technology is the television, microwave oven and the computer. We can derive a plenty of fun and relaxation from these inventions. Yet the danger lies in the radiation which we absorb from these items, especially the microwave oven and the color television. But we do not mind. We use them anyway, with some care some times.

On the other hand, we are worried constantly about our children's use of the television and the computer. The "My Space" website has really gotten parents in a tirade as they fear their children may become involved with sexual predators. The use of nuclear has the world in a tirade as the use of nuclear weapons could be 'the beginning of the end' of this world as we know of and about it.

The small country, North Korea which was a main player in the Korean Conflict in the 1940s has announced that it has tested a nuclear device. As a member of the United Nations, this country has violated the Partial Test Ban Treaty (1963), the Treaty on Non-Proliferation of Nuclear Weapons (1968), the Strategic Arms Limitation Treaties (SALT) of 1972 and 1979, and the Strategic Arms Reduction Treaties (START) of 1991 and 1993, which were negotiated between super powers (Funk & Wagnall New Encyclopedia.)

The United Nations has appealed to the United Nations to impose sanctions upon North Korea and the head of this country have announced that they are prepared to go to war with the United States. We must not forget that just a few weeks ago, President Bush was called the devil by the President of Venezuela. We must get 'in cinque' and figure out if there is a revolution aimed at the United States by a con-glomerate of small nations. We do not need another war.

IDENTITY THEFT
First published Mar 7, 2007

Each year becomes more of a major threat to personal security, as our population becomes more and more astute in the use of technology. Technology is good and in many cases now a vital part of every part of our lives. And just as technology has it quirks, there are more criminals than we care to think about who are preying on an unsuspecting population every chance that they get or take.

We hear about identity theft each and every day. The cyberspace thefts are now out-numbering the regular, normal kind of theft that we are acquainted with. The irony is that thieves outnumber the cyber police and often go undaunted. There may be the chance to stop the activities of the cyber thieves, but seldom are they caught. Damage to our personal security may be limited and sometimes eradicated, but we as individuals must keep an alert eye on activities that involve the revelation of our identity.

One of the recent events in identity theft is the rise of notorious ethnic gangs that seek to *place their wives and girlfriends in jobs* **in banks, stores**

and businesses that have access to your personal information, especially if you make transactions that call for a credit check where your personal information is needed. We write checks which bear our information and we shop on credit, using credit cards that have our information and these thieves are securing access to our personal information and when we find out about it, it is often too late.

Some credit card companies keep a vigilant on our transactions and know when there is foul play before we know it. A company like that can be appreciated and there is often a fee for that kind of credit card. Be that as it may, it appears that it is time for us to get 'in cinque' and return to paying cash on all the items for which that is possible, especially in light of the fact that our economy is seemingly entering a downturn. We need to pay off what we can and 'maybe' just maybe, get a shoebox for our valuables.

COMPUTERS IN OVERDRIVE
First published April 6, 2007

Our world is changing fast, and so is technology. It has come to the point where technological programs of the computer types are out pacing themselves. Changes are occurring faster than technicians can accommodate them.

About thirty years ago, the words Univac, COBAL, FORTRAN and keypunch were common computer terms. Ten years later, one needed to know the terms, 'boot-up,' floppy disc,' 'write,' 'graphics.' 'hard copy,' 'Macintosh,' 'IBM,' 'compatible,' 'software,' 'hardware,' and the magic word 'Windows,' soon to be followed by another magic word, 'Internet.'

In finally making it to the 'Internet,' I have personally been the owner of five computers trying to stay in touch with the latest technology because a job at some time or another deemed it necessary for me to keep my skills up to date.

I was first introduced to computer programming, earning credit at Illinois Institute of Technology using the Univac, which was a modified teletype machine using a foreign language,' COBOL and FORTRAN for which keypunch cards had to be used to get a program through the computer and typed. I was too happy to use the more modern machine which had to be 'booted up' and you could actually type sentences with a

178

mixture of other symbols. A great improvement, but not until 'Windows' came into being did computers take on a new easier life to understand and use. All one needed was a compatible software program to do wonders on the computer.

Real wonders were not seen until the Internet became available to computer users who had a version of Windows, called Windows 95. By now, I was into the use of my third computer and felt content. By the time Windows 2000 appeared, it became difficult to open some of my e-mail, but I continued to use my convenient version of Windows until I was forced to purchase Windows XP. Things went along fine until I ventured into a job where the only way to save anything on a computer required the use of a front-loaded 'Flash or Jump Drive.' There was something new. My XP used 'USB' cords but they were all in the back of the 'CPU' and were being used. I needed a computer which would be compatible to my work. Windows Vista Home Basics was what I needed; so I thought!

B.B. King sang, "Don't Make Your Move Too Soon," and I now know what he meant. Getting drivers for my printer was easy. It is time consuming to attempt to transfer files on a floppy disc to a computer which does not accommodate anything but a CD/DVD or Flash Drive. Furthermore, I had no idea that the Internet Security Suite which I purchased with my DSL connection *would not work* on Vista. I also learned that the new Microsoft Office Word 2007 cannot be opened by users of an older version of Word. Therefore, one needs to know if your Internet Carriers is prepared to accommodate your new computer for security purposes and will your friends with older computers be able to open the e-mail.

THE BIG SWITCH
First published June 14, 2009

The big switch has taken place. On Friday, June 12, 2009, the National Broadcasting Service switched from analog to digital television. The switch was supposed to take place around the beginning of the year, but it was postponed because the President felt that too many people were not ready for the switch and too many people had not taken advantage of the two coupons that were issued for the asking, to secure free converter boxes in order to be able to watch high definition digital television.

Those individuals who had cable or satellite service did not have to worry about getting a converter box as their signals would be sent in a digital format when the switch came about. With all of the warnings about the date for the end of analog broadcasting on television, many people were still not ready to change. It is similar to getting ready to go to Heaven. Some of us just are never ready to change. We wait until the last minute when sometimes it is too late to do any good even if we do change. Those persons, who waited too late, just missed their favorite broadcasts.

The converter boxes are doing a pretty good job if we also have digital antennae to hook up with them. Without cable or satellite, many of us will see the programs that we watched daily with analog in high definition digital instead. The real problem comes when you try to hook up a new DVD player or VCR to your old television that has been converted to digital. Most old televisions have just one outlet, for cable or an antenna. There is no place to plug in a digital coaxial cable. Some televisions manufactured as late as three years ago, still do not have a digital tuner, or outlets for digital equipment.

Digital may be the way today, but fiber optic equipment is on the way. As fast as we make one hurdle there is another to confront us, and when we cannot conform, we find ourselves in some miserable situations. It pays to stay informed about the changes that are taking place.

Some of us elderly people are really caught up in cultural lag, big time. We are frustrated with the television, DVD, wireless telephone service, the Internet, debit cards and the like. Most of us are familiar with credit cards and have a little knowledge about the Internet, but so much about these things escape us. Some senior centers offer courses to help the elderly. If you are totally lost, get one of your grandchildren to show or tell you what and how to deal with the new-fangled things that leave us behind. We must get 'in cinque' and make our way to the mainstream of our culture. That may mean buying a new high definition digital television so we can record our favorite soap operas.

SENIOR CITIZENS AND TECHNOLOGY
First published August 28, 2011

I have learned that as an older citizen and member of our current society, that older citizens need to learn the language and train of thought of the younger generations. We have a difficult time trying to figure out what makes them tick and why are they so different in so many ways than us older citizens.

I have learned that in order to understand my grandson, that I must learn to speak his language which is often an abbreviated form of the English language. The younger generation uses it's own vocabulary with their objects of technology. To us, their written words often look like a foreign language, but if we take time to read it and ask a few questions here and there, we may come out a winner in understanding what they are saying. I have found that they can text faster on an itty-bitty cell phone than I can on a full scale typewriter.

I forgot, many young people fifteen years old and younger have no idea what a typewriter is. A few about twenty years old have some idea as many of them had to take Typing as a prerequisite to their computer classes. The word "Qwerty" is more familiar to them than a typewriter keyboard.

I have come through just about all of the transitions of the computer from the old teletype machine of the fifties to trying to master COBOL and FORTRAN working with the Univac and Apple, McIntosh and IBM Windows to Word 95 and finally the confusion of multiple browsers, multiple operating systems and the powers of Yahoo and Google.

The most frustrating part of all of this is the fact that there are hackers out there who are into the secrets of our government and poor citizens have no more privacy. It makes you wonder if a good thing has gone really bad. Our young people, who came into this world with the existence of all of these things, definitely know more about the operations of them than those of us who witnessed the onset of today's technology. They do not have the baggage that we have, so they can grasp the details much quicker without having to dump any previous knowledge. The older we are, the more we have to dispose of and that makes learning slower and less effective. Most of our young people know more about technology than many of us will ever know.

As an example of what I am talking about, when my granddaughter was in high school, after each computer class, the teacher sent for her to come back and fix the computer she used so someone else could use it.

The teacher sent for her because she did not know to reset the machine and could not tell the next student what to do.

I admit that I have no desire to use those new cellular telephones which I call miniature computers and currently do not have a camera on the one that I do have. I have been thinking about getting one of the Jitterbugs on which all you do is talk; large numbers; no text, e-mail, messenger or any of that stuff for which one would need a data plan to operate the full extent of the apparatus. But if I do that, I will miss out on the text messages from my grandchildren and my friends who are too tight-budgeted to talk at certain times. It seems that there is no way around technology, so we may as well get 'in cinque' so we can understand the S, Y and Z generations.

PORTABLILITY AND TECHNOLOGY
First published December 18, 2011

There is no doubt in my mind that we must admit that we are definitely in an age where communication with a computer of some kind is the most prevalent means of achieving that goal. The latest cellular telephones are miniature computers and the monthly cost to maintain one is sometimes quite expensive even when your actual telephone is free. One has to pay for a data plan. Lately, it is almost impossible to secure a cellular telephone without a data plan. Most companies offer some kind of bundling, that is another telephone or internet services in one package, usually with a two year contract. When changing from a single service to a bundling, you enter into a _new_ contract whether the old one is up or not. Comparatively speaking, you are supposed to be saving money with the new contract and services.

A compact laptop computer and the desk model used to offer more applications than a cellular telephone, but because the cellular telephone is so much more portable, they now have almost as many applications as a laptop or desk computer. They are so convenient until many people no longer have a landline home telephone. Instead, they are bundling their cellular telephone, internet services and television services. You can get an arrangement wherein you can receive your e-mail on your telephone, see whose calling you on your television and program your television and computer from your telephone. With all of these applications and data plans, I am still wondering why there is a need for Facebook or Twitter. Frankly, I am a holdout.

I have had so many invitations to Facebook and other social networking sites until I once sent a memo to all of my contacts that I was not participating in a social network. The last invitation I received came from a cousin with whom I have a family group connection and who is on my personal e-mail list. I asked him what would be the advantage of being on Facebook. He stated that current events in the lives of your friends are not missed. You know what all of your friends are doing and when and where. I am sorry. I am from the old school where I learned **in** school, how to write letters, invitations, thank you notes, announcements *etc*. I still use the 'snail mail' for such things even though I may send a quick e-mail first. I feel that my friends tell me what they want me to know. If I have to go to Facebook to find out something, they did not want me to know it in the first place. So be it.

I wondered why large department stores did away with their catalogs. It later dawned on me that if you want to order something, you MUST us the computer! I was dumbfounded when I wanted to order filters for my humidifier from a store within easy traveling distance. I had to order on the computer to pick it up at the store! I thought it was ridiculous! And I still do. Truth is, some stores have items which you can **only** purchase online. Yet, you either go to the store to pick up the items or pay to have them shipped to you. I consider these instances computer waste.

Computers have taken too much compassion out of our lives. Machine socialization is not reality. It is too cold and dry. You cannot wrap your arms around a computer and feel the warmth of someone you care about. We need to get 'in cinque' and put more of the old fashioned ways into our socialization and things of the heart and leave the computer for more mundane things as we have a ***Merry Christmas 2011.***

SOCIAL MEDIA
First published January 23, 2012

About four years ago a young man in Mississippi invited me to join him on Facebook. At the time of his invitation, I was shown pictures of people in Mississippi with whom I had a nodding acquaintance and one lady whom had been my co-worker in Chicago whom I had not seem or corresponded with in a very, very, long time. I was puzzled as to why her picture would show up and I could not understand the logic. In addition, I could not recognize the young man from whom the invitation came and I was very skeptical about accepting such an invitation.

As time moved on I continued to get invitations from people whom I had no knowledge and some friends, to join Facebook and LinkedIn. I did not respond to any of the invitations because as fate would have it, I was getting negatives vibes from the media and other sources about the pitfalls and adverse effects of participating on Facebook, so I vehemently decided that Facebook was not for me. I felt so strongly about this until I wrote an e-mail message to all of my contacts that I did not do social media and please do not invite me to join.

Some people paid no attention to my message and continued to invite me to Facebook and LinkedIn. I continued to ignore invitations and delete them as fast as they came. Then, less than a week ago, I received an invitation from a family member and responded by e-mail for him to tell me the advantage of being Facebook. His response was that he was able to keep up with the activities of his friends and family members who participated, such as weddings, funerals, other gatherings, *etc.* My response to that was, "Whatever someone wants me to know, they will tell me."

Less than a week ago, I received ***another*** invitation to join Facebook from the young man who sent the very first invitation. I decided that if he was that persistent, that perhaps I should check it out. *Voila!* Before I could finish registering, and it was very late at night, I was getting messages and pictures and through the frustration could not find my way immediately but managed to stay afloat. One message or post was from one of my classmates from graduate school's daughter; sending pictures and words of encouragement. Another message was a high school and college classmate advising that this is the way to keep up with the younger generation; her children and grandchildren.

I am still trying to find my way, but surprised that most of my friends who seldom e-mail are on Facebook and responded right away to joining me. Now I know why they seldom e-mail. They are busy posting on Facebook on a daily basis. They get to e-mail when they have time or would rather chat on the telephone than respond to e-mail.

Facebook is an adventure for me and I have not yet decided to explore Twitter, but I have a feeling that it will not be long. Time and technology are moving at a pace which makes cultural lag an outdated content of vocabulary to be replaced by technology lag. We must get 'in cinque' and find out how the world is moving on without us if we are not in the mix.

VI-HEALTH AND HAZARDS

CAN YOU HEAR ME?
First published February 17, 2005

Every day, it becomes more and more important that we hear and then understand what we hear. There are many people who have problems hearing and too often we are not aware of it until something goes really wrong because we did not hear what was intended for us to hear.

It is important that the person speaking speaks clearly in order to be head and understood. Some people like the limelight and want to be out front speaking in public and having their say. This is all well and good if they speak distinctly and can be understood. Speaking and hearing are both important.

Some of us, who do not hear well, have the practice of asking someone who does hear well, to tell us what we are supposed to be hearing when it is not clear. That way, much confusion can be avoided. When a speaker does not speak clearly, there is no harm in asking to have something repeated. When you find more and more that you do not understand something that you have heard, it is time to have your hearing checked. On the other hand, when someone repeatedly asks you to repeat something you have said you need to be more careful in speaking.

Care is needed in church meetings when announcements are made, especially when they are concerned with members of the church, such as the sick and shut-in lists. One such misunderstanding had family members of a certain elderly lady, usually a very active member, on the bereaved list rather than the sick list. Her family members in other states were called to prepare to travel to the funeral.

Because the lady's telephone was being answered by an answering service, out of state family members thought they were away from home making funeral arrangements. On the second day of busy telephones, family members in other states were becoming very frustrated. It was decided to call a family member in the particular city to see what they had heard about funeral arrangements. This telephone call yielded some helpful information. *The lady was not dead!* She was in a hospital out of state receiving treatment for her ailment and her husband was with her. They had contacted their church and paid their tithes. Someone heard that they *had lost their lives!* Immediately, out-of-state family members were contacted. We must get 'in cinque' and be more careful in our listening and speaking, especially if the conversation or message pertains to a person or persons.

HIV and AIDS
First published May 24, 2005

A few days ago, I was fortunate to be involved in a conference which focused on ways to eradicate HIV and AIDS, as well as how to help individuals whom have been infected with HIV. Several HIV positive individuals were present at this conference and they spoke to the group present. It was an enlightening experience. I would like to have seen more people present whom could have derived as much from this encounter as I did.

These people appeared to us and we did not know that they were HIV positive until they told us. One of these people stated that they had AIDS. Just looking at them before they told us anything, we had no way of knowing that they were HIV positive and would not have given the first thought to treating them any differently than anyone else. We learned that this is exactly what the HIV positive wants; to be treated just like everyone else. They want to be hugged, kissed, and accepted as a sociable human being, one whose hand you can shake without misgivings. These are the kinds of casual encounters in which they find themselves being treated differently. They want us to know more about their disease and how it affects them and you.

In order to know more about HIV and AIDS, we need more education about the disease and the people suffering from it. We have watched Magic

Johnson for a number of years now; since he announced that he was HIV positive. He appears healthier than ever, however, that remains to be seen, as being HIV positive does not mean that one has AIDS, but none-the-less, is a carrier of the disease and may never get a full-blown case of AIDS. There is medicine to treat AIDS and patients under medical care are living longer, stronger.

In order for HIV/AIDS patients to live longer and stronger, our churches and community organizations need to get 'in cinque' and establish a medium for allowing HIV/AIDS victims to identify themselves without retribution and find help for their physical and social needs and work toward educating the public on prevention of the disease through abstinence, and periodic testing among sexually active individuals.

Every community needs a 'safe place' for HIV/AIDS positive individuals. The more we know, the more positive help can be found or developed.

SNORING
First published March 15, 2006

Do you snore? I do. It has taken a lifetime for me to find out that *snoring is not a normal body reaction when sleeping.* I can recall laughing when my grandfather snored and on the exhale, he whistled. I used to tease my mother about her snoring being so loud that I could hear her when I turned the corner coming home and we lived in the middle of the block. My husband has told me that I snore so loud that when I am asleep upstairs, that I can be heard downstairs. I have also been told that it seems that I stop breathing sometimes when I am snoring. For this reason, I have been diagnosed as having ***sleep apnea.*** Apnea means, not breathing.

We have heard of sleep apnea and often heard that someone died because of it. This has been a very rare occurrence, but none the less, a life-threatening situation. I never associated myself with having this disorder because so many people I know snore and think nothing of it. But more and more attention is being paid to this situation. There are many people whom I have been acquainted for quite some time to learn after I mentioned that I had the sleep apnea, to find that they had it too, but had never mentioned it to me or anyone else that I knew. It seems that once you discover that you have this disorder, you find that there is a whole neighborhood sleeping with the mask, just like you.

Sleeping with a mask connected to a CPAP machine (continuous positive airway pressure) is the current most common treatment of the day for sleep apnea. There is also surgery, which may or may not cure apnea. It may improve the air intake, but may not necessarily eliminate snoring completely. Sleeping with a mask can be quite uncomfortable, but necessary to sustain life. To know for certain if you are affected with sleep apnea, you need to participate in a sleep study.

A sleep study is usually conducted at a sleep center where you are connected to wires which are glued onto your head and attached to various parts of your body along with a rubber cord around your waist and chest to monitor breathing. The wires are connected to a machine which records all of your movements and what your brain is doing and how your lungs are functioning while observing your movements by an infrared camera. The end result determines if you have sleep apnea. An index of 15 or above indicates a positive case of sleep apnea. An oxygen level of 94 and above is considered normal. If your oxygen level drops, this too, is an indication of the presence of sleep apnea. Not treating sleep apnea can lead to heart attack, stroke, hypertension, and lung problems, among the known consequences. It is time for us to get 'in cinque' and check out our snoring. Avoid unwanted health problems taking steps to eliminate snoring.

'AGE OF TERROR:' PHYSICAL AND MATERIAL
First published May 8, 2007

It is becoming clearer each day that we are living in an *'Age of Terror.'* We are terrorized by the harsh weather that is clobbering the United States and by guerilla style assailants in the various phases of our daily lives. Cities are being wiped out by storms that have the power of deadly explosives. These are acts of nature, but it makes one wonder if we, the human beings on this planet are doing something to give impetus to these storms.

There is a lot of information being disseminated and a lot of dialogue about global warming which may or may not have anything to do with the deadly destructive storms. Though there is suffering in the United States, there are other countries which are experiencing deadly forms of weather in the form of tsunamis, earthquakes, wild fires, flooding and pestilence. If global warming has something to do with it, we need to hurry and find out what can be done and get started doing it.

There is a need to find out how and why our food supply is getting contamination. First the pet animals became very sick and many die from consuming commercial food which was contaminated with a substance which was harmful. Then can the contaminated food and vitamin items for human consumption, which have been reported to the Food and Drug Administration. Recall of too many food items is at an all-time high. Tainted cough syrup which could make its way to the United States from Europe is another example of an item which can kill you. This type of terror has not existed since the Tylenol Scare of a few years ago.

As a result of the Tylenol Scare, packaged items have seals now. It is more difficult to open anything which contains consumable good than ever before. However, when goods are imported that is another story. The United States does not have enough manpower to examine every item entering this country which is consumable, especially if it is already prepared for consumption. Sampling will not solve the problem. It is time for us to get busy, get 'in cinque' and return to growing more of our food and getting back to the old home remedies for medicines, especially since germs are becoming more resistant to current medications which used to work.

FIRE PREVENTION
First published October 21, 2007

Born in Chicago on the anniversary of the great fire of 1871 which has provided the impetus for Fire Prevention Week, I am compelled to make us all aware of the seriousness of fire prevention. ***October is Fire Prevention Month.*** Like all other causes, fire prevention has a whole month now.

Though fire prevention awareness is emphasized in October, we need to be aware of and prevent fires all the year. Sometimes the wind is very high in October in many states of the union making October one of the dangerous months for difficulty in controlling fires, as it was alleged that Mrs. O'Leary's cow kicked over a lantern in the barn and the high winds spread the fire all over the business section of Chicago. This was one of the reasons initially given for how the fire started, but native Chicagoans blame the fire on boys attempting to smoke tobacco and accidently set the fire.

Many fires are started accidently. Some are due to carelessness and others to a lack of knowledge about what can ignite an unwanted fire. Believe it or not, many fires are caused by cigarettes and other tobacco products or products used to light a tobacco product. We worried about keeping matches out of reach of children, but very few people really use matches now since the invention of the cigarette lighter and the utility lighters used to ignite gas and charcoal barbeque grills. Some people use utility lighters for their kitchen stove when their pilots no longer work. These can be dangerous in places where there are "No Smoking' signs. You may think, "I am going to smoke," but just igniting the lighter may cause an explosion or a fire. Turning on an electric light where there is gas, can cause a fire and explosion.

Most homes where oxygen of some kind, liquid or gas, is in use, may or may not have a sign on the door indicating that oxygen is in use, so it is very important that you do not light us a cigarette or cigar where there is oxygen in use or in anyone's home without first checking to see if the use of smoking materials is acceptable.

We keep a lot of hazardous materials in our homes without even thinking about what is capable of igniting a fire, so we need to take this month to check out what we need to get rid of to prevent a fire. We will soon need fire to keep warm as winter approaches, and more caution is needed because more homes burn in winter than any other time of year due to the need to keep warm. Let us get 'in cinque' and be as careful as we can, because we cannot be too careful, and prevent fires. They cause damage and take lives.

TATTOOS AND PIERCINGS
First published November 10, 2007

One of the greatest fads in this day and age is the tattoo and piercing of body parts. Some individuals have both the tattoo and the piercings in places where one would never imagine. There are however, may visible ones displayed on individual bodies that make one wonder how and why they are there. We have seen tattoos throughout the ages, but never so many on so many people and in so many places as now.

Some entertainers have so many tattoos until one wonders which line defines the tattoo and which the clothing. It appears that our younger generations have the idea that the movie stars, singers, dancers and rappers set the trend for the nation and if they have tattoos and piercings all over the body then that is what they are supposed to do also. Piercings have the same effect on our youngsters.

We used to pierce our ears in order to keep up with our one and only pair of expensive earrings; a tradition handed down from an African culture probably for some religious reason. Pretty soon our younger generation decided that they needed two holes in their ears since they had more than one expensive pair of earrings. Men, often sailors whom had been across the equator, wore one small earring in one ear signifying their accomplishment. This was probably a tradition among pirates and later picked up by some young gangsters to signify that they were 'Bad.' But what do the numerous earrings that the young ladies wear now, signify? Why do the young men wear the same number of earrings as the girls and often large studs instead of small rings?

The tattoos are markings which have different meanings for different individuals. We see a lot of butterflies, flowers, hearts, lace, names, chains and labels on the exposed parts of bodies where the tattoos can be seen. God forbid we see the ones not visible to us. Many youngsters are making tattoo memorials to their dead friends on part of their bodies. Men used to have a tattoo of their sweetheart on their arms or back. Now, there is no limit to what you might see.

There is one danger which many youngsters do not take into consideration when getting tattoos and piercings and that is the danger of getting infections of the HIV and/or the SUPERBUG, Staphylococcus, which is resistant to antibiotics; keloids and blood contaminations. The effects of an unsterilized tattoo or piercing are life enduring and one should think about it several times before tying it and make sure that is what they want and ponder the consequences. Parents need to get 'in cinque' and monitor their children's tattoos and piercings.

OXYGEN PATIENTS IN JEOPARDY
First published February 22, 2009

Just when we think things are looking up and the economy is about to blossom, you find a cog in the wheel. The excitement or lack of it surrounding the latest *'Stimulus Bill'* has over-shadowed the **Rule of October 30, 2008,** passed during the Bush Administration, before the November 4, 2008 election, which went into effect on **January 1, 2009.**

The CENTER FOR MEDICARE & MEDICAID SERVICIES, referred to as CMS released the rule on October 30, 2008 which affects about 1.5 million oxygen patients in the Medicare program who receive oxygen therapy in their homes. This rule has not only jeopardized the vendors who supply the oxygen, but the patients who need the oxygen. The rule caps Medicare reimbursements for home oxygen suppliers at 36 months. In simple terms, a patient is eligible for 36 months of payments from Medicare for oxygen. After that time, a patient needing oxygen may have to pay the total cash price for therapy, which can run into thousands of dollars per month depending on the need.

Tom Price, a medical doctor and a member of Congress cited the four weaknesses or inadequacies of the rule as follow:

1. The rule establishes inadequate maintenance and service payment Equal to two 30 minute visits annually at a pay rate of approximately $30.00 per visit.
2. The rule requires the original oxygen provider to continue to provide oxygen therapy for those patients who move out of the original oxygen provider's service area. Thus, the Ohio provider whose patient moves to Florida is still responsible for the provision of care to the patient in Florida.
3. The rule does not recognize the 24/7, unscheduled emergency care the providers currently furnish their patients; and
4. The rule requires the oxygen provider to continue to provide all supplies and parts for non- routine maintenance necessary for the proper administration of oxygen therapy for a period of 2 years.

Due to the fact that the lives of patients and the livelihood of vendors are in jeopardy, there is a nationwide need for patients and their families and everyday citizens to contact your Senators and Representatives and the Ways and Means Committee, Energy and Commerce Committee and Leadership asking them to urge CMS to provide adequate payment throughout the beneficiary's period of medical need. Please get 'in cinque' and help as you never know when your time of need may arise.

UNHEALTHY PASSIONS
First published February 13, 2010

America is such a diverse country with a multiplicity of ethnic groups, skills, interests, ability and capabilities until it is a unique situation when one can find an individual who has no passion about anything in life. There probably are a few in existence, but so rare until the number rest in obscurity.

As there probably does exist a few people without passion, there are also a few who have no idea where their passion should take them. Some people work hard at turning their passions into profitable endeavors. There are others who just seek to delight and make other people happy with their passions. Singing, playing music, acting, dancing, volunteering to help others, teaching, ministering, being an advocate for worth-while causes, doctoring and nursing, athletic endeavors, business adventures, traveling and even gambling are passions for some people. In all of these areas, there are individuals whom have made a profitable and often charitable endeavor following their passions.

Some passions have a negative effect on society and the individuals who engage in them. There are the pro-life groups whose passions are so deep until the only way they know how to save a life is to *take a life*. Some of these individuals have actually attacked and killed doctors and nurses and other health care workers who perform abortions. They do not give the individuals who want the abortions a chance to make a choice with their bodies. They are not able to discriminate between what their passion means to them and how it affects other human beings. The irony here is that in most instances, the pro-lifer does not have any type of acquaintance with the person seeking abortion or the medical professionals performing the deed. They are passionately against abortions, but most have **_no plans to care for the child if it were born._**

There exists in America the anti-fur group. They do not want animals killed for the purpose of making fur clothing; coats, hats, _etc._ They forget that this is all that early man had besides the fig leaves, to wear. Sometime, I feel that this trendy group was launched by someone who wanted a fur coat and could not afford it. Never-the less, there are people who are passionate about the use of fur as a garment. Fake fur *is just **not as warm** as the real thing, no matter how you line it!!*

If the Winter Olympic in Vancouver have not been scarred enough by the death of a luger, an American skater's life has been threatened because he has fur on his skating costume. It is time for us to get 'in cinque' and take inventory of our passions and put them in perspective of the rights of others as they relate to our passions. GOD HELP!

VII-MEDICARE AND
HEALTH INSURANCE

THE PATIENT SELF DETERMINATION ACT
First published June 1, 2005

Just about every meeting, workshop or group gathering which I have attended in the past few months, have had, in some fashion, a discussion, or 'how to' topic on 'Living Wills,' 'Advanced Directives,' 'Power of Attorney for Health,' and end of life 'Personal Instructions.' The subject has been in the forefront ever since the Terri Schiavo cases a short while ago.

Terri Schiavo's husband had her oral 'Personal Instructions' which gave him the final victory in the court decision to withdraw her life support system, after twelve years of fighting with her parents about it, which it seems was more apparently about the money her husband had received for her care, rather than love for their daughter. *He did not give them any of the money.*

Too often, money is the 'root of all evil' displayed in family disputes centered on a gravely ill or terminally ill family member. It is widely believed that if one has a Living Will, that end-of-life disputes can be avoided. This may be true in most cases, if the laws of the state involved are followed.

In 1990, The Patient Self Determination Act was passed by Congress, making it a federal law. It is often called the "PSDA." It imposes on states and health care providers, certain requirements about advance directives and a person's rights under state law to make his own decisions concerning his medical care, especially end-of-life care. A Living Will in one state may not be recognized in another state, so if you move, you may need to change or update your Living Will. Some states will not recognize your Living Will unless you have executed a *Durable Power of Attorney for Health Care.*

It appears that whatever route you choose, the most acceptable document you can complete is the Power of Attorney, as in some cases where there has been no Living Will, the representative who had the Durable Power of Attorney for Health Care had the authority to disconnect a patient from life support (Living Will-Attorney Jes Beard: www.jesbeard.com/56.htm). This was a case in Tennessee. Texas, California and Virginia have 'futile care' laws which can overturn decisions of family members *(AARP Bulletin,* May, 2005). The state of Mississippi recognizes two types of advance directives: Individual Instruction and Power of Attorney for Health Care.

If you do not see an attorney in your state to execute these documents, you need to get 'in cinque' to be sure that whatever you choose, that it meets your state's legal requirements.

HEALTH INSURANCE FINES
First published September 25, 2009

The idea of medical coverage for everyone is a brilliant idea and a necessity. The idea about charging a fine, or a more appropriate word, tax, to anyone who does not purchase the insurance is ludicrous. Someone needs to tell Senator Max Baucus and President Obama that the people, whom have not purchased medical insurance, cannot afford medical insurance.

The people who receive SSI or Supplemental Security Insurance also benefit from the Medicaid program. They receive free medical services, but some states have imposed a dollar fee for services and limited the amount of service which an individual can receive in any one calendar month.

Poor people who have worked all of their lives and had low paying jobs or were unfortunate enough to be robbed by the WEP(Windfall Elimination Penalty or the GEP (government Employee Penalty) of their Social Security benefits because they worked on a job with a pension plan and did not pay Social Security taxes while employed on that particular job but had enough quarters to qualify for benefits. The people in these categories include professional workers; teachers, social workers, policemen, medical professionals, other public employees and veterans.

The irony of this is, Congressmen DO NOT PAY INTO SOCIAL SECURITY *but get a lifetime pension that closely equals their salaries and their wives get a lifetime pension also.* It was Congress which passed this law in 1984, the WEP and the GEP, and Congress is happy about it. If a bill to eradicate the WEP or the GEP is introduced in Congress, it never makes it out of the Committee. Giving hard working retirees the benefits that are due them, even if it is not retroactive, would reduce the amount of money that Congress has to spend for other things that they do not necessarily benefit the citizens of THIS COUNTRY! It would reduce the available *monies* for health insurance for people whom have *not worked* and are unable to purchase health insurance. It would appear that rather than tax people who are unable to purchase health insurance, to add them to the Medicare rolls or give them their rightful amount of Social Security benefits. They would not get an SSI check, just medical coverage. We need to get 'in cinque' and write to our Congressmen and women to forget the tax and add those persons who are unable to purchase the insurance, to the Medicaid roll. WE NEED TO HURRY before we have another TAX to pay! If the IRS collects it, it will be a TAX!

MEDICAL INSURANCE AND FRAUD
First published August 12, 2012

The Republican Party, Tea Party and various individuals who are disgruntled about "Obamacare,' (The Affordable Care Act) need to take a look at the institutions and businesses that take care of the financial arena for medical entities and doctors. There need to be a crackdown on fraud.

My first encounter with fraud was with a certain medical facility which treated my mother and did not get their billings to the insurance companies in the required amount of time and I eventually paid that bill after she died to eliminate any 'estate' problems. Later, I learned that the same facility was sending claims to Medicare for another person using my mother's Medicare information. I did inform Medicare and they took care of that. Now I have found myself in a ridiculous situation regarding Medicare wherein I have been charged for things which Medicare paid for and the medical entity took assignment, meaning that they accepted what Medicare paid as the final bill.

This has not just been a case of me being overcharged, but refusing to let me be seen by the doctor because I refuse to pay what I do not owe. My appointment was cancelled after I offered to pay $98.00 of the $269 which I could not fathom where it came from and refused to sign a payment plan which would permit the financial entity to withdraw from my account that which I did not pay. I was also told that they did not have to tell me where the $269 originated as I was to keep tract with my Medicare statements. The problem being was the fact that the itemized items did not match Medicare billing numbers. Naturally, this infuriated me, so I went home and pulled up my supplemental insurance information on the computer because even if they do not pay on a claim, they send me a statement about what was paid, and took it to the doctor's office. It was received warmly by one of the receptionists and it was now closing time. I still did not sleep very well that night.

The next day, I decided to go into my Medicare file on the computer from the first day of my being under this doctor's care; a period of three years and four months. I pulled up my entire file of claims from day one to the present and recorded what Medicare had paid to this particular doctor and what I was supposed to pay. In addition, I went through all of my cancelled checks by number and recorded what I had paid this particular doctor for each year. As it turned out, I was overcharged $273.72 the first year; charged $6.41 less charges the second year and overcharged $25.85 the third year. No charges for the current year have been billed yet, as it takes about a year to receive a bill, though payment is expected at each visit. I took all of this information to the receptionist who told me that they would give it to the financial administrators and if they find that they owe me, they will give me my refund, but I would not see the doctor until I paid what they said I owed.

I like my doctor and I advised of this, stating that I have options: I can find another doctor; sue for fraud and putting my life in jeopardy or be given appointment. An appointment was made for me for two weeks later after telling me that the next available one would be in October and this was August.

We need to get 'in cinque' and check those medical facility bills against our Medicare HMO, PPO and supplement statements and put an end to fraud and overcharges. It is a federal crime and we senior citizens can put an end to it. Trust Medicare records. Keep up with your statements from Medicare, your advantage plans and your supplements. ***Do not pay bills for which you have not received an explanation of benefits from your insurance company.*** Your bill and insurance date of service as well as claim numbers should match. Do NOT be afraid to dispute a bill that cannot be substantiated. If you have a problem, consult with someone who can help you discern your status; an intelligent friend or a lawyer if necessary.

THE AFFORDABLE HEALTH CARE LAW
First published November 10, 2013

No matter how old we become or how 'smart' we become, here is one thing about lies and deceit'... The truth always comes out,' even if it is too late to rectify a wrong done long ago. Someday the history book, CDs, electronic records or whatever mode of technology exists at the time, is going to reveal the truth about all of the problems that are occurring with the roll out of The Affordable Health Care Law, callously referred to as Obamacare.

This law was intended to basically help young people who could not afford individual health care insurance. It was not intended to affect older people who were eligible for Medicare. Older individuals who were not eligible for Medicare could otherwise be eligible for Medicaid if not financially able to purchase Medicare.

However, the law was written by Congress, Republicans as well as Democrats putting their signature on it and it was sent to President Obama who had wanted it passed and he put his signature on it. The Republicans never wanted this law passed because they felt that the government would be 'wasting money' on indigent individuals through expanding Medicaid to those who could not afford health insurance. Forty years ago the state of Illinois had such a program referred to as MAING or Medical Assistance to the Indigent Grant. A person only needed to show the inability to meet their medical needs to be eligible. No check was issued with this assistance, just aid for medical purposes.

The Supreme Court cleared The Affordable Health Care Law as constitutional. There are new attempts to have it declared unconstitutional. When the Republicans who voted for the law cast their vote, most of them felt that the bill would go the same way all of the other attempts to have an affordable health care law would go, so there was no worry. They had not said a prayer before they voted. Some Congressmen, who cared, had prayed! The law passed, so the movement has been one to stop it from going forward. With the help of the insurance companies who are lobbied by the Republicans, they are working to make certain that President Obama's promise that individuals who had insurance would not lose it is a lie. Technically, and according to the law, they should not lose their coverage, but the impact has not only affected younger people, but the elderly on Medicare as well. ***<u>Individual policies have been cancelled.</u>***

I had an individual HMO with Aetna and I was advised in September that my coverage would not be available in 2014, so I should seek other coverage. I had a free supplemental coverage with Aetna through the Texas Retired Teachers program and switched to full coverage with Aetna a couple of years ago. Aetna is still offering full coverage to individuals who are a part of group coverage. Texas teachers can still purchase full health coverage under Aetna as long as it is though the Retired Teach program or any group program. Being in a group testifies that you are currently or have in the past worked for this organization. *This program costs more than the individual Medicare program.* I believe that the insurance companies are part and parcel of the rollout problems with the 'Obamacare' website and the telephone system. Call it hacking or whatever, we need to get 'in cinque' and keep a close watch on the progress or lack of it, with regards to The Affordable Health Care Law.

MEDICAL NEGATIVITY AND THE AFFORDABLE HEALTH CARE LAW
First published March 23 2015

It is very observable that when something is said about the new law which was passed to help individuals obtain health insurance, that it is referred to as The Affordable Health Care Act when the message is positive. When the message is ***not*** positive, it becomes "Obamacare."

The other strange thing about these views of the act is the fact that there seems to be an underlying culture to make certain that the Affordable Health Care Act is viewed as a disaster by all rather than just a few people who have no faith in it. The new trend with some insurance companies is simply <u>not</u> to insure individuals but only groups. An individual who is a part of an insured group may have coverage, but not as a separate entity. Some companies such as Aetna made that decision before the Supreme Court made their ruling.

The companies which make drugs for sick people have also taken a lead in making the Affordable Health Care Act a farce for many seriously ill individuals. Drugs for people with cancer, debilitating illnesses and chronic conditions are finding great increases in the cost of specialty drugs. The costs are enormous and quite unreal. Personally, one of the specialty drugs was prescribed for me at a cost of $1250.00 after the insurance company paid its share. I inquired of the generic price and was told that the $1250.00 *was* the generic cost; the brand name was $5000.00. I explained that it was cheaper to die and refused to buy it. When I returned to my physician, I was given a prescription for another drug which cost me $7.00. What a relief! The insurance company paid $1.00 as the drug cost was $8.00.

It is evident, that doctors are really not aware of the cost of the drugs which they prescribe for their patients. The drug representative gives the doctors samples and explains to them all the benefits of the drugs they are pushing, along with all of the perks which they allow the doctors and unfortunately, the patient does not always get the true benefit of the expected results. In addition, some pressure needs to be put on drug companies regarding their horrific drug costs. There is no way that these specialty drugs are really worth their asking prices. The irony is that some do not really perform as stated for everyone. Some cheaper brands do a better job.

As a patient, we need to open up and tell our doctors our true medical circumstances and ask for possible alternatives to our medical journeys. We are the ones looking for a cure and too often we forget what our expectations are and feel that we must accept what we are told by medical professionals without question. This is not true. We seek medical care to maximize our livelihood, while at the same time doing the same thing for our medical professionals, but we need to realize that the life that we are trying to preserve ***is ours.*** Therefore, we need to get 'in cinque' and survey and research all of the avenues to a better YOU and when necessary, seek a second opinion. It could be the right choice.

RACE TO REPEAL THE AFFORDABLE CARE HEALTH ACT
First published April 13, 2014

More than ever before, the Republicans in the U. S. House of Representatives have confirmed my belief in God. The Republicans in the House of Representative have brought legislation to the floor and passed a bill 50 (fifty) times to repeal The Affordable Care Act or some parts of it. So far, the Senate will have no part of it, and naturally, a piece of legislation which is considered one of the President's key signature pieces, that he would naturally veto any bill which would repeal the Affordable Care Act.

Fifty times a repeal bill has passed in the House of Representatives and for the three years that the Affordable Care Act has been passed, approved by the Supreme Court as a tax and so far, purchased by approximately 7 (seven) million individuals, the House Republicans would like to dismantle the law. It seems amazing that approximately 250 United States Representatives, mostly Republicans, feel that they have the best interest of seven million American individuals at heart.

Somehow, it appears that the allegations that the Internal Revenue Service has unfairly focused on certain individuals, especially members of the Tea Party, that since the Affordable Care Act has been labeled a tax by the Supreme Court and that the IRS will be the agency which will collect that tax, that the law should be repealed, and in essence, calling it a waste of taxpayers' money.

The House Republicans also want to change the work laws to making a 30 hour week changed back to a 40 hour week to be considered as full time with regards to how employers will pay and /or provide insurance for employees.

There are so many avenues that we could take in regards to why the law is so dreaded and why House Speaker John A. Boehner is dead set on repealing the Affordable Health Care Act, which he and everyone who wants the act repealed, refers to it as "Obamacare.' Somehow it seems that the name "Obamacare," which is often referred to as "No Care" by some representatives, hinges more on their dislike for the President, than it does for the law itself. This is the most obvious viewpoint of the call to repeal the law.

Passing the repeal bill some fifty times also remind us that there have been as many as fifty times, for fifty different decent causes, which the Representatives have had the opportunity to pass legislation for which Americans could profit. The Representatives have clearly been wasting time and money with their actions. House Speaker Boehner stated that the "House Republicans will continue to work to repeal this law." This seems senseless and is not making any point to many Americans and especially to those individuals whom have purchased the insurance.

After the mad rush to sign up for insurance coverage by the deadline, it was postponed but the Republicans would like to cancel it. We need to get 'in cinque' and let our representatives know how we feel about their actions.

VIII-ETHNIC AND BLACK

EARLY BLACK EDUCATION
First published September 22, 2005

Long before Black students in the South were allowed to attend public school, home school by a generous member of a reading family was the way Black children learned to read write, spell and do arithmetic. In states where Negroes were free, they were attending public schools and college **_before_** the Civil War. **_John Russwurm_** is recorded as the first Black man to graduate from a college. He graduated from Bowdoin in 1826. As time went on, during the era of Reconstruction, religious groups or missionary societies established schools in Southern states for minority students. As early as 1861 The American Missionary Association, often referred to as "Aunt Mary," was in the forefront of the establishment of many of the historically Black colleges, as well as The New England Freedman's Aid Society (_From Slavery to Freedom: A History of Negro Americans,_ John Hope Franklin.)

Churches are responsible for two historically Black colleges which are still functioning today; Lincoln University in Pennsylvania and Wilberforce University in Ohio (_Black History: A Reappraisal,_ Edited by Melvin Drimmer.) Lincoln University was founded by the Presbyterian Church and Wilberforce University by the African Methodist Episcopal Church.

Land Grant Colleges were established by the states under the 1862 Morrill Land Grant Act. Alcorn University of Mississippi was the first such college for Black students in Mississippi when Hiram Revels, an A. M. E. minister and one of the first two men of color to serve in the United States Senate, was appointed its first president in 1871. By 1878, it was renamed Alcorn Agricultural and Mechanical College with emphasis in those two areas. By 1974, it was renamed Alcorn State University (*Alcorn State University Mini Catalog, 2002-2004.)*

As churches and church organizations played a great role in the establishment of minority schools in the South, it would appear that churches have lost their touch. There is something in the way which is keeping the churches from supporting some of the schools that they had a hand in establishing. Most historically Black colleges are now integrated and accepting students of all races. Why are the churches *not supporting* their own? Every year, many of the well-known historically Black schools are closing their doors because the churches are not supporting them. It is time for our churches to get 'in cinque' and re-evaluate their programs. We sing the songs and pray the prayers but we are not 'walking the walk' when it comes to supporting youth education, and we wonder why they do not attend church.

BLACK HISTORY EMPHASIS MONTH
First published February 8, 2006

Once again, the month of February has arrived. This is the shortest month of the year but it has more causes to celebrate than any of the other eleven months. It was during this month, on Abraham Lincoln's birthday, February 12, 1909, that the Lincoln Day Call went out to organize the National Association for the Advancement of Colored People. Most of the organizers were of the Caucasian persuasion. Two outstanding persons of color, Ida B. Wells and W. E. B. DuBois were among those responding to the call. Therefore, the N. A. A. C. P. celebrates its founding in February.

Aside from the N. A. A. C. P. celebrating February as founder's month, the African Methodist Episcopal Church also celebrates its Heritage Day in February. Due to these two events being celebrated in February, it appeared to be natural and right for the month of February to be chosen by Dr. Carter G. Woodson in 1926 to be the time to celebrate Black History Week.

Black History Week was established to dramatize the achievements of Black Americans. This was sorely needed, as history textbooks left out anything about Black people that was not connected to slavery. The accomplishments of Black people took place during the same time that other Americans made accomplishments, but it was not until 1964 that a few history books intended for use in public schools surfaced with a little information about Blacks in America. Textbooks have gradually included _some_ of the achievements of Black people in the last twenty years due to the Civil Rights Movement of the early sixties. The Black History Week was expanded to include the whole month of February.

Aside from that, the United States Postal Service has taken an active role in memorializing influential Black people on postage stamps. The latest Black Heritage stamp to become available is that of Hattie McDaniel, an actress, whose face graces the 39 cents stamp; the new first class postage rate.

Black History Month is important to impart to the younger generations of Americans, the often hidden accomplishments of Black American because the information is not printed in the accessible history books. Many organizations and groups seek to impart information on a regular basis all during the year which is marvelous. Because of this, there are those who feel that Black History Month is no longer necessary. We know all about Jesus but the Christians want to hear about *Him* every week of the year. There is so much about Black Americans that we do not hear about until Black History Month. Let us get 'in cinque' and push for _all_ Black American history to be included in textbooks for American students and then emphasize Black History every February of every year!

IGNORANCE IS NOT BLISS
First published March 23, 2008

It has been over fifty years since the case of **_Brown v. The Board of Education_** was heard by the United States Supreme Court and rendered a verdict which in essence said that the public schools of the United States **_were not equal,_** though they were separate. Since that time, little has changed. What we have now is more of the unequal, though some have to go deep into their pockets rather than benefit from tax dollars to maintain the state of being _not equal_ even though they want the government to 'foot the bill' and in some instances it does.

The 'not equal' status is what many Americans want. They want to be set apart from the masses because they feel that they are superior to the masses, both in intellect and social status, whether they have finances or not. As my grandmother used to say, "They have the aire, but the millions are not there!" This is not an ethnic group or race 'thing.' There are people of every social status who have this notion. These are also the people who wish to think in their hearts and heads that history never happened. Only what happens today matters to them and how they want things to be. They do not want to know how history has affected the lives of others. The Holocaust and slavery do not exist in their vocabularies. They personally have not experienced either disaster, nor do they know or care about anyone who in any way has.

Today, we are raising a generation of brilliant but insensitive individuals. When you speak of the Holocaust, they think of *The "Diary of "Anne Frank.* It was a novel to them; nothing to believe that they can in any way relate, though they may have worked side-by-side with someone with a number tattooed on their arm and wondered why they always wore long sleeved shirts. When they hear the word 'slavery,' they think of something that happened a long time ago to Black people in America who are now free. They see *Roots* as a novel; nothing to be taken seriously. Little do the so-called liberals of this day and age have any idea of the frustrations of a people and their descendants whom have suffered these experiences, unless they have read *Black Rage* by Grier and Cobbs, two Black psychiatrists.

Brown v. The Board of Education has not made anything equal, or more accessible for that matter. It has opened some doors for Black Americans, but not enough. We cannot legislate morality, sensitivity, love and brotherhood. Only when we look deep into our hearts and realize that the things of the past that were unpleasant when they occurred and continue to be unpleasant when we talk or think about them now, or try to do something about it, will not go away because we try to ignore them. Ignoring the truth only keeps us ignorant and prejudiced. Ignorance is ***NOT BLISS!*** We need to get 'in cinque' and see to it that our youth know about their past and the effects that it has had on the current generation and will have on future generations. Too many mistakes need to be rectified.

RACISM TODAY
First printed February 1, 2009

I have been requested to address unfounded racism. Those of you who frequently read what I write, by now should have discerned that I believe in Justice, Equality, Honesty, Righteousness and the Commandment that says, "***Do unto others as you would have them do unto you.***"

These beliefs can often cause much heartache, pain and suffering because the world is full of people who have no conscious, morals, ideals or wholesome goals. Too often their goals are to bring heartache, pain and suffering to others. They live to make others unhappy. It has come to the point in life where they have formed organized groups to target ethnic groups, races religious groups, people with non-conventional sexual preferences, immigrants and some instances just plain evil terrorism for the 'fun of it.'

There seems to be a tendency among some younger members of the African American ethnic group who feel that since there is a Black man in the White House now, that they can have an open field day on harassing members of other ethnic groups and races. Tolerance begins at home, just as does charity, love patience and other attributes that we hope for in our young children. The absence of these characteristics is the reason our children are so difficult to teach during these modern times. What so many young Black boys and girls do not realize is that it has taken almost two hundred years of tolerance for a Black man to enter the White House as the President of the United States.

God made every human individual and once the color is removed, every one of us who entered this world as a normal human being has the same physical anatomy and can and will die from the same kinds of harmful encounters and if nothing else, eventually old age. We come in different sizes, heights, complexions, emotional, physical and mental capabilities, but whatever can kill one of us, can kill any of us. Therefore, we need to learn to "love, live and let live as we only go this way once."

Schools have taken on so many roles of the home, especially meals, discipline and often clothing and baby-sitting, but it definitely needs to begin to do more in the area of teaching tolerance. I made an overture to a discussion on organizations that seek to eradicate hate groups in the

United States in my last article. It is called The Southern Poverty Law Center (www.splcenter.org) and it publishes material on Teaching Tolerance as well as an *Intelligence Report* in which it keeps track of racist groups and individuals who target other groups for terrorist acts and often takes these groups to court. They operate on donations and memberships. Both publications come with a membership. Get 'in cinque,' join me and become a member to help to stop racism. Our new President would be proud.

"JIM CROW" - SEGREGATION
First published October 2011

It has been a very long time since I have been to a theatre and sat and watched a movie on the big screen. I believe that the last time I went to a movie was to see *Color purple.* We know that was a long time ago. My daughter decided to treat me to a movie for my birthday.

Going to the movies took me back to my childhood days when I seldom missed a Saturday night 'shoot 'em up' and the cliffhanging series that preceded the movie. Living in town meant that you attended the 6:00 P.M. movie because the matinee at 3:00 P.M. was mostly attended by children from the rural area who had to be back home by 6:00 P.M. Since I was 'colored' in those days, I had to ascend the stairs in the theatre because colored people sat in the balcony while the first floor was for 'whites only.' That did not bother me because I could see the film better in the balcony and I did not have to be concerned about popcorn, gum or peanuts falling on my head.

Of course, the theatre in my hometown had a ticket booth which was located between the two doors for entry. One door led upstairs and one door led downward to the first floor. It was not until I attended a movie in another town to learn that you did not go in the front door if you were colored; you went around to the side of the building to a set of rickety stairs which led to the balcony. I was insulted because I could not go in a front door, but I wanted badly to see *The Bells of Saint Mary's.*

Ironically, the movie which my daughter took me to see was *The Help*; a movie set in Mississippi circa the nineteen fifties. The early scenery showed a theatre in the capital city where the stairway on the outside led to the balcony where colored people sat. There were also scenes wherein the colored people sat in the back of the city buses, especially the maids on their way to and from their job as *"Help.'*

This film not only shows the segregated lifestyles of the Black and White people in this setting, but how the maids raised and loved White children as a part of their jobs. The sad part of this scenario deals with how some of the White families could not see that the colored help were really flesh and blood human beings with feelings and some of the same needs and desires as their White employers. Though set in Mississippi, this film rings true for most of the southern states which used colored help. It is focused on household maids and their duties, but the attitudes and social life of all colored help had the essence of the prevailing Jim Crow era.

For many young people of all ethnic persuasions, this is a history lesson to take note. It gets to the inner working of some of the things that took place, though were never really expressed in any textbooks, including many books on African American history. Let us get 'in cinque' and become aware of what we need to know about racial relationships and how to avoid the pitfalls of the past.

ONE GREAT AMERICAN NATION
First published February 5, 2012

This is February, 2012 and once again it is time for the Super Bowl, number 46 or XLVI if we think in Roman numerals. It is also Black History Month which once was just Black History Week. This is the shortest month of the year, but it has the extra day this year because it is leap year and the year of a presidential election.

There are so many things taking place in this month until if you wish to be a part of many of them, you can meet yourself going and coming. This particular weekend, however is culminated with the football game known as the Super Bowl.

The television and the internet is ripe with information about the Super Bowl, the players, the coaches, the teams, their history, projections about which team will win and an onslaught of advertisements to lure you to purchase all of the things you *need* to really enjoy the game whether you are at a party in Indianapolis, in a box seat at the stadium, at a friend's house for the Super Bowl party or just home 'chillin.' It seems that the Super Bowl has taken on more importance than Christmas. The celebration does not take as much time for planning because there is the wait to know which teams will be playing in the game.

We know, however, that this is Black History month and each year there is more and more to celebrate. Above all else and especially this election year, we can celebrate working toward re-electing the first Black President of the United States of America! He has done and still is doing a great job in resurrecting economic stability in this country, fostering peace in the world and keeping America on a steady and profitable path as the greatest nation in the world.

The birthdays of two former celebrated President of the United States are this month as well' Abraham Lincoln and George Washington. They both figure in the celebration of Black History. Abraham Lincoln has been given credit for freeing the slaves in this *Emancipation Proclamation of 1862* which was to be effective on January 1 1863 though the actual emancipation came with the enactment of the Thirteenth Amendment to the *U. S. Constitution* in 1865.

Many slaves were freed after the *Emancipation Proclamation,* but many were still in bondage because of slow communication. One such state was Texas wherein the emancipation news was not learned until June 19th. Consequently, Texans have been celebrating June 19th and it is called Juneteenth and is equivalent to July 4th to Black Texans. In the past decades other states have begun to celebrate this date as well. Louisiana, Arkansas and Mississippi are among those celebrating the Juneteenth holiday.

George Washington is hailed as the first President of the United States and one of America's first Black poets, Phillis Wheatley who was born in Africa and brought to America as a girl in 1763, wrote a poem to George Washington, *"His Excellency General Washington"* before she died in 1784. She had some questions for Washington about slavery.

Elijah Muhammad, the founder of the Black Muslim movement often said that this country was taken from the Indians, owned by the White man and built by the Black man. As a free people, we all have our duty to get 'in cinque and celebrate our progress as one GREAT AMERICAN NATION.

VERNON JOHNS: A REAL HERO
First published February 27, 2012

February, 2012 has been a month of awards. There have been several Gospel Award Shows, a couple of BET award Shows, The Stellar Awards, The Academy Awards, The Emmy Awards, UNCF Awards and perhaps some awards that I missed. In addition, there was the entertainment presented as memorials to Don Cornelius and Whitney Houston.

February is Black History month and anyone who has not heard of some of America's notable Black citizens, had the opportunity to take a view into their lives as well. It would have been very difficult to miss Martin Luther King, Jr. in February or January as his birthday is in January and as a part of Black History, he could not be omitted in February. Any mention of MLK and the Montgomery bus boycott cannot omit Rosa Parks, but it **SHOULD NOT OMIT** the *Reverend Vernon Johns* who was replaced by Rev. M. L. King, Jr.

Rev. Vernon Johns was born in 1892 in Virginia and was the grandson of slaves. He attended Oberlin Seminary and the University of Chicago's graduate School of Theology. He was the pastor of the famous Dexter Avenue Baptist Church in Montgomery, Alabama from 1947 to 1952 and by all rights should be called the *Father of the Civil Rights Movement.* He laid the foundation upon which Rev. Martin Luther King, Jr., his successor, Ralph Abernathy, Wyatt Walker and many others who were a part of the Southern Christian Leadership Conference built its strategies. Rev. Vernon Johns was a mentor to those involved in that organization.

You do not hear very much about Rev. Johns and his influence in the Civil Rights Movement, but he had already started a movement when Rev. King arrived in Montgomery. He had been arrested, taken from the pulpit because of his sermons which depicted how people of color were not given the respect of hunting prey. Colored people were always in season.

Rev. Johns advocated Black business and tried to encourage the Black citizens to go into business and provide the items that they needed for a comfortable livelihood. He was looked upon by many as an eccentric individual and by the White community as a trouble maker. His influence was felt in his home county as he is believed to have advised his niece, Barbara Rose Johns to lead a student strike for better school conditions.

The NAACP pushed the cause of the students on to the Supreme Court as a part of the ***Brown v. the Board of Education***.

We have a tendency to grab and celebrate the notable Black Americans every year, but too often we leave out many individuals who played a larger part in an achievement, or who sacrificed more for a cause, simply because the 'noisy wheel gets the oil.'

There was a movie for television released around 1994 that tells the story of Vernon Johns, entitled *Road to Freedom: The Vernon Johns Story.* All students should see this movie. It does not detract from the accomplishments of Rev. Dr. Martin Luther King, Jr., but it will reflect on the roots of the King experience and enlighten the observer. The movie is based on an unpublished biography written by a member of the **Vernon Johns Society.** Let us get 'in cinque' and explore more Black History than what is brought to us on the television screen each February.

OUR RIGHTS NEED PROTECTION
First published August 19, 2013

Sometimes the spirit gets ahead of the body and the desire to have a say makes it impossible to be quiet. The body has not come full circle yet, but the spirit decided that so much has transpired in the last month for which I have taken careful inventory but have kept quiet.

I watched the court hearings of the Zimmerman case in which he was on trial for the Trayvon Martin killing. As I watched, it appeared to me that the prosecution at no time attempted to derail the defense on the premise of the reason for that trial. It took several hearings before it was concluded as to what the charges were. They allowed self-defense to be a premise using 'stand your grounds.'

The flaw in this case which was plainly seen by all of the evidence, clearly pointed to a teenager, walking, trying to get to his destination, on foot and yet an unknown person, to him, got out of a car to confront him, was accosted and killed. Those were the facts: plain and simple. Trayvon was walking and talking on his cell phone. Zimmerman *was in a car.* There was no reason to apprehend Travon.

The reaction of the average Black teenager or Black adult when apprehended by a person of another race especially, their gut reaction is:

"If they interfere with me and I am not doing anything illegal and they attempt to hurt me, my gut says that If I want to live, I must hurt him bad enough to make him leave me alone."

The marches, the demonstrations, the screaming and yelling and speeches will not do very much except call attention to the situations at the current time. We need to become more active in organizations which fight racism and hatred such as the Southern Poverty Law Center and the National Association for the Advancement of Colored People (NAACP.) Another young teenager has been killed since Trayvon Martin and a bright young lady as well. There was no excuse for either death and justice has NOT been served. It is my hope that the spirit is awakened to do the right thing. Some of us just need to mind our own business and leave others alone. Volunteer security personnel should be **DOUBLE-CHECKED.** Many of them are renegade racist terrorist and use every opportunity to offend members of a group they hate.

We need more EDUCATION for ethnic groups in this country. We have plenty of religion, but education is needed for the spirit to work right. America has to learn that we are all ___human___ and have God-given and government given rights. We also need to get 'in cinque' and ___ELECT___ representatives to ___pass laws that will protect ALL of our rights.___

IX-LIFE, LOVE AND HAPPINESS

'LOVE MAKES THE WORLD GO AROUND'
First published March 21, 2006

What the world needs more of, and tons of it, at that, is love. I do not recall who wrote the song, "What the World Needs Now Is Love, Sweet Love,' but they had a real handle on life in this world. Rarely does a day pass by when the 'breaking news' on the television, radio and in the newspapers is violence. It would be so nice, to be able to turn on the radio or television for news and hear about all of the wonderful things that are taking place in our neighborhood, our town, our society, our state, our nation and with the rest of the countries in the world.

It is human to err. We all err from time to time. We do not err intentionally and for the most part, we are dearly sorry about our errors. Too often we do not seek to apologize or seek to correct our errors. Much confusion can be eliminated when we are honest and full of love in our erring ways.

"Love Is a Many Splendored Thing' and I am not just referring to romantic love. When we love each other as brothers, children of God, we can see life in a completely different light. When we walk in another's shoes an unseen dimension comes into view. When we treat others as we wish to be treated and have this thought in mind each time we take action on things which affect our lives we may have a change of mind and heart on many occasions. Even impulsive people will have heart and mind changes if they can see themselves in the place of others with whom they have transactions.

No matter which religion one confesses or possesses, love for humankind all over the world, is the key to peace in this world. There are some mean people and nations in this world, but if they can witness the love of mankind, their numbers will shrink. We may never have peace all over the world at the same time, but we certainly can work on having peace in our little corner, most of the time.

It does not take a rocket scientist or a professional psychiatrist to understand that everything acts better with a little love, because 'love does make the world go around.' Some snakes understand and appreciate love. Then there are some which do not, but if we love those who let us love them we will have more friends and fewer enemies. It is time for us, each individual, to get 'in cinque' and show more love in this world, and work toward world peace.

REUNIONS
First published September 20, 2009

As the years go by and we become older and older and finally the day comes when we have the opportunity to meet and greet once again the people with whom we shared our childhood, high school and college days. There is a kind of anxiety which is connected to such reunions.

In our early years, just after college and our early adulthood, we are eager to meet our old friends and anxious to know how successful we have become as young adults. We want to know who got married to whom and how many children they have accumulated and the kind of career which has been launched. We also wonder how our lives compare to those of our counterparts. Is there anyone among us who has an inside track on the quickest sure way to becoming more successful than we already are?

After all the questions are answered and the doubts removed, we go back to our little bailiwicks and often re-evaluate our stature in life. We may feel validated or have a need for further future validation. Either way it is usually a learning situation. We may even be bemoaned over the loss of a once-upon a time very close and dear friend. This, too, may make us grateful that we had some time together. As the years go by, life and things do change.

During the middle years, reunions almost become a dreaded affair for some individuals who feel that they have not been especially blessed with material things or the aging process. These are the times when ladies secure every cosmetic they feel will help them to look young again, and hope that the old high school beau whom they put aside for the man they married, still think they rate a '10.' They are not necessarily interested in him, but want to know if they *'still have it.'* The men are more concerned about how large their bellies have become and wonder how people will look upon their extended faces because the beautiful curls and waves of their hair has gone away. Once seeing their old friends, the fears usually vanish because by now everyone is just happy to be able to get together, rehash the fun or the older days and go back home with pleasant memories.

Finally, we become senior citizens and reunions become a luxury. We are blessed if we have lived long enough to be able to attend a reunion. We will be more than happy to meet and greet anyone among us who is able financially or physically to attend. We rejoice in the sight and presence of our old friends, who by now seem like family. We dine, laugh, sing, praise and worship together. Let us get 'in cinque' and cherish all of our old acquaintances and friends when and wherever we meet, and call it a **_blessing!_**

LOVE AND HAPPINESS
First published November 27, 2009

Fortunately, I took psychology long enough to learn that human beings and some other animals need love to develop, grow and survive. In Psychology 101, one learns that a new born baby needs love to survive. Babies, whose mothers' were not available, but were given the needed attention by someone else in a caring manner, developed and grew at a normal rate. Babies, who were left unattended without adequate care, did survive, but did not develop or grow at the same rate as the babies who were loved and nourished.

As a social worker, I learned that babies and children whose mothers were with them and did not give them adequate love and attention, also did not develop and grow at the same rate as babies and children whose mothers gave them love and attention. As we grow into adulthood, we find that we still need love and attention, but usually not as much because as we mature, we find other means of making us happy.

Love and Happiness are definitely a state of mind once we become adult. As we mature, we learn that nothing in life is infinite; we grow older and we die. Nothing in life lasts forever. Family members usually die in the order in which they have been born, but sometimes it does not happen that way. We learn that life **should go on** in spite of the fact that we lost someone dear and near to us. As a mature individual, this is normal and acceptable. Immature individuals have a difficult time and often need psychiatric care to overcome losses.

Losses are especially difficult for some people around holidays like Thanksgiving and Christmas. Research has found that way too many people commit suicide during the holidays because of loneliness and the feel of not being loved. This is tragic and could not be the situation if most people learn first of all to **LOVE and RESPECT THEMSELVES!**

Being narcissistic is not loving one's self, but a mere reflection of the fact that one is a consumer of love and affection. Love is a two-way affair. You give love and receive love, that **IS _love!_** If you only receive love and it remains with you, then you are a consumer of love. When there is no one to give you the love that you consume, and then self-hate kicks in, often followed by thoughts of hurting one's self. As a last resort, when self-hate kicks in, instead of having a pit party, one should get 'in cinque' and think of the greatest love of all, God's love for the world and for us individually, and see our way clearly to a brighter day.

LOVE AND MARRIAGE
First published August 15, 2010

I am certain that I am not the only person in this day and age who feels that marriage is no longer sacred. The sanctity of marriage seems to have slipped into the abyss. It no longer signifies the union of two individuals, a man and a woman, whom have pledged themselves to each other for life; to love, cherish, have and hold until 'death do we part.' Even when expanded to include those individuals of the same sex, the essence of marriage is lost.

Originally, a marriage was a union of a man and a woman to beget children; to start a family. This is possible with a man and a woman, but not so with two men or two women. If the marriage, regardless of the denomination of the couple, is not to increase the population of the world, it is not really a marriage of the ilk for which it was intended.

We are aware that many couples are childless and in most instances, the reason does not lie in the fact that they did not intend to have children, but the fact that for some biological or other physical reason, no children were forthcoming. Their hearts were united for the intent of the purpose. When couples unite with no intention to having children, they are not married; they have a business arrangement which they call marriage.

On the other hand, there are couples who live together, have children and never bother to get married, or do so very late; late enough for their children to take part in the wedding ceremony. These are instances when the ceremony should have been secluded and kept very quiet. These are the examples which show that marriage is a social symbol with no sanctity.

To some couples, the amount of money spent on the wedding is representative of how much they 'love' each other. The more expensive the wedding, the more they 'love' each other, especially if they pay for the affair themselves instead of their parents. Too often, too much is spent on the wedding, after which they begin life as a married couple in what amounts to a kitchenette instead of a home.

It appears that the wedding is now more important than the marriage. It seems that we love a *good show*. Weddings can be beautiful, but they should entail the substance of a marriage. There are many more weddings now than marriages. We need to get 'in cinque' and plan more marriage than weddings. Weddings make merchants rich, but marriages with LOVE, makes families healthy, and morally rich.

INTERNET MATING
First published April 10, 2011

A few months ago, as I was surveying the reasons why an individual could or possibly should venture onto an internet website to meet a possible mate, I decided to give it a try myself, since I have been a widow now for about two years and thought that perhaps a male acquaintance would put some spice into my life.

It was not difficult to sign up for this adventure, which is what it has become for me. You can elect to view for free with limited contact to the opposite sex or you can pay for basic service communication for a flat fee, per month or several months at a time, or you can upgrade for another fee to find out if the persons you communicate with reads your messages *etc.* You can send what is called a flirt, which is a programmed one-liner if you do not pay, or a message that you choose to write if you have paid for that privilege.

After your account set-up, you are assigned a pseudonym and you have the option to post your pictures and create your profile which will include, your age, location, height, color of your eyes and hair, your gender, race, occupation, income, marital status, number of children and if you live with any. In addition you have the opportunity to describe yourself and the characteristics of the mate you are looking for. Some questions about your personality are also included. Once you have taken care of these items, the adventure begins.

If someone flirts with you, sends you a message or views your profile, you will be notified online or the information is sent to your e-mail address, if you are not online. You can chat with individuals online and if you have a webcam, you can look at the individual with whom you are chatting if both of you have a webcam. You can view any person's profile who views your profile.

Many individuals do not post a picture for many reasons: some are really married and do not want their faces recognized or they want you to give them your e-mail address to send you a picture of them. That way, they will have a means to contact you offline. This is your decision to respond. However, some may have a legitimate reason for not wanting their picture posted for job security purposes if they are in the public sector, and/or, if their job does not want their pictures on public display online. Many discreet viewers will not respond to a profile without a picture.

We worry about our young teenagers with the i-phones and sexting, but we need to heed the internet daters with the webcams. They are used for sexting as well. It is not illegal for adults, but for youth, it is called pornography. Many users on these sites are not looking for a mate, but are perpetual seekers of sex. Sincere seekers of mates attempt to get acquainted with you without discussions of the three letter word.

Should you decide to meet a prospect, you should tell at least one responsible person, who, when and where you will meet and possibly have a picture of the person you are meeting. We must get 'in cinque' and keep it real.

Renetta T. Womack Howard

MAY/DECEMBER AFFAIRS
First published May 22, 2011

Throughout history, Homo-sapiens, the scientific name for human beings or modern man, has tended to be homogenous and homologous. Any deviation from the norm was looked down upon by society as taboo. Deviation could render one to be ostracized from society.

Couples, who decided to be wedded, were expected to wed someone in their own age group; a couple of years' difference in age was the norm. Decade or generational differences were strictly taboo and for the most part, this is still the norm. For some members of the latest generations of our society, the whole idea to them is taboo. Some of them feel that 'age is a matter of mind over matter; if you do not mind, it does not matter!'

As a consequence of this thinking, every day, teachers, men and women in public schools are being arraigned and fired from their positions because of illicit relationships with their students. It would seem that they would be intelligent enough to realize that a non-platonic relationship with a student under 18 years of age is a crime, punishable by law.

Many books and movies have been written about May/December love affairs and marriages such as _The Graduate, How Stella Got Her Groove Back, All That Heaven Allows, Casablanca, Pretty Woman, Breakfast At Tiffany's_ and many others, some of which have been banned by some public schools and public libraries. It appears that the banning has intensified the desire for such relationships. Could it be true that non-platonic love has no division line? Can it be so strong as to cause individuals to disrespect the law?

This is a real concern for schools. Should there be some educational orientations for prospective teachers regarding respecting the law when it comes to underage students who could possibly seduce them? This is not a new area of interest in the realm of education; it just has not been properly dealt with. It may be a matter of teaching self-control to teachers and students to resolve this issue. I believe it is time for us to get 'in cinque' and gather some conclusions about this matter. I personally would like to have some input regarding May/December affairs as it is not exclusive to schools and education. Contact me at: rhowrite@yahoo.com.

LOVING OUR CHILDREN
First published June 3, 2012

We have entered the month of June, 2012 and the first day of June has come and gone. I remember celebrating _Children's Day_ as a child. In the church of my family's choice, this day was as important as Mother's Day and Father's Day. We had a program to celebrate each day with the children of the church performing in the celebrations.

As an adult, I have not heard very much about _Children's Day_ and at one point I was beginning to wonder if it had been a figment of my imagination. Reality did set in and I realized that _Children's Day_ had made me feel that children were somebody and actually important in our society. In our church, it was also a tradition to serve the sacraments to the _children first_, inviting us to come to the altar while the choir sang the song, "I think when I read that sweet story of old, When Jesus was here among men, How he called little children as lambs to His fold, I should like to have been with them then," and the minister would be saying, "Suffer the little children to come unto me, and forbid them not; for such is the kingdom of God."

Following the sacraments, there was a handshaking in a circle of some kind where everyone in the church shook hands with everyone else. Children were equals in the handshaking ceremony. These activities helped to boost self-esteem in children. It made us look forward to church activities and the celebration of our special day.

Children's Day was first observed in the United States in 1856 in Massachusetts by the pastor of the First Universalist Church of Chelsea for the dedication of children to a Christian life while helping to dedicate parents to bring their children up in Christian nurturing. The Sunday which was first set aside for this purpose was the second Sunday in June. Other churches set aside a Sunday for this purpose as well. This is the Sunday which my denomination celebrated as well, historically.

President Bill Clinton established October 11, 1998 as _Children's Day_ in response to a letter written to him by a six year old boy inquiring about a Children Day for him. President George W. Bush proclaimed June 3, 2001 and the first Sunday in June in subsequent years as _"National Child's Day."_ Most state governors have proclaimed the _second Sunday in June_ as _Children's day_. The second Sunday in June is a few days away and I feel that we need to activate that day, not just in churches, but everywhere so that our children can feel more worth and respect from their elders.

Celebrating children hit me hard because I have recently read about and seen instances where mothers and some fathers, are giving up their children because their significant others do not want their children in their lives. Children should always come first in a parent's eyes and life. We MUST get 'in cinque' and value our children. They are our future. We cannot afford to throw them away *for anything or anybody*!

LOVING OUR ELDERLY
First published June 16, 2013

Today is Father's Day and though mine is no longer with us, I did contact several fathers to wish them a happy day. Happy days are sometimes few and far apart when the majority of your years are behind you. One father called me today who is the father of eight children. The only one he had heard from today was the one who resides with him. He told me of his chronic illnesses and was disappointed as it was not after six o'clock P.M. I told him that the day is not over and he should think positively.

It is difficult in this day and age when old age has become a real burden. We are living longer but the quality of life has changed tremendously. An elderly person with a small family knows that as the years go by and their health fails rapidly, that they will most likely spend their last days in a nursing home. Ironically, elderly people with large immediate families also have to consider life in a nursing home.

I have always been anti-nursing homes because I have seen so many people whom I knew placed in a nursing home and instead of their quality of life improving, it deteriorated. I will not place all of the blame however, on the nursing home, as it appears that in some instances, the family deserted their family member once deposited in the nursing home. It appears that family love vanished or perhaps never existed.

On the other hand, there are elderly individuals living with family who would in some instances be much better off in many ways if they were in a nursing home. An adequate nursing facility, would assure the resident of a reasonable amount of cleanliness and nourishment as well as medical support. Some homes fail to provide those adequate features and it is as if they were just waiting for their family member to keel over and die. This is sinful especially where there are able-bodied family members in the home who are capable of providing the care needed.

It is true that giving adequate care to an elderly person can be a chore, no matter how much you love them, especially if you have no one to help you do the chore. A healthy, hardy and handy individual caring for an elderly person who has dementia and is incontinent alone is a chore. When they have diabetes and blood/heart related problems it can wear you down. Some relief like daycare several days a week can be helpful, but a caregiver needs respite time especially if they have no other relief during the week.

Caregiving takes a physical toll on one's body. One's back can give away from lifting and pushing and pulling. The back problems affect the upper and lower limbs causing pain and incapacitation. It is as this time that a caregiver without any help should consider placing their family member in a nursing home. It is a grievous situation. The caretaker can end up in the hospital long before the one they were caring for. A caretaker must take care of themselves because *they cannot care for another if they are not well themselves.* On this note, I will say that we need to get 'in cinque' and weigh the decision carefully to place a loved one in a nursing home. Is your health at risk if you do not do it?

X-NATURE

SEASONAL BODY ENERGY
First published February 14, 2006

Amid all of the excitable happenings during the early part of each year, it makes us wonder where do we get all of the energy that we need to enjoy everything that is going on. There is Mardi Gras or "Fat Tuesday," the last day before Lent, a tradition which had its roots in the Mobile, Alabama and New Orleans culture, but has spread to other cities and other states.

Because of Hurricane Katrina, it is believed by many that the festivities of years gone by will no longer be the same in New Orleans since so much of the city was damaged. There are those hopefuls who like some of the former residents, still have heart and plan to carry on just like they did before Katrina and Wilma. The crews are getting it together and many of the revelers simply think of Mardi Gras as party time, but many of us are aware that it is the carnival before a sacred holiday season, Lent.

Lent is the season from Ash Wednesday until Easter. During this time, many Christians make sacrifices of money for their religious organizations, or give up some unhealthy or obnoxious habit, praying that the willpower of this period will enrich their lives and the lives of those whom they love. Some people use this period of time as an intense period of prayer leading up to the time in which Jesus was crucified on the cross of Calvary, to rise again on Easter Sunday.

There are many things that we Americans can pray for intensively and that is for all of the ills of this country and our relationships with other countries; our domestic policies that prohibit us from achieving our inherit rights as citizens; challenges to our freedom, here and abroad; blockades to financial comfort or success; access to medical competency; honest politicians and elected officials in government. Let us get 'in cinque' and pray for positive changes in our local communities, states and our federal government which will permit us to use our body energy efficiently.

BROTHERHOOD NEEDED
First published May 11, 2008

Springtime is a time of year which is plagued by the kinds of storms we do not wish to see. It is also the same time of year that we celebrate a very important day, World Day of Prayer. This is a time when we definitely need to pray for more love in the world and brotherhood. We experience storms throughout the year, throughout the world, but it just seems that God is trying to tell us something with all of the devastation that we have experienced in the past few years which have been natural disasters, not manmade disasters.

We know that the victims of Hurricane Katrina are still trying to recuperate. We know that the city of New Orleans was almost washed away as well as coastal cities and towns in Mississippi and Alabama when that storm hit those areas. This was one of the most unexpected and unbelievable occurrences to take place in the United States in decades.

While coastal cities and towns are still on the mend, states away from the coasts within the country have recently experienced deadly tornadoes and thunderstorms along with high levels of flooding, especially along the Mississippi River way. The river flooding this year has not been this devastating in thirty-five years. Many homes and lives have been lost due to the storms and flooding. In addition to flooding, fires are again taking tolls in the Western part of the country where people are still attempting to recover from the most recent ones last year as well as the landslide losses.

Most recently, residents of the Twin Cities in Minnesota are in court to recover the loss of properties and lives due to the collapse of the bridge over the Mississippi River. Money cannot replace lives, but they can lay blame here on faulty bridge construction for which there may be a monetary settlement.

There is no monetary settlement when natural disasters occur unless you have insurance to cover the cost of what is lost. There is no one to blame for the storm which struck Myanmar or former Burma, where over 200,000 lives have been lost. Prayer is needed, though the surviving residents do not seem to really want any outside help. We need to get 'in cinque' and pray in earnest for world brotherhood. Without brotherhood, speaking of 'going green' to combat global warming will mean nothing.

HUMAN RACE: NATURE SHAPED
First published March 13, 2011

The Ides of March had not yet arrived and destruction struck. The earthquake that hit Japan with a force of about 9 on the Richter scale left a path of destruction which touched the western shores of the United States. Earthquakes and tsunamis have left paths of destruction in Haiti, New Zealand and now Japan. All of these nations are islands which probably had their origins due to an earthquake.

As a Social Studies teacher, I have always had the notion that the entire world was at one time, one mass of land, which due to earthquakes and other calamities, was broken up into various masses of land. This was an exercise in which I challenged my students to cut out the land areas of the world and put them together as one mass. One can easily see how islands tend to be fragments of a part of the whole. Of course, the *Bible* contends that the destruction was a flood. Who am I to disagree, as it appears that two thirds of the world is water any-way?

It is also my contention that the people of the world, who are oceans apart and have some of the same customs and traditions, were at one time, one people. The differences in appearances and modifications of customs can easily be justified due to the climate and zones of where they live now. We are different because of location and in-breeding, but ***we all came from the same place, Africa***.

Because we are all human and of one race, the ***human race,*** we rush to help others in need when disaster strikes. This is human nature and this is the way it should be. The only problem with that is the fact that we are crisis oriented and have not learned to practice on a daily basis what we do in a crisis. As people, and as nations, we have no choice but to try to get along with each other. If we do this, many of our crises would not arise.

For all we know, these hard hitting earthquakes may very well be the result of some of the scientific research that we are conducting in an attempt to one-up each other. Brotherhood week should be fifty-two weeks of the year. There should never be a reason for civil discontent which affects the world.

Natural disasters may not be avoidable as only God has the last say on that, but the people of the world, who are closer to each other and aware of the circumstances in all of the world nations, need to come together and work on world peace. The United Nations needs to take a greater role in peace keeping. Citizens of the world, need to let them know that we are all brothers and sister, children of the Almighty and we need to get 'in cinque' and work on making this world a better place for us and future generations. If the manmade and natural disasters continue at the rate in which they are going, we may be coming to the end of this world.

UNREST: PHYSICAL, POLITICAL, ECONOMIC AND SOCIAL
First published March 21, 2011

Strange things happen every day in this world, and ye they are really not that strange after all. The twenty-first century has come into full bloom with the trends in history that will not be soon forgotten. There is subtlety in what is happening around the world; the unrest, physically, politically, economically and socially.

The physical unrest caused by the earthquakes and tsunamis are uncontrollable by man, but they do produce economic and social unrest, leading to political unrest. A great number of lives have been lost due to these natural disasters in several nations of the world. As we are *one people,* the devastation of any one nation places undue hardship on that nation as well as others who attempt to help them. As the number of disasters rise, the economic toll rises as well. Suffering people think and wonder, "Why me?" But, life goes on and too often, how it goes depends on the economic and social as well as the political environment.

The social unrest is often due to political environments which are not conducive to a wholesome life. Oppression is somehow the culprit in social unrest which leads to political chaos and often to relief of some sort. When Apartheid was abolished in South Africa, the world was on the threshold of the acquisition of freedom. Nelson Mandela was the epitome of a freedom maker. He had served many years in prison to be released to

229

be elected the president of his country. People stood in line for days to have the opportunity to cast a vote for him. The people of the world witnessed this. Oppressed people everywhere wanted to be free. That was not the end. It was a great beginning. Then, a few years later, in the 21st Century, another Black man in another subtle apartheid, said, "Yes, we can!" We did, and the people of the world still wanted to be free. Barack Obama's election in America is tantamount to Nelson Mandela's election in South Africa. The world has seen it and everyone wants to be free. Those who oppose are in opposition; fighting freedom, attempting to hold on to the bastions of segregation, oppression, economic status, social superiority and plain meanness.

People of the world are more intelligent now than they were a few decades ago and now that we are in the computer age, news, good and bad, travels very fast; so do individuals who are on the move. The people of the world have seen what God can do and they want the same opportunities that other people of the world have and have had. That old song about "It is hard to keep them on the farm when they have seen Paris," works for keeping people oppressed when they have seen the commencement of freedom and know that it can be achieved. It is time to get 'in cinque' and realize that the world is changing fast and in order to keep up we will have to adapt and sometimes in some places, die trying.

TECHNOLOGY AND THE WEATHER
First published June 5, 2011

No one has to tell anyone today that times are hard and life is fragile. It is but the grace of God that we are here to hear all of the bad news around the world. It is heart wrenching just to learn about the tragedies surrounding us in the United States.

The *Bible* speaks to earthquakes, storms, wars and rumors of wars, (Matthew 24:6; Mark 13:7; Luke 21:9) as well as false prophets and we know historically, that these things have been occurring since the beginning of time. In my lifetime, and that of many of my contemporaries, we have witnessed the intensity of the earth' tragedies. One has to wonder: is the intensity of the tragedies that we witness more than previously, or is man's ability to measure and record better now than it was years ago or does it have something to do with man's advanced technology?

Have we or are we outdoing ourselves? Every day in the news, we hear of earthquakes, tsunamis, volcano eruptions, hurricanes, tornadoes and floods. Every prediction seems to be record breaking of an occurrence. We say that we pray and believe in God, so are our prayers not going through the roof?

Some areas of the United States are known to be situated for certain kinds of catastrophes, but what about the unsuspecting areas where tragedy falls? Some areas are called tornado alleys, hurricane paths, earthquake fault areas, area of an active volcano and the people who reside in these areas brace themselves and prepare for the time when tragedy might strike. Sometimes it pays off and sometimes one just cannot prepare for some of life's tragedies.

We have made such tremendous strides in harnessing some of the elements of this world to make our journey here much easier and in some instances safer, but are all of our new strides and developing technology doing something to our environment and atmosphere which causes tragic natural occurrences to be more intense than in past times? Was *Atlantis* real or a figment of Plato's imagination?

Atlantis was a utopia which had harnessed all of the modern knowledge of the then known world but it was believed to either have been destroyed by an earthquake or an overabundance of its technology. Are we moving too fast with technology? There is no more privacy. Identity fraud is rampant and new technology is making it possible. We need to get 'in cinque' and assess what is happening to us as individuals, families, states and a country in order to avoid some of life's tragedies.

SMOKE POLLUTION
First published July 26, 2008

There is a passage in the *Bible* which mentions "...and the rocks cried out," and I keep thinking that perhaps we must all hear them cry before we realize how much we civilized people are polluting this earth where we live. I can remember clear running streams when I was a child. The water was clear and you could see the rocks at the bottom of the stream

231

as well as the fish and other life forms which lived in the water. There was no guessing as to where the fish were, because you could see them. A few years ago, I returned to that stream and all I could see was the black, oily, murky substances that took the place of water. This was in a really rural area. So I hesitate to think about the streams in urban areas.

The streams are not the only things that we are polluting. The very air that we breathe is one of the most important areas of concern in this whole world. We may live a little while without water, but not for long without air. Is there any wonder that so many of us suffer from allergies, asthma, bronchitis, emphysema, tuberculosis, pneumonia, silicosis, asbestosis and other form of lung cancers and diseases?

It appears that the more there is a tendency to educate the public about pollution and especially smoke pollution, the more we smoke and pollute; not just our own lungs, but anyone else who happens to be nearby. So often, the polluter has no regard for those around him and if anything is said about it to the polluter, one may become the victim of a barrage of deleted expletives. I have witnessed a person connected to an oxygen tank puffing and blowing more smoke than one who does not need oxygen.

Because smoking, at a cost of about $4.00 per package, is not on the decrease, the companies who provide oxygen to those in need of it are now in Big Business. The reason for this is because more and more people are smoking and giving themselves lung diseases and also to the people around them from the second-handed smoke. People who never lit up are coming down with lung diseases at a greater rate than some of the smokers. Cigarettes are the greatest culprits in the smoke pollution arena. The paper wraps are dangerous. Pipe smoke is not bad, plus they tend to give the tobacco an aroma which makes it 'pleasant smelling.' Some cigars are supposed to do the same thing, except their odor gives me a headache.

Some businesses have established a no-smoking area or do not permit any smoke, but if you wander into the nearest smoking area, God forbid the aroma and the ability to breathe. E-cigarettes or electronic cigarettes are not the answer. We need to get 'in cinque' and do more to help cut down on smoke pollution. ***TAX THAT TOBACCO MORE!***

XI-SAME SEX MARRIAGE

WHAT IS SAME SEX MARRIAGE?
First published June 1, 2004

The media is having a field day with the passage of laws permitting same sex marriages. The President, on the other hand has requested Congress to pass an amendment to the _Constitution_ banning same sex marriages. A topic for debate in the upcoming presidential election has now been conceptualized. A few years ago, it was _Rowe v. Wade_ which was the issue, or to have or not to have an abortion.

There exists some medical reasons for an abortion, but the only medical reason for a same sex marriage is insurance. That gets into another whole new ballgame and into a zone of legal and illegal because there is no gray area. Some governmental entities have made same sex marriage legal on their official records, but every sensible, moral and Christian individual in these United States know that it is wrong from a biological, historical, and ethical, as well as a sociological standpoint. _**There is no justification for same sex marriages.**_

Ethically, the _Bible_ speaks of the destruction of Sodom (root word for sodomy) and Gomorrah because of their iniquity or sin. Sodomy is sinful and in some states it is a crime punishable by a harsh law. This was an historical event which according to the records took place about 1900 B.C. If God did not approve of it then, surely He does not approve today. According to "Little Richard' Pennington, "God made Adam and Eve, not Adam and Steve."

Biologically speaking, and according to the _Bible_, God did make Adam and Eve and Adam was a male and Eve was a female. Most animals on earth are of two varieties, male and female. We even make tools in those same varieties. There are some asexual animals and some dual-sexed animals, because the main objective of all living creatures is to propagate or have off-springs. There may be a record someplace like "Ripley's Believe It or Not' where there is documentation of a birth from two same sex entities, but I personally have no knowledge of it. If it exists, it is characterized as unique and rare.

Sociologically speaking, a family consists of a man and a wife or father and mother and some children. In the norm of things, the children are the off-springs, biologically, of the man and woman or at least one of them, in the household. This is also the usual definition for the Internal Revenue Service, as well. A husband and a wife, without children are a couple, ***not a family!*** Two women or two men living together make up a ***household,*** not a couple. ***They*** will not be the biological **parents** of any child.

Whether there is an amendment to the *Constitution* or not, we need to get 'in cinque' and realize what kind of message we are sending to our youth who will be tomorrow's adults.

SAME SEX MARRIAGES FALLOUT
First published May 18, 2008

It has often been said that California is the land of fruits and nuts and now I believe it. Just recently, the California State Supreme Court decided that it is OK, legal, that is for people of the same sex to get married. One would believe that after "Lil' Richard Pennington said that he found out that God meant' Adam and Eve, not Adam and Steve,' that the fusses over same sex arrangements were put on the back burner forever. The individuals who wanted this ruling from the courts could be seen dancing and hopping for joy on the television.

There may be some advantages to same sex marriage, though I for one will never be able to see or understand it. We know that morality cannot be legislated and that those people who are very happy now because of the California ruling would probably have continued in their mode of living even if the court had not ruled in their favor.

In this Christian society, it is and will be very difficult to reckon with legal, same sex marriages which by all means go against the grain of morality. This ruling comes at a time when our country's morality is about at the lowest peak of all times. It comes when our young people are completing a phase of their education at the elementary, secondary, college and graduate levels. This is something that will stick in their minds as they attempt to enter another phase of their education or join the world of work. This ruling will also have an effect on education as every phase of learning deals with a marriage being between a man and a woman. The components of a family entail a father, a mother and a child or children. How will the courts determine the 'she' from the 'he?' What will their children call them; Mom number 1 and 2 or Dad number 1 and 2?

How are regular communities going to accept these couples in neighborhoods where there are impressionable children? How will normal parents explain these couples to their children? How will children explain these arrangements to each other? How are textbooks going to address the very existence of same sex marriage?

The next question is how will same sex marriages affect business in this country as if it is not already complicated enough? Somehow, I just do not see how the existence of legal same sex marriages is not going to present some embarrassments and hurt feeling in daily lives. A lot of soul searching and patience will have to go into the acceptance of such marriages into the greater society. It is time to get 'in cinque' and hope that the court realized its error and then correct it.

OPEN MIND NEEDED
First published June 26, 2011

New York has become the sixth state to approve same sex marriages with the hope by many Americans of that persuasion that the idea will quickly spread to other states. One thing is certain; the provincial family which is discussed in the ***Bible*** will not be forthcoming from such unions. The word marriage implies that a family will possibly be established, meaning that there will be children at some future point in time. Strange is the only way to describe these marriages, and when they adopt children it still will not be the same. They will not have to practice birth control and how do children from such unions feel when they are with children of natural or possibly natural parents?

There were possibly problems with so called gay people being in the closet or coming out of it for that matter, but when such relationships are legalized and there can possible be children in such home, there is the possibility of another kind of discrimination being established for the children of these unions. It is the attempt to make a family out of these relationships which will have the greatest impact on society.

The idea of "My two dads" or "My two moms" is going to take a massive amount of open-mindedness for children with impressive minds to adjust in school and anywhere else for that matter. If the rush continues, it may become necessary to establish schools just for children from same sex marriages because the average Reading textbook is geared to the family of Dick and Jane, Baby, Mother/Mommy and Father/Daddy. How are the children from homes with two moms or two dads going to feel as a result of reading the text? What kind of modifications will teachers have to make when there is an influx of such students?

There is epic conflict now when students whose biological identification state that they are of one legal sex and they have decided that they do not wish to be what their identification says that they are and want to attend the prom as the opposite sex. In several states, students have sued for the right to be what they want to be when they attend the prom.

In some instances there have been no problems. My grand-daughter's best friend was a so-called gay boy. He attended the prom with her, dressed as a girl. There had been no broadcast that he would attend in that fashion and they both had a great time, I am told. Unfortunately, he was dead before his 23rd birthday because of his lifestyle. He had a promising career as a beautician which was cut shot. Aside from discrimination, harassment and outright cruelty, it just pays to be straight. There are hormones and psychological treatments to help those who have difficulty identifying their sexual orientation and we to get 'in cinque' early in the lives of our children to help them to stay on the straight path.

INDIVIDUAL CHOICES
First published July 15, 2012

Many people are talking about and asking questions about President Obama's statement regarding same sex marriages. There are interpretations and more interpretations on what he did or did not say and how it makes him look in regards to the upcoming presidential election in November and how voters will react then. Personally, how he feels or stands on the matter does not concern me as an individual.

I see same sex marriages as an individual choice of the individuals who will live that particular life style and their happiness. As of this date, no one has consulted me about their choices and I feel certain that the same is true for President Obama. Same sex marriage is an issue of morality and by now, we should understand that we cannot legislate morality. Making a law which makes a moral issue a crime, only makes criminals out of those individuals who choose to ignore the law. If they only do harm to themselves, it *should* be ignored.

One thing is certain: many states have made same sex marriages legal, but even in those states; there are still those persons with that tendency, *still 'in the closet.'* President Obama knows this and has voting focus on this fact. The National Association for the Advancement of Colored People (NAACP) has also accepted the fact of the existence of and respect of same sex marriages. This was done to appease the President. This is the result of the direction of the morality of this country and the irate church pastors need to take note and get busy understanding the logic.

The morality of this country has headed in this direction ever since prayer was taken out of the public schools. It is against the law to pray in school, so naturally a breakdown in morality ***HAD*** to follow. School was the *only place many children had a chance to pray* or hear a prayer. Surely there are many religions in the United States, but this country was founded on Christian principles and that foundation has been shaken! It is still rocking and in too many instances to the blasphemy of the Hip Hop culture. Female bashing and profanity are the main ingredients of what I have heard and even with diminished hearing, it was more than I wished to hear.

We discuss babies getting babies, but for sure same sex couples will not be having babies naturally. Further, we cannot ignore the fact that there have been same sex couples in this country for years but we kept it 'hush hush.' Now it is open on television talk shows, soap operas, internet and wherever you look. Just the other night I heard Wanda Sykes talking about *her wife* on the Jay Leno Show. Webster and other dictionary makes are going to have to change or modify the definition of ***'husband.'*** We may not like it and cannot do much about it, so we may as well get 'in cinque' and understand, even if we do not agree and /or accept it, that same sex marriage is a characteristic of our current moral dilemma in the United States of America.

UNDERSTANDING SAME SEX MARRIAGES
First published January 1, 2014

This New Year, 2014 has arrived. The dancing, shouting, singing, whooping and hollering are all over and the fat lady has sung. As we look back over 2013, so much has happened until it makes us wonder what will this year be all about. There is one thing that we can be certain of and that is the increase in the number of states legalizing same sex marriages. While I do not condone them or condemn them, I find it difficult to understand them.

Growing up in these United States of America in a Christian home where every member of the family was either male or female and where there was no discussion of any other kind of sexual orientation has made this a difficult situation for me to understand and I feel that I am not alone. Do not *misunderstand* me when I say that *I do not understand,* even as I matured and became an adult and learned of family friends who had a different identification, and learned that my family was not indifferent to these individuals, it still has not helped my understanding.

As an adult, I learned that one of my mother's closest male friends was of another persuasion, though at the time, it was a 'closet thing.' Since that time, I have learned that my grand-daughter's closet male friend was also of another persuasion. The two of them went to their senior prom as twins. He taught her how to groom her hair and match her clothing. He would later become a beautician but his life was cut short by AIDS.

From a scientific and Biblical point of view, God made two varieties of each species of animals. The only thing that I have learned about any other variety is the fact that some mistake has been made. There is the old saying that 'God does not make mistakes.' I suppose that we must have the notion that some other variable came into play that interfered with what God had planned. We are aware that there is a lot of that taking place, everywhere.

There are too many people 'coming out of the closet' these days.

Certainly, God did not make all of these mistakes! I am a firm believer that perhaps some of this is the result of some interference with God's plan, but I truly believe that too much of this is a ***learned behavior*** which has nothing to do with God or even an upset in the balance of hormones. Hormones can be balanced if they are out of sync. The world is changing rapidly and maybe we can blame some of what is taking place on skyrocketing technology, but same sex cohabitation? Our governmental units, founded on Christian doctrines are upholding beliefs which were not a part of the Christian heritage. There has to a rational explanation somewhere! If and when found, I would love to see it and know it. Lord, let us get 'in cinque' and get back to the Master' Plan in 2014. We need a whole lot of praying going on!

XII-MORALITY

DECEIT
First published January 9, 2011

"Oh what a tangled web we weave when first we practice to deceive." Life throws a lot of curves to us and some of them are ill-conceived. Some of these curves result from the tangled lives that we live. Tangled lives are often bedded in deceit and often would not be tangled if we were true to ourselves and especially family members with whom we live and associate and affiliate.

Personally, I believe in calling a spade 'a spade.' I have no hidden agendas and attempt to keep my life open, clean and free. The clutter that I have does not bother me or anyone else. It represents my sentiments, dear only to me, and once I have gone on to the great beyond or classroom in the sky, the value will disappear, whether it is today or tomorrow. There is nothing in my life that I have done which should or would cause anyone I have professed to love to think any less of me and perhaps to think better of me for not leaving them the kind of garbage that so many of us leave an undeserving family when we no longer grace this earth.

This past year, 2010, I lost a total of twenty friends, associates and relatives. I have observed the remaining families and they all have my deepest and heartfelt sympathy. Some are truly saddened by the passing of a loved one whom they cherished and will sorely miss and some are as angry as can be, mostly about 'What he/she left me!"

A good rule to follow is to do what you can for whomever you choose to do it with no expectations of some kind of reward when your beloved passes on. Do for, care for or be there for someone you care about simply because you care. Your reward comes from God's grace because you do what you do out of the goodness of your heart. If by chance you are not mentioned in the distribution of your beloved's earthly properties, you have a clear conscience that you did what you could when you could. There is no need to cry and feel betrayed, even if you should have been entitled to some wealth. You made it before the passing and you can still prosper after the passing, because ill-gotten gains will not make the holder as happy as they think they will be.

Parents, especially have a tendency to favor one child over another. Too often, this is deceitful and causes unthinkable problems after a parent passes, among the siblings. Parents who love their children, equally or not, should consider the fallout of their actions when they pass on. Parents get 'in cinque' and do not cause your children to wish you were cremated alive.

IDENTITY THEFT
First published May 1, 2011

Do you know people with whom you often communicate and just about every six months they have a different telephone number? Yes, we all know someone like that. We wonder why there is a regular change taking place, but never really bother to ask.

If we should ask why, there are several answers that we might receive. One answer is that they are being harassed by someone; either someone they do not know or someone they **wish** they did not know. Another answer is that they were late paying their bill and the service was cut off temporarily. One might notice that each new number has a different name on the account and caller ID. Another reason for the change of numbers is to avoid calls from creditors.

All of this may seem insignificant to those of us who pay our bills regularly and are not dodging creditors, or have not lived in such a way to have people harass us. But if you have ever worked in a job which demand that you get into the personal life of the people with whom you have some business dealings, you do become interested in what makes some people tick, especially with identity theft rising higher every day, sometimes in places unimaginable such as our money management sites and our job personnel sites which has access to our vital statistics.

Identity theft is not just being practiced by strangers who target us, but the worst case scenario is taking place in families. Parents are the main culprits in homes where the credit rating is low. Instead of building up their credit, they are using their children's names to secure credit for various items. I personally met a 'lady' who had six children and she had an account in each child's name somewhere. Each time the telephone was disconnected, she had it turned back on in a different child's name. Some people go so far as to use the name of a pet animal to get credit.

The problem with this kind of action is the fact that when the child is old enough to try to get credit in his own name, it will already be so bad until it will be 'mission impossible.' Children hardest hit are those children in foster care that have been moved from foster home to foster home and their personal information has been used and abused. This is an opportunity for schools to get 'in cinque' and become involved and help students to know how to establish credit and how to repair credit and make students aware of the need to have good credit.

MORAL MATURITY
First published July 12, 2008

We often discuss individuals needing to mature or 'grow up,' especially when we refer to something which they say or do. The latest snafu of the day came by way of the utterances of the Reverend Jesse Jackson about Barack Obama, the presumptive Democratic candidate for President of the United States. Of course Mr. Obama accepted Mr. Jackson's apology and left with a smile on his face. Why not? He is the chosen one. Mr. Jackson had an unsuccessful run for the office of President of the United States about a decade ago. We hope he was not feeling somewhat jealous.

One would think that when you decide to run for a public office that you would not only be mature, but *morally mature.* Anytime a person is in the public in the limelight for any reason, one needs to be aware that you are under the microscope and magnifying glass. It is best to choose carefully what it is that you want to say and most of all what you really say, whether it is written or verbal.

I learned at the ripe old age of 13 years old that what you say and especially what you write is very important. Too soon, I learned that disparaging remarks about another person can come back to haunt you before the ink gets cold. I allowed myself to write freely, my feeling about another person, in an Opinion Book. That act alone put me in a position to be expelled from school; not suspended; but expelled. Someone' good heart kept me afloat. From that day forward, I have been more than careful about what I say about others, but even more so about what I write about others. My Great-grandmother had always told me that "If you cannot say something good about a person, don't say anything at all."

For the most part, I have attempted to follow my Great-grandmother's teachings, but as a teacher and a social worker, my job has often called for me to make candid evaluations where the truth had to be told, and many times, especially in social work, it was not pretty and there were no words to clean it up. What I have learned, however, is moral maturation. Whatever I do or say, I have no regrets. I am able to make rational decisions about what I do or say. That is, thought has gone into making a decision. Even when the decision is wrong and I felt it was right at the time that it was made I accept the consequences. I am morally mature. We, the citizens of this country needs to get 'in cinque' and work toward moral maturity and encourage our leaders and our youth to work toward that end. It surely will end some of the governmental corruption.

BATTERED WOMEN
First published March 12, 2009

It appears that the media and several talk show hosts and hostesses are 'all shook-up' about singer Chris Brown's alleged brutal attack on his singer girlfriend Rhianna, which apparently took place just prior to an award ceremony at which they were both supposed to make an appearance. Pictures of the face of a battered female, allegedly Rhianna, appeared in newspapers following the incident and Chris Brown was arrested. The next news story told of Rhianna's forgiveness and reunion with Chris Brown and finally to his purchase of a $50,000(fifty thousand dollar) diamond ring for Rhianna. Blogs on her decision to reunite with Brown have again turned the media upside down. Oprah and Dr. Phil have addressed the issue of "Why Battered Women Remain with Their Abuser."

Some time ago, this topic was explored in this column. There are several tenets to why women remain with an abuser, whether it is a spouse or a significant other. One of the first reason is that a female feels that she is *'in love'* and the man in her life is *'in love'* with her. The first time that he hits her she is shocked and upset and ready to run away. She is hurt and during this time the abuser will usually apologize and promise to never hurt her again and tell her how much he loves her and does not wish to live without her. He is sincere and she believes him and forgives him and they reunite until the next time. Next time, in addition to the sincere apology, he will generally do something nice that she wanted him to do and once again, she reunites with him, her abuser.

The next part of this scenario deals with the low self-esteem of the female which is fueled by the abuser. He will tell her on a regular basis that no one cares as much for her as he does and no one else will take care of her like he does, and because she is committed to him, she buys into his line of reasoning. She fears that he is *'all that there is and after him there is no other!'* She stays with him out of *fear of the future.* She sees other males as a more dangerous version of him and therefore feels safer with him. If they have children together, the fear is twofold. She does not feel that any other male will be as loving to her children as their father.

A third factor involved in why women stay with their batterers stems from our homes and heritage. Did Mom and Dad fight? Some young men believe it is their duty to 'beat their wives.' Some women believe that their husbands have a right to 'beat' them. They believe it is *normal* and endure until the end. We need to get 'in cinque' and *teach our children* that it is *never alright* to be hit by our mates. Parents raise you, not husbands and boyfriends.

MORALITY AND SOAP OPERAS
First published April 20, 2009

I have been watching soap operas for a very long time and found them to be very refreshing as well as entertaining. They have been a help to ease tension, provide an outlet for stress of my own, provide critical observation of written materials and entertaining. Lately, there seems to be something missing in most soap operas which I have from time to time watched.

One of the most amazing things about today's soap operas is how many people come back from the dead. These rebirths have occurred on daytime and night time soap operas. Some have been believable while others have left much to be desired. We all know that with some of the unbelievable deaths that have taken place that there is no way that those persons could have survived and have the identical appearances that they had before the maiming.

The next thing that has puzzled me is the incest that occurs. One of the most loved characters on one of the soap operas has been married to two brothers and their father. Aside from that, she has five children by four different men. One of her husbands also married her sister for a while and her sister was at one time married to a man with whom she has a child. It seems that the producers could hire other people for these characters to cut down on incest, or is this really how some people live? Is this what is referred to as a tight knit family?

Everything is explored on the soap operas, including teenage sex, drugs, crimes and abortion. Sometimes, the outcomes are commendable, but there are times when the end results are unreal and unbelievable. The only thing which I have not witnessed is a sex change, but one story has come close by having two women, both mothers being so in love with each other and one of their husbands, to a point where a marriage between a man and a woman is stopped because of the feelings that the two women have for each other. For me, this is the last straw. It is time to cancel this show.

It is my sincere hope that the writers of soap operas will keep in mind what is morally correct for their viewers and not cave in to what people are actually doing all the time or show the moral values triumphant over the lower values IF they must be dealt with. Aside from that, we need to get 'in cinque' and let the writers of these shows know how we feel about soap operas and morality.

BABY MAMA
First published May 25, 2009

It is Memorial Day; the day in which we remember those persons whom have put their lives on the line for our country in order to preserve freedom and democracy. Many of us observe religious ceremonies to commemorate the ideals and sacrifices which have taken place for us. Then, on the other hand, this is just another day in which many of us did not have to check in at the job. It is a day when we can just kick back and rest or try our hands at the art of grilling on the patio, having a few friends over and 'party hearty.'

Young people, teenagers and young adults find this is time to spend more time with their significant others. The only problem is that the significance does not last very long. Too often, the significance ends after nine months with the birth of a child and then the young lady becomes a 'baby mama' because the young man in her life no longer finds her significant. Then the 'Baby Mama' drama begins. Many of these young ladies had some grandiose idea that if they became a mother, the young man would make them their Mistress, legally.

The young fathers do not want to be husbands and fathers at this juncture in their lives. Many of them want a child, but all they want is visiting rights when they feel like it. The baby may or may not be cared for by the father, but he expects the mother to care for the child on a daily basis, physically and financially. If and when he is ready to settle down to be a husband and a father, it is not usually with the 'Baby Mama.' Some young men take pride in having more than one 'baby mama.' They become amazed at the conflict between the young ladies as most of them are always up for drama, either with another 'baby mama' or the young man's newest significant other. It was bad enough when out-of-wedlock babies came into the world because of a lack of knowledge about birth control, but it is devastating when they are brought into the world on purpose for selfish reasons which often lead to child abuse and neglect.

Virtuous young ladies and young men are having a difficult time finding each other in this day of casual sexual activities. Most virtuous young ladies have a difficult time finding a nice young man who ***does not*** have a 'baby mama.' This generation in the making has no wholesome role models. They do not know the definition of 'family' and virtue. Our President Barack Obama and his family are setting good examples of what a family should be like, excluding the million dollars, and it would be wise for adults to point the way that our young people should go and walk in the paths themselves. We must get 'in cinque' and educate our youth on the values, virtues and vitality of Family.

WORKPLACE ETHICS
First published June 2, 2009

In times like these, more people are becoming members of various churches. Times are hard and many people are not just looking for a church, but in essence, a welfare station. Others want some kind of support system for their general wellbeing. With the media on a fast track to let us know that this deep recession in which we are experiencing has not hit a turning point just yet, makes one wonder just how much harder times are ahead and how long hard times will last.

Discussions of cut backs on employment opportunities as well as current jobs, paints a bleak picture for the new college graduates. Because of this, we will probably see an increase in graduate school enrolment, which is good for the future outlook on employment. This will be a positive aspect of the lack of employment opportunities.

Current employees, white collar and blue collar are experiencing difficulties on their jobs as employers know that there are probably hundreds of possible employees for every job that they have. Bosses are pushing a hard line since they are aware that they have the upper hand. Some have even put themselves in a position to make decisions about life or death situations of some employees. As an example, a lady whose husband died took off a little time from her job to bury her husband, take care of business which needed attention and mourn her loss. She was away two weeks and when she returned to her job, she no longer had a job. She was told that she was away too long. Her boss was a staunch churchgoer and choir member.

In another instance, a middle-aged lady who is a receptionist at her job, has a daughter who is in intensive care because she had a difficult pregnancy which threatened her life and caused her physicians to have to deliver her fetus prematurely in hope of saving her life. As a result, the lady's daughter and grandchild are both in intensive care. Because workers whose job description it is to do back-up for this lady when she is absent from work, do not want to do it, her boss does not want her to have time off, though she has accumulated sick time, annual leave and compensatory time which is available for her to be off from work with pay. In times like these, the church goers and hallelujah hailers seem to have forgotten their god-fearing, god-loving ideals and heart-felt empathy for their co-workers. 'Friends' are complaining about co-workers to their bosses instead of speaking with their 'friends' about the quality of their work. Care and concern are lost in the workplace. We need to get 'in cinque' and practice the love we preach in the workplace.

XIII-VOTE

CONTACT CONGRESSMEN
First published March 16, 2005

In instances where you cannot vote directly, contact your Congressmen. I was not surprised when I read an article by U. S. Senator Trent Lott praising the merits of President Bush's plan to privatize Social Security and persuade young workers age 55 and younger to buy into the idea of the new plan. He did mention that the new plan would be voluntary. According to him, his 91 year old mother who worked until she was 75 years old cannot live on her Social Security benefits which will remain the same for the rest of her life, though his 35 year old daughter has a chance to be a part of the new plan.

The new plan will allow his daughter to "begin contributing to one of these personal accounts and then select from a variety of funds which to invest and grow her retirement. Though she'd have more control over her money, it is not a privatized system as many people have suggested. Like the Thrift Savings Plan, these retirement funds still would be managed by the federal government. Because they would be publicly administered, participants could not withdraw the funds at any time or for anything they wish."

The information that Senator Lott left out is the fact that the investments may take a drop in value, depending on the stock market, just as any other stock investments. If there is a loss, the investor loses. Senator Lott stated. "Now, I don't take Social Security reform lightly. In fact, I've worked to stop major Social Security changes before, back in the 1980s, but times have changed...my elderly mother cannot live on her meager Social Security income. She worked until she was 75, for a small return. It wasn't fair."

Senator Lott failed to mention that as late as 2003; he worked to stop Social Security changes such as the GPO or Government Pension Offset and the WEP or Windfall Elimination Provision. As a teacher who taught in three states, Illinois, Texas and Mississippi, I wrote to all of the senators in these states and the appropriate representatives requesting them to support the House and Senate bill which would repeal these legislative acts.

These acts reduce Social Security benefits for teachers in states who pay into a pension plan, but do not pay Social Security taxes during the time of their employment. Though the teacher worked in other areas and paid Social Security taxes and eventually earned the required quarters to qualify for a Social Security check, the amount is reduced by about one-half. In addition, a married recipient is not eligible for a spouse's benefits upon death of the spouse and vice-versa. The only negative response that I received was from Senator Lott. He assured me that the program was working as it was supposed to and there was no need to change the provisions. If he believes that his mother's income is meager, I wonder what he thinks of mine.

It is time for all working American to get 'in cinque' and bombard their senators and representatives with letters letting them how they feel about the proposed changes to Social Security, keeping in mind that the Congressmen will have a lifetime pension and personally do not have to worry about the 'meager' Social Security benefits.

The GPO and WEP need to be eliminated and workers earning six figure salaries need to pay more into the Social Security treasury; Social Security funds should not be 'lent' to other departments of government either. When possible, make your vote count in these matters.

PRESIDENTIAL POLLS
First published October 25, 2004

On the eve of this presidential election, the daily newspapers have the result of a poll on the presidential candidates. Following the debates, the polls showed that Kerry won all three debates and he was leading in the polls. The most recent polls show that Bush is ahead a few percents over Kerry. All of this can be confusing to the electorate.

Polls as we know them can reflect whatever someone wants them to reflect depending on the sample they take and use. We do not have to be concerned about the election polls to see how social polls work. We can look at the results over a period of time for instance about the advantages for butter or margarine.

The poll for butter reflects all of the positive aspects of eating butter over that of eating margarine; it is a natural product which the body can easily digest with no long term side effects to your health, though we know that it is loaded with calories and it tastes good. On the other hand, margarine lacks all of the ingredients of butter. It is difficult to tell it from butter and it has low or no cholesterol and very few calories compared to butter. The fact that margarine has substances in it which are not really digestible is not mentioned. So, we switch from butter to margarine and then back to butter and finally decide if we want the natural extra calories of butter or the less fattening margarine.

The difference in our choice-making between butter and margarine is not as difficult as making the choice for president because we can only make one choice there, whereas with butter and margarine, we may decide to use both. We are being prompted to which choice to make regarding Bush and Kerry and if we are not careful, the polls will be a deciding factor in the vote which we cast.

Some people who look at the polls showing Bush as a leader in election choices may decide not to vote at all because if they would choose Bush, will feel that he will be elected anyway, so why bother to vote? On the other side of the coin, voters who would vote for Kerry, may feel that he will not win anyway, so why bother to vote? We do not need to let any poll sway our decision to vote or not vote. ***Apathy should not be a consideration in this election.*** There will be enough voters claiming that they were not able to vote or feel that their vote did not count, to make up for the lack of votes. We should use our franchise constructively and make the choice that **_we want,_** not what the polls say we want. Each of us who has registered to vote, has some idea as to which candidate will be the lesser of the two evils for this country, based on our own situations and relationships. It is time for us to get 'in cinque' and make that choice on **NOVEMBER 2, 2004,** regardless to who we are or where we are. ***VOTE!!!***

THE POWER OF A VOTING CITIZEN
First published June 23, 2005

The old South has changed. This is what we hear now, that an 80 year old *'former'* Klansman has been convicted of manslaughter for the gruesome murder of three civil rights workers forty years ago in Mississippi. It took a jury only two days to decide that he was guilty of manslaughter, **not murder.** The other conspirators involved in the murders, as well as key witnesses are reported to already be dead.

Convicting an 80 year old man of manslaughter or murder, at this date, does perhaps make some people feel that justice has been served. Has it? According to the life expectancy of man, as recorded in the <u>BIBLE,</u> an 80 year old man is already living on borrowed time. And in the case of this man, he is in a wheel chair with broken legs and uses portable oxygen for breathing and has a nurse nearby because of his blood pressure. Some would view this situation as 'one foot in the grave.' With his strong will, however, he may live 20 more years. Chances are, *IF he goes to prison,* the hospital or nursing home will be where he will spend his time. He will not be physically able to perform any useful service in a prison. Has justice been served?

There have been more than many unlawful acts which have been committed in Mississippi and the other Southern States; lynching, arson, theft of real estate and services, burning of churches and crosses, to name a few, are acts which are not as common as they used to be, but never the less, still occurring in the United States of America, not just in the Southern States.

The outward evidences of racial segregation in these United States have definitely shrunk, but if it were really gone, there would be no need for organizations such as the National Association for the Advancement of Colored People, The Urban League, The Push/Rainbow Coalition, Operation Breadbasket or Southern Poverty Law Center. There also would not be any evidence of the existence of the Ku Klux Klan, the Young Nazis, Anti-Semitic or any other group whose main purpose for existence is to prevent certain ethnic groups from celebrating life in this country with all of the inalienable rights afforded citizens of this country, especially voting.

There are citizens in the Southern States who believe in equal rights of all citizens, but are afraid of being ostracized by the powers that be which do not see things their way. Every individual of voting age has a voice in the government and if they are afraid to speak out verbally, they can have their say at the polls and in the courthouse. We need to get 'in cinque' and **_realize the power of being a voting citizen_** and let those people whom we elect to office, know how we feel. We need to make sure that Mississippi is not *still burning!*

APATHY
First published December 2, 2007

This year, an off year has been filled with the elections of state and local officers and this has been a prelude to the upcoming presidential election next year, a leap year. The candidates have been campaigning on every level. Signs have dotted the landscapes on vehicles that pass by, on the highways and byways, many lawns and businesses, as well as billboards and the media; television, radio and the newspaper. There is no way to escape, but many people do.

Many people, in spite of all of the coverage for candidates in all of the right places, just **do not get out and vote!** **_Voter apathy is very serious._** We sit down and refuse to vote, yet we have complaints on top of complaints when the people whom have been elected to office, do not fulfill our wishes. When we fail to vote, we fail to have our voices heard. We take whatever others want us to have; a good clean government for the people or an 'iffy' situation where the officers please themselves and forget about the people. When only one third of the eligible voters elect someone to office, the other two thirds take whatever they get. They should not argue about anything that goes on in the government because they failed to have a voice in the government.

A vote gives us power. Too few of us use our power. We hurt ourselves when we fail to vote. We permit unscrupulous individuals to abuse their power in various ways as well as misuse government finances for their own selfish desires. When this happens, we sit back and complain and feel helpless. If we get out and vote, we can make our desires and voices known. People have died to make it possible for some of us to vote. We should show our appreciation.

As a voting citizen, we have a right to attend governmental meetings and see and hear what our officials are doing. We also have the right to voice our opinions and take action with petitions to change things which we feel or know are not right. Tax dollars speak loud and sometimes just as clear. Voting does not mean that you choose a candidate and suffer the candidate's desire for his/her term of office. It means that as a voting citizen that there is something you can do beside sit, grumble and just 'take it.'

All over the world there are citizens action committees and just as citizens rally to put an officer into the government, they can rally to put them out. Often, an election sends a loud and clear message to government when an incumbent loses by a two to one margin. It usually means 'goodbye.' It **should mean 'Goodbye.'** Good government has its rewards. The people are rewarded when government is good. When citizens vote instead of being apathetic, government is usually good. We must get 'in cinque,' put apathy aside and VOTE.

VOTE IN PERSON: PREFERRABLE
First published September 23, 2012

There is no doubt in anyone's mind that the upcoming presidential election is a crucial one. With all of the mudslinging, deceptions, attacks and counter attacks, it makes one wonder what the final outcome could possibly be. It also brings to mind the number of illegal and underhanded things that can and probably will take place at the various polls on and before the Election Day. History has shown us the inadequacies which have been recorded in several states with regards to vote counting. Some of it has been due to rigging of voting machines to register the vote for one candidate for the other especially when there has been a favorite in that particular precinct. There have been many instances of not counting the absentee votes or simply discarding them as though they never arrived.

Not counting votes is one problem, but keeping certain people from voting is yet another problem. The Motor Voter ID situation, having a valid ID in some places and failure to receive an election card in other places has presented problems for voters. In cities famous for having election 'machines' (people groups) one's name can quickly be removed from the registry, denying the right to vote with the proper ID. This is a year that when you go to vote, to make sure that all of your 'T's' are crossed and your 'I's' are dotted.

This is also the year, in which I suggest that you go to the polls even if you are in a wheel chair, walking with crutches or in any way have limited mobility, go. If you have limitations, solicit someone that you can trust to get you to the polls and assist you. This is a year in which I have negative suspicions about absentee voting. I am somewhat uptight about some voting machines, especially those where a person at the poll has to overlook the registering of your voted ballot.

One of my suspicions is rooted in the fact that I received an application for voting by mail from a politician who is running for an office. I looked at it and put it with the items which I planned to put in the trash. Before I could finish looking at it, I received a telephone call from the office of the politician inquiring if I received the card. I replied that I had received it the very same day, but had not intentions of using it. I thought about this and just wondered what the big idea is? Why now? Many things went through my mind, but the main thing is, that I plan to cast my vote, put my slip in the machine and see it register in the machine. Mail can get lost at the post office and at it destination, resulting in a ***lost vote!*** It is my most humble suggestion that we get 'in cinque' and ***get out to the polls November 6, 2012 and cast our votes! Let us make sure that it counts!***

XIV-PRESIDENT BARACK OBAMA

THE WORLD APPEAL OF OBAMA
First published January 25, 2009

The inauguration of Barack H. Obama is over and some of the celebrating has ceased. As his first acts as President, he quickly reversed some of George W. Bush's orders with his own Executive Orders, one of the first, by ordering the closure of Guantanamo Bay torture prison. He apparently believes, as does many Americans that inhumane torture is not acceptable.

It appears that Mr. Obama is attempting to try to live up to some of his campaign promises. We all know that he cannot correct overnight what has been wrong for many years. He is the first man of color to become President, but that will not be enough for him to right all of the wrongs of the American society. His election alone speaks to the fact that there are some people in this world who are not race conscious and look and work toward a state of harmony among races and ethnic groups in this country.

The campaign and election of Barack Obama has had a world following from its outset. Countries around the world had supporters who made a video of their feelings on bridges, called "Bridges of Obama." It gives us the feeling that Obama will and can bridge the racial, political, social and world divides that exist. The same fervor of the campaign translated into the election and now into the inauguration. Countries around the world celebrated as Barack Obama became the 44th President of the United States. The world sees _hope_ in the presidency of Barack Obama.

Only since the advent of Jesus Christ has the hope of Obama had such a worldwide impact. His following is worldwide, but we must remember that he is a _man,_ not a saint or a god. And though there are parallels, such as 'no room in the inn," when he wanted to enroll his children in Washington, D. C. schools on time, attempts to deny that he is who he is; attempts to place his birth in a foreign country to deny his access to the presidency; attempts on his life by radicals who do not want peace in this country or the world and feel that he not worthy of the position because of his color.

Racism in America still lives and there are many strongholds that pursue those ends unto death. There are also organizations in America that are determined to eradicate such groups and it behooves us all, who want peace and prosperity, to get 'in cinque' and seek out the groups that would help to make America stronger and less racist; they need our support: words, deeds and money

PRESIDENT OBAMA'S SPEECH TO STUDENTS
First published September 5, 2009

For some time now, it has puzzled me as to why some of the courses in Social Studies in the public high schools are being deleted. It just occurred to me that it is the undercurrent of the political movements to the left that have infiltrated the public schools in hope of making sure that political ideology is not taught. The lambasting of the occurrence of a United States Presidential speech to students in schools, which has not been made yet, is the fruit of such ideas.

Presidents of the United States have made speeches to students in schools for the past thirty years that I am aware of and there have been no loud cry-outs from parents or the public. As a matter of fact, these speeches have been welcomed by any and every one affected. There has been no backlash following the speeches either, but President Obama had only to announce that he **planned** to speak to students regarding staying in school, and in some instances, especially in **'dense'** Republican areas, parents are having their children 'opt out' from listening to the speech or harassing principals and school districts not to allow the speech to be heard or seen in their schools. Some have decided to record it for a later viewing and listening time. If they only knew that years ago, a classroom was lucky if it could *borrow a radio to listen to the President speak!* Where have our morals and desire to learn gone?

One would think that in schools where motivational speakers are hired at the beginning of each school year to speak to their student bodies and pay much more than the electricity for a televised speech, or the cost of a high definition television, that a speech from the highest office in the United State, that of the President, would be welcomed. But it seems that some folk just 'can't get over it!' The irony of it all is, that President Obama has acquired ***more education and experience*** than the average motivational speaker hired by school districts. He has more to offer and has been constantly encouraging not just students attending school to stay in school, but is encouraging parents who dropped out to ***return to school.***

We are busy contemplating what the health care reform will be like in the end, and how Medicare and Medicaid will be affected, but we also need to become interested in an overhaul of the educational system in this country, as we are still encountering separate and unequal education, fifty-five years after *Brown v. The Board of Education.* Perhaps a better funded and better personnel filled educational system in this country would increase the thinking and moral skills of its products, our children. We need to get 'in cinque' and revamp our values.

OBAMA'S PEACE PRIZE
First published October 11, 2009

We live in an inquisitive world. Many of the things which we inquire about are necessary in order to solve problems that once rectified, will enhance our lives. There are some things however, that need no inquiry. In that category of unnecessary inquiry falls much of the rhetoric which deals with the opinions of other people and their lives. Some of the things that we inquire about are none of our business. Some of the things that we are told about, especially in the live media, are none of our business either. Who is marrying or divorcing who, or where some celebrity spent their vacation and how much it cost should not really concern most of us, unless we like to throw a pity party because we did not have the kind of money that was spent for the occasion. Most of us do not care how much Michael Jordan is spending for his new home in Florida or his cigar smoking in California. That is not the kind of news one can use.

On the other hand, it is good to know when your President, the president of your country has won a prestigious award like the Nobel Prize for Peace. That is a world accomplishment, especially when it is GIVEN to you, not purchased, borrowed or stolen. It has always been this writer's belief that when something ***is given to someone,*** that someone was meant to have it. It was not a sale, a loan or a robbery. In addition, individuals or groups have the right to give whatever they have control over, to whomever THEY CHOOSE!

In 1901, the first Nobel Prizes were given at the request of Alfred Bernhard Nobel in his will, that the initial $9 million estate be set up to fund prizes in physics, chemistry, medicine and physiology, literature and world peace (*Funk and Wagnall's Encyclopedia.)* The first United States President to receive the Nobel Prize for peace was Woodrow Wilson, in 1919 most likely due to his work in establishing the League of Nations of which the *United States never became a member.* Our country displayed a narrow view of the president's leadership and broke his heart and body, but not his spirit in his efforts to bring peace to the world. He did not live to see his dram realized in the United Nations which we have today. The same kind of people who criticized Woodrow Wilson and had no knowledge of the depth of his actions, are the naysayers of today, of Barack Obama, led by the news media on the radio and television and some major newspapers. HE WAS GIVEN the NOBEL PEACE PRIZE. The people who did not vote for him to become President are trying to make his tenure unbearable. Let us get 'in cinque' and put the naysayers behind us.

AMENDMENT FREEDOMS
First published March 4, 2012

This is America; land of the free, home of the brave! There is a lot packed into those three phrases. Many Americans are now more aware of what is implied in *The United States Constitution* especially since this country has a Black President. The American Civil Liberties Union intends to make certain that every citizen knows what is in the *Constitution.* Each time they send out a survey now for a citizen to complete they include a small copy of *The CONSTITUTION of the United States of America.*

The Constitution includes the 27 Amendments and the first two are currently being used frequently because of our current President. The First

Amendment grants freedom of religion, speech, and the press; rights of assembly and petition. In spite of these rights, President Obama's religion is constantly being questioned. He claims that he is a Christian, but members of certain anti-Obama groups claim that he is a Muslim. What difference does it make?

At this juncture of our country, America that is, the use of the *Holy Bible* and prayer have been banned from our schools, public places, governmental offices and agencies, so this so-called Christian foundation of this country no longer exists. About the only place you can find prayer and the *Bible* now are in Christian churches, private gathering places and individual homes. Therefore, if President Obama is a Muslim and we have FREEDOM of Religion, what difference does it make? Is this not the land of the FREE? Is every citizen who is not in a prison FREE? Prisoners have freedom of religion.

The First Amendment also grants freedom of speech. There is so much freedom there until an entity has been brave enough to purchase an advertisement in a public place in Washington D. C. which spells out in no uncertain terms stating "Go to Hell Obama!" He has the right to say this and it is protected by the *Constitution!* According to the director of the transit system because it is political and they cannot refuse political advertisements. He has been asked to remove it because it was disrespectable to the President, but this has made no impression upon the transit director. The advertiser fears that the government is taking over medical care.

Many individuals, who fear that President Obama will be re-elected, are busy trying to make certain that they will have arms to bear even if the Second Amendment which gives the right to bear arms is abolished by the passage of some other laws. They are currently giving the gun shops more business than they can handle in gun purchases because they expect President Obama to tighten the ownership and use of guns.

We all know that guns are made to *kill.* Is there a quiet storm gathering for some kind of revolution? We know that his country is now polarized into the rich and the poor, the haves and the have nots, but must there be a war? We need to get 'in cinque' and start some rational thinking, praying and strategy to keep American the land of the free and the home of the brave.

OBAMA RE-ELECTION
First published January 20, 2013

Our President Obama and Vice President Biden have been sworn in to begin their second four year term as the leaders of this great nation. The inauguration is set to take place on the same day which has been set aside for the observance and celebration of the birthday of Dr. Martin Luther King, Jr. This means that Americans and especially Black Americans have a dual reason for celebrating the 21st of January, 2013. We know, however, that King's birthday is really January 15th.

In order to give workers long weekends, so many holidays have been set on Mondays instead of the regular day. The continuance of this trend is going to have people confused about which day to really celebrate. One of the few days where there are not mix-ups is Thanksgiving because it is always slated for a particular Thursday in November. It is also difficult to misplace Ash Wednesday as well.

The 20th of January is the traditional Inauguration Day. It will be a day late this year and is being held on the day set aside for observing Martin Luther King, Jr.'s birthday which permits individuals whom would ordinarily be working to have the day off to witness the Second Inauguration of President Barack Hussein Obama. Many of us who were not able to attend in person had the opportunity to view it on the television or a website on the Internet.

Young men and especially young Black men do indeed have a role model. The excuses are all gone now. This Black man has been elected President of the United States ***TWICE!*** It is time to put the excuses behind and use this inauguration as a starting point and building block for the socially and ethically correct upbringing of young men. Parents, young and old, have a framework within which they can teach boys and young men how to be decent, respectful and honorable men. It is time that they learn that the 'baby mama' drama is old, stale, unhealthy and in no way a desirable trait for any man.

If this country is to go forward in a healthy and wholesome manner, it demands that the men of this country be healthy, wholesome and respectful. Moms Mabley said about fifty years ago that during the war, the men classified as 4F's were left to carry on the country. She may have been correct, but by now most of those off springs should have produced some healthy descendants. We have some good stock now that *can carry the torch for* improvement; growth, physically, mentally, emotionally and socially. Let us get 'in cinque' and put our best positive foot forward to make our communities and our country what it should be.

EPILOGUE

February 28, 2017

This work was completed on the above date, twenty eight days following the inauguration of President Donald Trump, the 45th U. S. President, who has in this amount of time, attempted to reverse the work of President Obama creating confusion and chaos around the world and in America with his Executive Orders which are ethnically and religiously discriminatory. His election was marred by evidence of interference from Russia causing him to be elected instead of Hillary Clinton who won the most popular votes. As President, Mr. Obama expelled the Russian officers in this country and initiated an investigation of the alleged election hacking. At this time, a special prosecutor has not been named and no results are coming from the media. Mr. Trump attempts to exclude the media from government information at this time and calls the news FAKE.

The Executive Order banning people from countries believed to have a large number of Muslims was blocked by a federal judge. Many people were deported or turned away at entry before the blocking of the order.

Mr. Trump also has plans to build a wall between the United States and Mexico and intends for Mexico to pay for it. As of this date however, a number of cabinet offices have not been filled due to candidate withdrawals and nomination withdrawals. Assistants have been fired as well as the Attorney General; a trait which Mr. Trump was known for on his Celebrity Apprentice television show; "You're fired!" There are those who wish to hear him on the receiving end of that statement.

Printed in the United States
By Bookmasters